THE *ALL-NEW* OFFICIAL
TAILGATING
COOKBOOK
GREAT FOOD · LEGENDARY TEAMS · CHERISHED TRADITIONS

THE *ALL-NEW* OFFICIAL TAILGATING COOKBOOK

GREAT FOOD · LEGENDARY TEAMS · CHERISHED TRADITIONS

BY THE EDITORS OF Southern Living

Oxmoor House®

, a division of Meredith Corporation
Published by Oxmoor House, an imprint of Time Inc. Books
225 Liberty Street, New York, NY 10281

Writer: Cassandra M. Vanhooser
Executive Editor: Katherine Cobbs
Assistant Editor: April Colburn
Project Editor: Lacie Pinyan
Design Director: Melissa Clark
Photo Director: Paden Reich
Designer: AnnaMaria Jacob
Executive Director, Business Development
and Partnerships: Megan Pearlman
Photographers: Antonis Achilleos, Iain Bagwell,
Caitlin Bensel, Jennifer Causey, Greg DuPree,
Kelsey Hansen, Alison Miksch, Victor Protasio,
Linda Pugliese, Hector Manuel Sanchez,
Time Inc. Food Studios
Prop Stylists: Cindy Barr, Ginny Branch, Kay E. Clarke,
Audrey Davis, Lindsey Lower, Mindi Shapiro Levine
Food Stylists: Mary Claire Britton, Margaret Monroe Dickey,
Emily Nabors Hall, Anna Hampton, Katelyn Hardwick,
Ana Kelly, Karen Schroeder-Rankin, Chelsea Zimmer
Recipe Developers and Testers: Allene Arnold,
Sheri Castle, Kathryn Delaney, Southern Living Test Kitchen,
Time Inc. Food Studios
Assistant Production Director: Sue Chodakiewicz
Senior Production Manager: Greg A. Amason
Assistant Production and Project Manager: Kelsey Smith
Copy Editors: Donna Baldone, Jasmine Hodges
Proofreaders: Adrienne Davis, Julie Gillis
Indexer: Mary Ann Laurens
Fellows: Holly Ravazzolo, Hanna Yokeley

ISBN-13: 978-0-8487-5539-3
Library of Congress Control Number: 2018941156

First Edition 2018
Printed in the United States of America
10 9 8 7 6 5 4 3 2 1

We welcome your comments and suggestions
about Time Inc. Books. Please write to us at:
Time Inc. Books
Attention: Book Editors
P.O. Box 62310
Tampa, Florida 33662-2310

Time Inc. Books products may be purchased for business or
promotional use. For information on bulk purchases, please
contact Christi Crowley in the Special Sales Department at
(845) 895-9858.

Front endsheet photo credit: William DeShazer/The New York Times/Redux

TABLE OF CONTENTS

HOW TO USE THIS BOOK

Flip through these pages and you'll find 150+ crave-worthy tailgating recipes, including those specifically developed for each of the 14 NCAA Southeastern Conference football teams. For each team, there's a menu of four recipes, plus a customized spritzer, jalapeño popper, and whoopie pie, so you can make dishes perfectly suited for game day no matter who you root for. You'll find more than recipes here, too. Each SEC team is profiled with information on school traditions, iconic football moments, legendary coaches and players, and photos. At the end of each school profile, a full-spread image shows the dishes from the team menu on a table decked out in school-spirited decor. Decorating tips on the image will help inspire you to recreate the look. Finally, football trivia is presented throughout in Tent Talk sidebars so you can entertain those at your tailgate or in your kitchen with a fun round of Q&A!

A NOTE ABOUT ORGANIZATION

The book begins with a chapter on setting up your tailgate that includes advice on grilling, food safety, crucial supplies, and lighthearted rules for successful tailgating. After that, the book is organized into recipe chapters for breakfast and brunch; drinks; appetizers and snacks; soups, stews, and chili; entrées; sides; and desserts. The team profiles and tablecapes are featured alphabetically, two schools per recipe chapter (see the Table of Contents for where each begins). Each recipe from a team's menu can be found in its appropriate recipe chapter, with page references listed on each team tablescape. The customized team spritzers, jalapeño poppers, and whoopie pies start on pages 71, 106, and 257, respectively. Tent Talk trivia questions are found within each chapter, and the answers are on page 269.

FOREWORD

IT FEELS LIKE I HAVE BEEN TRYING TO EXPLAIN THE PASSION OF THE SOUTHEASTERN CONFERENCE SINCE I CAME OUT OF THE WOMB.

Perhaps, the most difficult moment came on April 23, 2007, when I was a guest on NPR's *Morning Edition.* The host, in a steady, cerebral voice, asked: "Can you possibly explain how and why 92,138 people showed up at Bryant-Denny Stadium yesterday to watch Alabama's preseason inter-squad scrimmage?"

I stuttered and stumbled. There really wasn't an explanation other than these two words: SEC football (and, well, perhaps two others: Coach Saban). People think the SEC is about football. The SEC is really about people—the average fans who show up in droves every Saturday, driving across the city or cross-country to celebrate life through the game. You see, college football is a religion in the South and Saturdays are High Holy Days— even in April. One of the most important events on game day actually occurs before the coin toss—it's called the tailgate.

On my first trip to the Holy Grail of tailgating—The Grove in Oxford, Mississippi—I was shocked to see Mercedes and BMWs backing up and unloading fine china that the Rockefellers would have envied, along with an array of food like I'd never seen served on white tablecloths that seemed more Buckingham Place than Delta lawn party. The Rebel motto puts it all into perspective: "We may not win every game, but we've never lost a party."

Of course, every great party needs people, and nothing compares to SEC fans. After all, the league's official motto is quite simply: "It just means more." For many, Saturdays in the South are everything.

How else do you explain Dick Coffee, who recently died at 91, attending 781 consecutive Alabama games, starting in 1946, including four in Hawaii. His final game was in 2012 in Miami, where he watched Alabama beat Notre Dame for the national title.

Freeman Reese, another super fan, saw his streak come close but ultimately stop at 701 games. Reese and his wife, Betty, once missed his daughter's wedding to see Alabama play Tennessee. "We warned her," he said. But they did make it to the reception.

Like all SEC fans, I can't wait to see what the 14 schools will look like on the field this season. I'm equally anxious to see the competition before the game. Everyone tries to, and usually does, top their previous tailgate. There are certainly no losers in this competition—except in the pocketbook, where no expense is ever spared.

Paul Finebaum,
sports author, television and radio host, SEC football fanatic

PREGAME RITUALS

YOU'VE COUNTED DOWN ALL WEEK. FINALLY, IT'S SATURDAY, AND THAT MEANS FEASTING, FRIENDS AND FAMILY, AND OF COURSE, COLLEGE FOOTBALL. TO MAKE THE MOST OF THIS FAVORED DAY, A LITTLE PREP IS IN ORDER. HERE, YOU'LL FIND TIPS FOR GRILL READINESS, FOOD SAFETY, TAILGATE-PACKING PROWESS, AND EXUDING THE TRUE SPRIT OF THE SOUTH AS AN SEC TAILGATER.

FIRE IT UP!

A great lineup of grilled foods can transform your tailgate party from ho-hum to humdinger. Here's how to get fired up for the big game!

// KNOW THE RULES

Before you leave home, check the rules of the campus where you'll be tailgating. Most schools regulate where you can park, how early you can set up for tailgating, how late you can stay, where you can place a grill, and the types of fires you can build. A little research before game day goes a long way toward heading off problems.

// CHECK YOUR LIST

A pre-tailgate checklist will help ensure that you pack everything you need to properly set up and tear down your grill.

It's a good idea to keep a box of grilling essentials clean and ready to go. Fill a clear plastic container with an array of items such as long-handled tongs (one pair for placing raw items on the grill and another for removing cooked items), a long-handled spatula, grill brush, oven or grill mitts, meat thermometer, grill basket, and long matches for lighting the grill.

If you're using a charcoal grill, be sure to take plenty of water. You'll want to extinguish the coals before you go into the stadium to minimize the risk of fire. Pack a fire extinguisher in case of an emergency.

And be sure to clean up after yourself. It's the ultimate show of good sportsmanship! A generous stash of trash bags is essential for discarding paper plates, cups, and other refuse, but you will also want to bag up and discard the ashes from your grill after the game. Nobody wants to make the long drive home with an ash-filled grill rolling around in the back of the SUV.

// GRILL SETUP

Companies make a variety of portable grills these days, from propane to charcoal. While some serious grillmeisters swear by charcoal, you might not want to haul it to the game. Propane grills minimize the amount of cleanup required. Personal taste and ease of transport to the tailgate will dictate your choice.

Calculate your travel time, potential traffic delays, and the amount of time you need to set up and cook your grilled items. If you're grilling burgers you've prepared ahead of time, you won't need to arrive as early. If you're roasting a whole chicken or pork shoulder, you'll need to arrive well ahead of the crowd.

When setting up the grill, position it so that smoke blows away from your tailgate (and your neighbor's). If you're using a charcoal grill or have foods that need some extra time to cook, such as grilled ribs, get the grill started while you finish the rest of the unpacking and setting up. It's fun to play cornhole or toss around a football before you eat. Take a radio, a portable TV, or a tablet so you can monitor the pregame show while you cook.

// GET YOUR GRILL ON

Before you grill, preheat your grates to incinerate any remaining residue from the last cookout. Then brush the grates vigorously with a grill brush until they are free of any rust or food particles. Once they're clean, let the grates heat up for a few minutes. Then dip a paper towel in high-heat cooking oil and, using an oven mitt and tongs, swab the grates. Preheating and oiling the grates will help keep food from sticking and give you those handsome grill marks.

For gas grills, simply ignite the burners and preheat the grill to the temperature specified in the recipe.

If you're using charcoal briquettes, light the coals about 30 minutes before cooking. A chimney starter is indispensable for charcoal grilling. Stuff newspaper in the bottom, place charcoal in the top, and light the paper. Now wait until the coals catch fire.

When the coals turn ashy gray with a bright red center, bank them in the center of the kettle. Sear food in the middle, where heat is highest (direct-heat cooking), then move it to the outer edges of the grill (indirect-heat cooking) to finish cooking without burning.

A meat thermometer gives the best results for determining doneness. Remember, food continues to cook after it's removed from the heat. Remove your grilled items just before they reach the desired doneness and let them rest before serving.

FOOD SAFETY PLAYBOOK

Tailgate parties at home or on campus can last for hours, but this is no time to ignore the basic tenets of food safety. Follow these rules for maximum tailgate success.

- Don't let your food sit out for more than two hours. If it's above 90 degrees, reduce that time to one hour.

- Pack raw meat and poultry separately from vegetables and the side dishes you'll be serving without heating.

- Contaminated hands and prep areas can easily spread bacteria, and you likely won't have ready access to a sink and hot water. So pack disinfectant wipes and other products for cleaning your hands and wiping up messes.

- Keep hot food hot and keep cold food cold. Pack food in a well-insulated cooler with plenty of ice or ice packs to keep the temperature below 40°F. Transport the cooler in the back seat of your air-conditioned car instead of in your hot trunk, and keep your cooler closed tight. For hot food, keep and transport in a casserole carrier, slow cooker, or thermos.

- Remove from the cooler only the amount of raw meat, fish, or poultry that will fit on the grill at one time.

- Take food in the smallest quantity needed. Pack only the amount of food you think you'll eat. Consider taking along nonperishable foods and snacks that don't need to be refrigerated.

- Nestle platters and bowls filled with mayonnaise-based deviled eggs and potato salad into larger bowls filled with ice.

- When the tailgate is over, discard all perishable foods if there is no longer sufficient ice in the cooler or if ice packs are no longer frozen.

- Be sure that foods are fully cooked before you eat them. Use this chart to the right from the US Department of Agriculture, along with a meat thermometer, to determine if food is at a safe temperature to be eaten.

SAFE MINIMUM INTERNAL TEMPERATURE CHART

BEEF, PORK, VEAL & LAMB 145°F	**HAM, FRESH OR SMOKED** 145°F
GROUND MEATS 160°F	**ALL POULTRY** 165°F
FISH & SHELLFISH 145°F	**EGGS** 160°F
LEFTOVERS 165°F	**CASSEROLES** 165°F

TAILGATE ESSENTIALS

Smart tailgaters get to the party with all their food and equipment by crafting a well-thought-out checklist of things they'll need and then marking the items off as they pack their vehicles. Don't worry! The more you tailgate, the easier it gets. Here's a checklist to get you started.

✕ TAILGATING STAPLES ○

- ☐ Bungee Cords
- ☐ Chairs
- ☐ Coolers
- ☐ Extension Cords
- ☐ Extra Batteries
- ☐ Flashlights
- ☐ Folding Tables
- ☐ Freezer Packs or Ice
- ☐ Paper Towels
- ☐ Permanent Markers
- ☐ Sanitary Wipes
- ☐ Tailgate Games
- ☐ Tent
- ☐ Tickets
- ☐ Tool Kit
- ☐ Trash Bags

✕ FOR YOUR COMFORT ○

- ☐ Antacids
- ☐ Binoculars
- ☐ Blankets
- ☐ Bleacher Seat Cushion
- ☐ Bug Spray
- ☐ First Aid Kit
- ☐ Hats
- ☐ Jackets
- ☐ Rain Ponchos
- ☐ Sunglasses
- ☐ Sunscreen
- ☐ Umbrellas

✕ GREAT FOR GRILLERS ○

- ☐ Aluminum Foil
- ☐ Aluminum Pans
- ☐ Basting Brush
- ☐ Chimney Starter and Newspaper (for charcoal grilling)
- ☐ Cooking Oil/Grilling Spray
- ☐ Cutting Board
- ☐ Fire Extinguisher
- ☐ Fuel Source
- ☐ Grill Basket
- ☐ Grill Brush
- ☐ Grill Mitts
- ☐ Matches or Lighter
- ☐ Meat Thermometer
- ☐ Portable Grill
- ☐ Skewers
- ☐ Utensils
  - ☐ Carving Knife
  - ☐ Meat Fork
  - ☐ Spatula
  - ☐ Tongs
- ☐ Water

✕ MEALTIME NECESSITIES ○

- ☐ Bottle Opener
- ☐ Can Opener
- ☐ Condiments
- ☐ Cups
- ☐ Food Covers
- ☐ Freezer Bags
- ☐ Napkins
- ☐ Plastic Wrap
- ☐ Plates and Bowls
- ☐ Utensils (Forks, Knives, Spoons)

✕ ADVANCED TAILGATING ○

- ☐ All-Weather HD Television
- ☐ Cornhole Game with Team Logo
- ☐ Generator for Electricity
- ☐ Heavy-Duty Coolers
- ☐ Linens in Team Colors
- ☐ Melamine Plates and Serving Platters
- ☐ Monogrammed Chairs
- ☐ Outdoor Pizza Oven
- ☐ Personalized Cups
- ☐ Portable Heaters
- ☐ Portable Radio
- ☐ Portable Satellite Receiver
- ☐ Professional Grill or Smoker
- ☐ RV with Attached Tent
- ☐ Tent Chandelier
- ☐ Wireless Speakers

TEN COMMANDMENTS OF TAILGATING

In the South, it's often said that college football is religion and every fall Saturday is sanctified. Whether you're attending the game or watching at home, following these rules of engagement will guarantee your game-day fun.

I. THOU SHALT ARRIVE HUNGRY AND LEAVE WITH BELLY FULL.

Tailgate parties—no matter where they occur—are eating extravaganzas. No one should leave craving more.

II. THOU SHALT NOT ATTEND A TAILGATE EMPTY-HANDED.

Ask what you can bring or simply pack your favorite nosh. If you don't cook or it's inconvenient to transport food, ask if you can contribute drinks or paper products. If nothing else, bring an inexpensive team-themed gift.

III. THOU SHALT BREAK BREAD WITH FRIENDS AND FOES ALIKE.

One admirable Ole Miss tailgater bases her game-day menu on the traditions and culture of the opposing team of the day.

IV. THOU SHALT LEARN EVERY SINGLE WORD OF THY SCHOOL'S FIGHT SONG.

And be ready to sing it loudly on demand all day long come rain or shine. This separates the true fans from the wannabes.

V. WHERESOE'ER THOU DOST TAILGATE, THOU SHALT OBEY THE RULES.

Nothing ruins a party faster than being booted from campus—or hauled to the hoosegow—for violating school policy. Know the rules and keep 'em.

VI. THOU SHALT REMEMBER THY MANNERS.

You're modeling behavior for the next generation of fans. Don't blow it.

VII. THOU SHALT NOT BE A FAIR-WEATHER FAN.

It's impolite to boo the opposing team, but it is incredibly bad form to boo your own team. Notable exception: when a team member's name rhymes with boo.

VIII. THOU SHALT WATCH THE GAME, NOT THY MOBILE DEVICE.

It's fun to see what your friends are posting, but wait until after the game or during breaks in the action. Be in the moment!

IX. THOU SHALT NOT ENGAGE IN BEHAVIOR THOU WOULDST NOT WANT TO GO VIRAL.

Nobody wants to be the meme of the week. As a rule, if it would disgrace the football legends of yore, don't.

X. THOU SHALT REMEMBER THE REAL REASON FOR TAILGATING: MAKING MEMORIES.

Enjoy the journey as much as the destination. College football is just a game. The world will go on if your team loses.

OPENING DRIVE

WHEN KICKOFF OCCURS BEFORE NOON, A SPECIAL GAME-DAY MENU IS IN ORDER, ONE THAT AWAKENS THE SOUTH'S LEGENDARY FOOTBALL FERVOR AND FUELS FANS FOR THE LONG DAY AHEAD. THE CHICKEN AND WAFFLES, CASSEROLES, SWEET ROLLS, AND MORE INCLUDED HERE DO JUST THAT. AND DON'T THINK THESE DISHES ARE ONLY FOR THE MORNING; BREAKFAST AND BRUNCH FOODS SHOULD BE EATEN ALL DAY.

HOUNDSTOOTH HEAVEN

Crimson. White. These are the colors that stir the blood of an Alabama fan. Disrespect them? You might as well wave a red flag at a bull.

But there is an unofficial "third color" associated with the Alabama football program—which is not actually a color at all. It's an ancient Scottish checked pattern favored by sleuths and hunters. The story of how houndstooth check has come to symbolize one of the greatest football programs on the planet is the stuff of legends.

In 1964, while courting favor with coveted Alabama senior quarterback Joe Namath, flamboyant Jets owner Sonny Werblin gifted Coach Paul "Bear" Bryant with a houndstooth fedora. When the coach sported his new chapeau at a game, delighted Crimson Tide fans took note. Soon Bryant had a hoard of hats, and the Bama faithful had a brand-new tradition. Since then, many have referred to the pattern as Alabama Houndstooth.

Today, houndstooth remains a symbol of greatness, both team and individual. Since 1892, when The University of Alabama first fielded a team, the school has claimed 17 national titles. Six of those championships came during the Bear's 25-year tenure, from 1958 to 1982.

Bryant's original hats are on display at a Tuscaloosa museum that bears his name. You'll even find in the exhibit hall a houndstooth hat crafted of Waterford crystal that was commissioned by a local jeweler to pay homage to the iconic fixture.

But you don't have to go to a museum to see a houndstooth fedora in Tuscaloosa. You'll still find them very much in fashion at Bryant-Denny Stadium, worn by students, alumni, and other Bama lovers, especially on the many days when the Crimson Tide is commanding the gridiron.

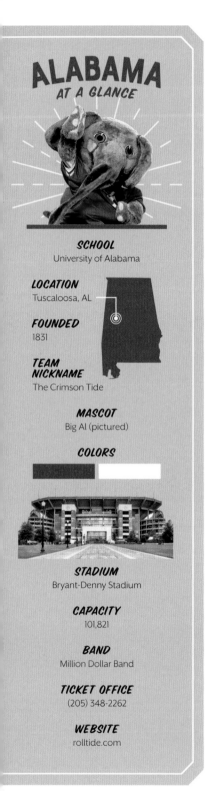

ALABAMA
AT A GLANCE

SCHOOL
University of Alabama

LOCATION
Tuscaloosa, AL

FOUNDED
1831

TEAM NICKNAME
The Crimson Tide

MASCOT
Big Al (pictured)

COLORS

STADIUM
Bryant-Denny Stadium

CAPACITY
101,821

BAND
Million Dollar Band

TICKET OFFICE
(205) 348-2262

WEBSITE
rolltide.com

// TITLE TOWN

They stride with purpose—these modern-day warriors—as they make their way toward Bryant-Denny Stadium on the Tuscaloosa campus of The University of Alabama. Each and every player here today is aware that he walks in the shadow of greatness.

Two hours and 15 minutes before each home game, large motor coaches slide to a stop on University Boulevard to let members of the Crimson Tide football team disembark. From here, they venture through a gauntlet of cheering fans along the redbrick Walk of Champions to the stadium's north end zone.

Embedded in the bricks are granite monuments that bear the name of every player who suited up for one of the school's first 16 national championship teams. Not yet included are the names of the players for Alabama's 17th national championship team, who secured a hard-won victory over the Georgia Bulldogs in Atlanta on January 8, 2018. There are markers for the SEC champs, and the winning coaches are here, too. Wallace Wade, Frank Thomas, Paul "Bear" Bryant, Gene Stallings, and Nick Saban are bronzed gods in this neighborhood.

Closer to the stadium stands a statue featuring two anonymous football players—one wearing the No. 18 jersey, the other No. 92. These numbers represent the beginning of football on campus in 1892. The older player points the way for the rookie, who, in turn, plants his flag at Bryant-Denny.

// DIXIELAND DELIGHT

Alabama's football stadium holds an astronomical number of seats—101,821, to be exact. And the university fills them for every game. If they had more seats, they'd fill those, too.

Ask Tide fans why they love to attend games here, and they'll put it to you straight. "Winning," says one alum. "Fans at other SEC schools go into a game hoping to win. At Alabama, we go into every game expecting to win. That's what sets us apart from other schools."

These words are more than just hubris. Over the years, Alabama has won more than 80 percent of its games at Bryant-Denny Stadium. Paul Bryant's record at the stadium that bears his name is 72-2.

// BAMA'S PLUCK AND GRIT

For every fan who comes to see Bama play, there are more who come just for the tailgating. The Quad, the green space at the heart of campus, is ground zero for game-day parties. Those not lucky enough to score a spot on the Quad stroll through to enjoy the atmosphere.

When the school opened in 1831, Tuscaloosa was the capital of Alabama, but it was still just an untamed outpost on the western frontier of a brand-new state. Pioneers carved this rectangle out of the wilderness and built a school around it. Bama's winning gridiron traditions were born right here.

Still, only four of the school's original buildings remain around the Quad today. The rest were burned by Yankees just a few days before the South's surrender at Appomattox, a parting insult to the many Alabama cadets who had served as Confederate officers. The remains of those early buildings lie beneath the Quad—buried, but not forgotten.

The picture-perfect Denny Chimes, named for a former university president, anchors the south side of the Quad. On game day, fans gather here to walk in the footsteps of their heroes.

Since 1948, the captains of the football teams have stopped by during the spring A-Day Game celebrations and placed handprints and footprints in the cement slabs at the base of the chimes. Lee Roy Jordan, Joe Namath, Ozzie Newsome, Cornelius Bennett, Shaun Alexander, Dont'a Hightower, and Derrick Henry are among the more than 175 of the best to play the game that have left their mark on this Walk of Fame.

// YEA, ALABAMA!

Wherever fans gather, there are many only-at-Alabama traditions. The team's nickname is the Crimson Tide, but the mascot is an elephant. Confusing? "Nah," fans say. Both are traditions instigated by sportswriters and are apropos for a school this dominant.

Before they were the Crimson Tide, Alabama's nickname was Thin Red Line. But the 1907 team changed that when they played a heavily favored Auburn team to a muddy 6-6 tie in the pouring rain. The surging defense resembled "a crimson tide" in "a sea of mud."

The team's prodigious size and stature caused a reporter to liken them to a herd of elephants. These days, the gray-costumed elephant Big Al bounces to the beat with the Bama cheerleaders.

Before the game, fans gather on the steps of the Gorgas Library for the famous Elephant Stomp. In old-school pep-rally style, Alabama's Million Dollar Band whips the faithful into a frenzy with plumes bobbing, horns blowing, and the drum line a-rat-a-tat-tatting. Inside the stadium, the revelry continues—until Bear Bryant begins his speech. Sure, he's been gone a long time, but a previously recorded pep talk from the legendary coach, broadcast before the team runs onto the field, drives the crowd wild.

For Bama fans, this is heaven on earth. As the Bear once said: "If you want to walk the heavenly streets of gold, you gotta know the password, 'Roll, Tide, Roll.'"

ROLL TIDE

FUN FACT
Until 1915, before moving to Denny Field and, subsequently, to Bryant-Denny Stadium, the Alabama football team played their games on the Quad.

CHOOSE A TABLE COVER WITH THE CRIMSON TIDE LOGO. FOR FLOWERS, MIX CRIMSON ROSES AND WHITE BERRIES.

CRIMSON-AND-WHITE PATTERNED DISHES WILL POP. HOUNDSTOOTH ACCENTS SUCH AS NAPKINS ARE A MUST.

ROLL TIDE

ROLL TIDE

ABAM

A

IMSON T

ALABAMA
CRIMSON TIDE

𝒜

Rammer Jammer
Coffee Punch
P. 70

Fried Chicken,
Green Tomato,
and Waffles with
Sriracha Syrup
P. 25

Cheese Grits and
Greens Casserole
P. 26

Sweet Crimson
Roll Tide Rolls
P. 41

SERVES 8

ADORN WITH MINI FOOTBALL
HELMETS. CREATE NAPKIN
RINGS WITH SMALL, PAINTED
WOODEN LOGOS AND STRING.

ROLL
TIDE

FRIED CHICKEN, GREEN TOMATO, *AND* WAFFLES *WITH* SRIRACHA SYRUP

SERVES **8** // HANDS-ON **30 MINUTES** // TOTAL **2 HOURS, INCLUDES 1½ HOURS CHILLING**

This *Southern Living* Test Kitchen favorite is worthy to be eaten on SEC campus grounds, where some of college football's most legendary figures have walked. A maple-sriracha syrup coats crunchy, spicy chicken while the fried green tomatoes add pleasing tang. The Belgian waffle is the perfect vehicle for the rich toppings.

2 cups whole buttermilk

2 teaspoons paprika

1 teaspoon kosher salt

½ teaspoon cayenne pepper

½ teaspoon black pepper

8 (3-ounce) chicken cutlets

4 large green tomatoes, cut into ⅜-inch slices

8 thick-cut bacon slices, cut into 1-inch pieces

2 cups crushed cornflakes cereal

2 cups panko (Japanese-style breadcrumbs)

¼ cup cornstarch

4 to 5 cups peanut oil

8 frozen Belgian waffles (such as Van's)

2 cups pure maple syrup

2 tablespoons sriracha chili sauce

EXTRA **POINT**

Assemble this dish at your tailgate site after prepping everything at home. If you have a way to fry at the site, you can even do that step on location.

1   Stir together the buttermilk, paprika, salt, cayenne, and black pepper in a large bowl. Divide the mixture between 2 medium bowls. Place the chicken cutlets in one of the bowls, and place the sliced tomatoes in the other bowl. Chill both 1 hour.

2   Cook the bacon pieces in a large skillet over medium-high, stirring occasionally, until crispy and golden brown, about 6 to 8 minutes. Transfer the bacon pieces to a plate lined with paper towels, and set aside.

3   Combine the crushed cornflakes, panko, and cornstarch in a wide shallow bowl; stir to blend. Remove the tomato slices from the buttermilk mixture, allowing the excess buttermilk to drain from the slices; dip each slice in the cornflake mixture, pressing to adhere. Repeat the process with the chicken, placing the coated items on a baking sheet lined with parchment paper. Discard the buttermilk mixture from both bowls. Chill the coated chicken and tomatoes 30 minutes.

4   Heat the oil in a deep Dutch oven over medium-high to 350°F. Fry the tomato slices and chicken cutlets, in batches, until the tomatoes are crispy and golden and the chicken is cooked through, about 4 to 5 minutes. Place on a baking sheet lined with paper towels; cover and keep warm.

5   Prepare the waffles according to the package directions. To assemble, top each waffle with 1 chicken cutlet and 2 fried green tomato slices; sprinkle with some of the bacon pieces.

6   Heat the maple syrup and sriracha in a small saucepan over medium, stirring to blend the flavors. Drizzle over each waffle stack just before serving.

CHEESE GRITS *AND* GREENS CASSEROLE

SERVES **8** // HANDS-ON **40 MINUTES** // TOTAL **1 HOUR, 10 MINUTES**

Balancing two classic Alabama foods—creamy, cheesy grits and savory, salted collard greens that take on heat from the red pepper—this dish is a terrific brunch accompaniment. Bake the casserole right before heading to your tailgate, and transport it in a casserole carrier to keep it warm.

2 tablespoons olive oil

1 cup finely chopped thick-cut bacon slices (about 5 slices)

1 small yellow onion, chopped (about 4 ounces)

3 garlic cloves, chopped

2 tablespoons light brown sugar

1 teaspoon crushed red pepper

1 (1-pound) package prewashed collard greens, stems removed, leaves coarsely chopped

7 cups chicken stock

1 cup heavy cream

1 cup half-and-half

2 teaspoons kosher salt

2 cups uncooked regular grits (not quick-cooking or coarse stone-ground)

¼ cup chopped fresh flat-leaf parsley

6 ounces Parmesan cheese, shredded (about 1½ cups)

6 ounces Monterey Jack cheese, shredded (about 1½ cups)

Hot sauce (optional)

1 Heat the oil in a large Dutch oven over medium-high. Add the chopped bacon, and cook until lightly browned, 6 to 7 minutes. Add the onion, stirring often, until softened and aromatic, about 5 minutes. Add the garlic, brown sugar, and crushed red pepper, and cook until the bacon is well cooked, but not crispy, about 2 minutes. Add the greens in batches, stirring until wilted. Stir in 1 cup of the chicken stock, and cover. Reduce the heat to medium, and cook, stirring occasionally, until the greens are slightly tender and wilted, about 8 minutes. Cover and keep warm over low until ready to use.

2 Preheat the oven to 350°F. Combine the cream, half-and-half, salt, and remaining 6 cups chicken stock in a large saucepan; bring to a boil over high, and whisk in the grits. Reduce the heat to medium, and cook, whisking often, until the grits are tender, 15 to 20 minutes. Stir in the parsley and 1 cup each of the Parmesan and Monterey Jack. Remove from the heat.

3 Using a slotted spoon, remove the greens from the Dutch oven, and stir into the grits. Transfer to a lightly greased 13- x 9-inch baking dish, and sprinkle with the remaining ½ cup each Parmesan and Monterey Jack. Bake at 350°F until golden brown and bubbly, about 30 minutes. Serve with the hot sauce, if desired.

MINI POTATO *AND* ONION FRITTATAS

MAKES **12 MINI FRITTATAS** // HANDS-ON **30 MINUTES** // TOTAL **45 MINUTES**

If you've been invited to someone's tailgate and are now wondering, "What should I bring?" these mini muffin frittatas are the answer. They can be made a day or two in advance and stored in an airtight container in the refrigerator.

2 tablespoons salted butter
4 tablespoons olive oil
1 large yellow onion, thinly sliced vertically (about 2 cups)
1 teaspoon kosher salt
½ teaspoon black pepper
8 ounces frozen shredded hash browns, thawed
½ cup chopped fresh chives
12 large eggs, lightly beaten

1 Preheat the oven to 350°F. Grease a standard 12-cup muffin pan with the butter, about ½ teaspoon per muffin cup, and set aside.

2 Heat 2 tablespoons of the olive oil in a large nonstick skillet over medium-high. Add the onion, salt, and pepper; cook, stirring often, 1 minute. Reduce the heat to medium-low, and cook, stirring often, until the onions are tender and caramelized, 12 to 15 minutes. Transfer to a large bowl.

3 While the onions cook, squeeze the thawed hash browns between paper towels to remove as much water as possible; set aside. Heat the remaining 2 tablespoons oil in the skillet over medium-high. Add the hash browns and cook, stirring often, until tender and starting to brown, 6 to 8 minutes. Remove from the heat.

4 Add the hash browns and chives to the bowl with the onions, and stir to combine. Let stand about 5 minutes to cool slightly. Add the beaten eggs to the hash brown mixture, and stir to incorporate.

5 Spoon the frittata mixture into the prepared muffin pan. Bake at 350°F until the eggs are set, 12 to 15 minutes. Serve hot or at room temperature.

TENT TALK

Which matchup is billed as the South's oldest college football rivalry?

A. Auburn v. Georgia
B. Alabama v. Tennessee
C. Alabama v. Auburn
D. Georgia v. Georgia Tech

BREAKFAST ENCHILADAS

SERVES **6** // HANDS-ON **20 MINUTES** // TOTAL **1 HOUR**

Remove the eggs from the stove-top while they're still a bit wet; they'll finish cooking in the oven. After baking, transport the dish to your tailgate site in a casserole carrier to keep warm, and bring the toppings in individual plastic containers. Set up a toppings bar where guests can serve themselves.

2 tablespoons unsalted butter
¾ cup chopped red bell pepper
½ cup chopped sweet onion (about 3 ounces)
12 large eggs
½ teaspoon table salt
¼ teaspoon black pepper
2 tablespoons water
1 (16-ounce) jar salsa verde
12 (6-inch) flour tortillas
10 ounces colby Jack cheese, shredded (about 2½ cups)
2 tablespoons chopped fresh cilantro

CHEESE SAUCE

¼ cup (2 ounces) salted butter
¼ cup (about 1 ounce) all-purpose flour
2 cups milk
6 ounces colby Jack cheese, shredded (about 1½ cups)
1 (4.5-ounce) can chopped green chiles
½ teaspoon table salt

TOPPINGS

Halved grape tomatoes, chopped fresh cilantro, chopped avocado (optional)

EXTRA POINT

To make this a day ahead, go through Step 3; cover and chill the casserole. Let stand at room temperature about 20 minutes before baking.

1   Preheat the oven to 350°F. Melt the 2 tablespoons unsalted butter in a large nonstick skillet over medium. Add the bell pepper and onion; sauté until tender, 4 to 5 minutes. Stir together the eggs, ½ teaspoon salt, ¼ teaspoon pepper, and water in a medium bowl. Add the egg mixture to the bell pepper mixture, and cook, without stirring, until the eggs begin to set on the bottom, about 1 to 2 minutes. Draw a spatula across the pan to form large curds. Cook, stirring occasionally, until the eggs are thickened, about 6 to 7 minutes. (Do not overstir.)

2   Make the Cheese Sauce: Melt the ¼ cup salted butter in a heavy saucepan over medium-low; whisk in the flour until smooth. Cook, whisking constantly, 1 minute. Increase the heat to medium. Gradually whisk in the milk; cook, whisking constantly, until thickened, 5 minutes. Remove from the heat, and whisk in the 1½ cups cheese, chiles, and ½ teaspoon salt.

3   Spread 2 tablespoons of the salsa verde in the center of each tortilla. Spoon about ¼ cup of the egg mixture over the salsa; sprinkle each with 2 tablespoons of the cheese and ½ teaspoon of the cilantro. Roll up; place, seam side down, in a lightly greased 13- x 9-inch baking dish. Add the Cheese Sauce and the remaining 1 cup cheese.

4   Bake at 350°F until the sauce is bubbly, 30 minutes. Serve with the desired toppings.

RAZORBACK BREAKFAST CASSEROLE

SERVES 10 // HANDS-ON 30 MINUTES // TOTAL 1 HOUR, 30 MINUTES

TENT TALK

Where is the
Southeastern
Conference
headquartered?

A. Birmingham, Alabama
B. Atlanta, Georgia
C. Nashville, Tennessee
D. Jackson, Mississippi

Here's a delicious new spin on a breakfast casserole sure to energize you for a full day of stadium-side fanfare. The hash browns give the dish substance while the pork sausage—a nod to the Arkansas razorback—adds a spicy kick and smoky flavor. You can make this dish the night before and bake it right before serving. Substitute halved cherry tomatoes for the diced vine-ripe pink variety, if desired.

1 (30-ounce) package frozen shredded hash browns
2 teaspoons vegetable oil
1 cup finely chopped sweet onion (about 5 ounces)
1 cup diced green bell pepper (about 5 ounces)
3 garlic cloves, minced (about 1 tablespoon)
1½ teaspoons kosher salt
1½ teaspoons black pepper
1 pound spicy pork sausage, casings removed
4 ounces sharp Cheddar cheese, shredded (about 1 cup)
10 large eggs
1 cup whole milk
3 vine-ripe pink tomatoes, diced (about 1½ cups)
2 tablespoons chopped fresh cilantro

1 Prepare the hash browns according to the package directions. Preheat the oven to 350°F.

2 Heat the oil in a large nonstick skillet over medium-high. Add the onion and bell pepper, and cook, stirring often, until tender, 4 to 5 minutes. Add the garlic, and cook, stirring constantly, just until softened, about 1 minute. Stir in ½ teaspoon each of the salt and pepper. Transfer the mixture to a large bowl.

3 Cook the sausage in the skillet over medium-high, stirring until crumbled, lightly browned, and no longer pink, 5 to 7 minutes.

4 Stir together the hash browns, onion mixture, sausage, and cheese. Pour into a lightly greased 13- x 9-inch baking dish.

5 Whisk together the eggs, milk, and ½ teaspoon each of the salt and pepper. Pour over the hash brown mixture. Bake at 350°F until the edges are golden and the center is just set, 50 minutes to 1 hour.

6 Toss together the diced tomato, cilantro, and remaining ½ teaspoon each salt and pepper. Sprinkle over the casserole before serving.

FUN FACT

Sooie is derived from Suidae, the Latin word for animals in the pig family. "Wooo Pig Sooie!" is the equivalent of calling, "Here! Piggy, piggy!"

WOOO! PIG! SOOIE!

If you're looking for Babe or Wilbur, you've come to the wrong place. The University of Arkansas is the home of the Razorbacks. Intelligent. Aggressive. Fierce. With razor-sharp tusks, bone-crushing jaws, and thick barrel-like bodies, wild hogs thrive in almost any condition. They roll, dig, and wallow, and they'll charge when cornered. Without question, a feral razorback is one of the most destructive forces in nature.

This is the unholy beast Coach Hugo Bezdek was imagining when he said his undefeated 1909 team was as tough as "a wild band of razorback hogs." And this is the ill-tempered creature fans summon when they "Call the Hogs" at Donald W. Reynolds Razorback Stadium in Fayetteville on a football Saturday.

"Wooo Pig Sooie!" Both arms go up, fingers wiggling on "wooo." Arms come down on "pig," and a fist pumps the air on "sooie." After the third call, fans shout the word "Razorbacks."

Before the band enters the stadium, before the team runs through the A, before anything happens on game day, fans call the hogs. When the team needs a rally and spirits are flagging, they call the hogs. When Lady Luck smiles and the game is in hand, they call the hogs.

It's hard to describe and hard to imagine, unless you've witnessed the spectacle or learned it at your papa's knee. The sound is eerie, a battle cry designed to chill the blood of opponents and fire the passions of the Razorback faithful.

Sure, it takes some serious chutzpah to embrace a mascot as homely as a hog. But to that, Arkansas fans simply say, "Wooo Pig Sooie! Razorbacks!"

// A IS FOR ARKANSAS

A ripple of excitement surges through the crowd at Donald W. Reynolds Razorback Stadium in Fayetteville as the final notes of the University of Arkansas alma mater hang in the air.

Without missing a beat, band members scramble into a new formation. Fans cheer wildly when a giant A locks into place. Playing their signature "Arkansas Fight," the Best in Sight and Sound Band marches the length of the football field, bringing the top of the A to a rest at the back of the end zone nearest the Razorback locker room.

"This is the most exciting part of the day!" yells one fan, clapping as the band launches into the William Tell Overture.

Smoke soon billows from the end zone, and the announcer whips the crowd into a frenzy. "Let's welcome to the field your Arkansas Raz-z-z-z-zorbacks!" With that, the team bursts onto the field and runs through the A.

// GIVE A CHEER! RAH! RAH!

No matter their opponent, Razorbacks fans get an A for school pride. Few schools in the country have embraced their mascot as thoroughly as Arkansas.

True fans own and wear Hog Hats, red plastic headgear fashioned in the shape of a running Razorback. Wherever Arkansas graduates go in the world, they find like-minded alums—in San Francisco, graduates ham it up with the Hogs in the Fog. Other alumni chapters have their own porcine names.

The university has a small herd of mascots on the sideline. In addition to Tusk, a live Russian boar, there's a costumed boar named Big Red and his female sidekick Sue E. Pig. Pint-sized fans favor the kid-friendly Pork Chop, plus there's Boss Hog in his 9-foot inflatable suit. Fans find Ribby hanging out around the baseball diamond in the spring.

Game-day festivities focus on food, and pork is always on the menu in the

LETS CALL THOSE HOGS!

FUN FACT

Before they were the Razorbacks, Arkansas was known as the Cardinals. Ties not fully severed, cardinal red remains one of the university's official colors.

form of ribs, pulled pork, Boston butt, and sausage. Anything wrapped in bacon is welcome. Those looking to work off some calories may stop by the Janelle Y. Hembree Alumni House, where fans can ride Buckingham, the bucking mechanical hog, upon reservation.

// HOG HEAVEN

The University of Arkansas is cradled in the folds of the Ozark Mountains on what was once a hilltop farm. From the beginning, founders praised the area's natural beauty, graceful oaks, and commanding views. The clock towers of Old Main, the oldest building on campus, can be seen for miles.

A carillon atop Old Main chimes the hours from 8 a.m. to 8 p.m. and plays the university's alma mater at 5 p.m. But until recent years, students couldn't look at the clock to tell the time. Funds ran low during its construction in 1875 and there was no money to buy a clock. A faux face was painted on the tower, where it remained until 2005, when a clock was finally installed.

Old Main anchors the University of Arkansas Historic District, which encompasses the 25 buildings that once formed the campus core and an

arboretum containing every one of the state's native species. It's also the beginning of the famous Senior Walk. Every Arkansas graduate's name is etched into the endless slabs of concrete, a length that now stretches more than five miles. It's not unusual to find alumni and their families staring at the ground on game days.

// HOGS ON THE FIELD

While many people have had a hand in shaping Arkansas' flagship university, few have had more impact than Frank Broyles. His tenure, first as coach, then as athletic director, stretched nearly 50 years. While he's credited with building the Razorbacks football program into a national powerhouse, he's also acknowledged as a stalwart supporter of the school's academic ideals.

From 1958 to 1976, Broyles coached the Hogs to seven Southwest Conference championships, 10 bowl games, and a record of 144-58-5. His 1964 team, considered the best in school history, was undefeated and untied. These boys also brought home Arkansas' only national championship.

Though Broyles stepped away from his duties as coach in 1976, he continued as athletic director until his retirement in 2007. The school's athletic programs won 43 national titles, 57 Southwest Conference championships and 47 Southeastern Conference championships under his leadership. And many outside the Arkansas family remember Broyles as the color commentator who worked alongside legendary ABC sportscaster Keith Jackson from 1977 to 1985.

A statue of Broyles sits outside Donald W. Reynolds Razorback Stadium, and the playing field bears his name. When Broyles passed away in August 2017 at age 92, the celebration of his life was held in the nearby Bud Walton Arena. At the end of the service, former players, coaches, family, and dignitaries called the Hogs.

Frank Broyles calls the Hogs with fans at the dedication of his statue at Donald W. Reynolds Razorback Stadium in 2012.

ARKANSAS
AT A GLANCE

SCHOOL
University of Arkansas

LOCATION
Fayetteville, AR

FOUNDED
1871

TEAM NICKNAME
Razorbacks

MASCOTS
Tusk, Big Red (pictured), Sue E. Pig, Boss Hog, Ribby, and Pork Chop

COLORS

STADIUM
Donald W. Reynolds Razorback Stadium

CAPACITY
76,000

BAND
Razorback Marching Band, Best in Sight and Sound

TICKET OFFICE
(800) 982-4647 or (479) 575-5151

WEBSITE
arkansasrazorbacks.com

USE A PLASTIC HOG-SHAPED HAT AS A CENTERPIECE. UP THE HOG-LOVING HYSTERIA WITH RAZORBACK BALLOONS.

BUTCHER PAPER MAKES A CLASSIC, SIMPLE TABLECLOTH, AND MAKES FOR EASY CLEANUP—JUST TRASH IT.

ARKANSAS
RAZORBACKS

Arkancider-
Honeybee
Grape Cider
P. 69

Razorback
Breakfast Casserole
P. 30

Ham-and-Cheddar
Pinwheels
P. 38

Mini Biscuits with
Chocolate Gravy
P. 38

SERVES 10

LEATHER FOOTBALL-
SHAPED COASTERS ARE
CHIC AND PRACTICAL
TABLE ACCESSORIES.

A CHECKERED TABLE RUNNER
IS A STATEMENT. HOG CHARMS
EMBELLISH NAPKINS AND
DOUBLE AS TAKE-HOME GIFTS.

WOOO
PIG SOOIE!

HAM-AND-CHEDDAR PINWHEELS

MAKES 12 PINWHEELS // **HANDS-ON 10 MINUTES** // **TOTAL 35 MINUTES**

The spicy-sweet mustard spread and smoky ham are sinfully delicious.

TENT TALK

On what yard line is the ball placed for a kickoff in both college and professional football?

A. 20-yard line
B. 25-yard line
C. 30-yard line
D. 35-yard line

1 (8-ounce) can refrigerated crescent dough sheet (such as Pillsbury)
2 tablespoons Dijon mustard
1 tablespoon honey
1 teaspoon hot sauce (such as Tabasco)
1 teaspoon black pepper

8 ounces smoked ham, thinly sliced (about 12 slices)
6 ounces sharp Cheddar cheese, thinly sliced (10 to 12 slices)
2 tablespoons salted butter, melted

1 Preheat the oven to 375°F. Roll the crescent dough sheet into a 16- x 12-inch rectangle on a lightly floured surface.

2 Whisk together the Dijon, honey, hot sauce, and pepper; spread the mustard mixture on the dough sheet. Top with the ham and cheese.

3 Roll up the dough rectangle from 1 short side; press the seam to seal. Cut the roll into 12 (1-inch-thick) slices. Place 1 slice into each greased cup of a 12-cup muffin pan. Drizzle the melted butter evenly over the top of each slice.

4 Bake at 375°F until golden brown, 20 to 25 minutes. Cool in the pan on a wire rack 5 minutes. Remove the pinwheels to the wire rack. Serve warm, or cool completely.

MINI BISCUITS *WITH* CHOCOLATE GRAVY

SERVES 12 // **HANDS-ON 30 MINUTES** // **TOTAL 45 MINUTES**

You've heard of biscuits and gravy, but biscuits and chocolate gravy is an Arkansas original that you don't want to miss. Don't forget to bring forks!

EXTRA POINT

Be sure to flour your hands and the biscuit cutter well. If you don't have a cutter, a small vessel such as a shot glass will work fine.

BISCUITS
2 cups (about 8 ounces) self-rising flour
½ cup (4 ounces) cold salted butter, cut into small cubes
1 cup whole buttermilk
3 tablespoons heavy cream

CHOCOLATE GRAVY
¾ cup granulated sugar
¼ cup unsweetened cocoa
2 tablespoons all-purpose flour
½ teaspoon kosher salt
1½ cups whole milk
1 teaspoon vanilla extract
¼ cup (2 ounces) unsalted butter

1 Make the Biscuits: Preheat the oven to 450°F. Place the flour in a large bowl. Cut in the cold butter using a pastry blender or 2 forks until crumbly. Using a wooden spoon, add the buttermilk, stirring until combined. Turn the dough out onto a well-floured surface, and gently press (do not roll) with floured hands to ¾-inch thickness. Cut with a 1½-inch round cutter, and place, with the sides touching, on a parchment paper-lined baking sheet.

2 Brush with the heavy cream, and bake at 450°F until golden, 8 to 9 minutes. Transfer the biscuits to a wire rack to cool.

3 Make the Chocolate Gravy: Whisk together the sugar, cocoa, flour, and salt in a medium saucepan. Gradually add the milk and vanilla, whisking until smooth. Bring to a boil over medium-high; cook, whisking constantly, until thickened, about 1 minute. Remove from the heat, and whisk in the butter until melted. Serve over the biscuits.

SWEET CRIMSON ROLL TIDE ROLLS

MAKES **8 ROLLS** // HANDS-ON **55 MINUTES** // TOTAL **4 HOURS, 30 MINUTES**

Even opponents will say "Roll Tide!" to these amazingly jammy breakfast rolls.

ROLLS

¼ cup warm water (105°F to 115°F)
1 package (2¼ teaspoons) active dry yeast
½ cup (about 2⅛ ounces) cake flour
⅓ cup granulated sugar
¼ cup whole milk
1 teaspoon table salt
1 teaspoon vanilla extract
2 large eggs, lightly beaten
2¼ cups (about 9⅝ ounces) bread flour
½ cup (4 ounces) unsalted butter, softened

FILLING

1 cup fresh or frozen, thawed blackberries
2 cups seedless raspberry preserves (from 2 [10-ounce] jars)
10 tablespoons (5 ounces) unsalted butter, softened
1 tablespoon cornstarch
1 tablespoon water
¼ cup granulated sugar

ICING

1 cup (about 4 ounces) powdered sugar
4 teaspoons whole milk
¼ teaspoon vanilla extract

EXTRA POINT

The dough at the end of Step 1 will be super tender and a bit sticky. Don't worry. That's what you want in order for each bite to melt in your mouth.

1   Make the Rolls: Combine the warm water and yeast in the bowl of a stand mixer. Let stand until the yeast is foamy, about 5 minutes. Add the cake flour, granulated sugar, milk, salt, vanilla, and eggs; beat on low speed with the paddle attachment until almost smooth, about 5 minutes. Gradually add the bread flour, and beat until the dough comes together, about 1 minute. Change to the dough hook attachment, and knead on medium speed until the dough is smooth and elastic, 13 to 15 minutes.

2   Add 6 tablespoons of the butter, 1 tablespoon at a time, beating until combined after each addition. Use 1 tablespoon of the butter to grease a large bowl; place the dough in the bowl, turning to grease the top. Cover with plastic wrap, and let rise in a warm place (80°F to 85°F), free from drafts, until doubled in size, about 1 hour and 30 minutes.

3   Deflate the dough by folding it over on itself twice. Cover and let stand in a warm place for 30 minutes.

4   Butter a 13- x 9-inch baking pan with the remaining 1 tablespoon butter, and set aside.

5   Make the Filling: Combine the blackberries, 1 cup of the preserves, and 4 tablespoons of the butter in a small saucepan over medium-high. Bring to a boil, and stir, lightly pressing on the blackberries to release their juices. Cook, stirring often, until the mixture thickens slightly, about 4 minutes. Stir together the cornstarch and water in a small bowl, and gradually pour into the saucepan, stirring constantly, until the mixture thickens, about 1 minute. Pour the mixture onto a rimmed baking sheet. Let cool to room temperature, about 15 minutes.

6   Stir together the granulated sugar, remaining 1 cup preserves, and 6 tablespoons of the butter in a bowl. Spread in the bottom of the prepared baking pan.

7   Using a rolling pin, roll the dough into a 16- x 12-inch rectangle on a floured surface. Spread the cooled blackberry mixture on the surface of the dough, and roll up the dough from 1 long side. Cut the dough crosswise into 8 even pieces. Place the rolls, cut side down, in the baking pan, spacing evenly. Cover with plastic wrap, and place in a warm place (80°F to 85°F) to rise until the rolls have doubled in size, about 1 hour.

8   Preheat the oven to 350°F. Bake in the preheated oven until the rolls are browned and the syrup is bubbly, about 30 minutes. Let cool 5 minutes, and then invert the baking pan onto a platter or plate lined with parchment to catch the syrup.

9   Make the Icing: Whisk together all the ingredients in a bowl; drizzle over the hot rolls.

OUR FAVORITE BUTTERMILK BISCUIT

MAKES **12 TO 14** // HANDS-ON **25 MINUTES** // TOTAL **50 MINUTES**

According to our Test Kitchen, these are the best buttermilk biscuits ever.

½ cup (4 ounces) salted butter, frozen
2½ cups (10 ounces) self-rising flour

1 cup chilled buttermilk
2 tablespoons salted butter, melted

1 Preheat the oven to 475°F. Grate the frozen butter using the large holes of a box grater. Toss together the grated butter and flour in a medium bowl. Chill 10 minutes.
2 Make a well in the center of the mixture. Add the buttermilk, and stir 15 times. (The dough will be sticky.)
3 Turn the dough out onto a lightly floured surface. Lightly sprinkle flour over the top of the dough. Using a lightly floured rolling pin, roll the dough into a ¾-inch-thick rectangle (about 9 x 5 inches). Fold the dough in half so the short ends meet. Repeat the rolling and folding process 4 more times.
4 Roll the dough to ½-inch thickness. Cut with a 2½-inch floured round cutter, reshaping the scraps and flouring as needed.
5 Place the dough rounds on a parchment paper-lined jelly-roll pan. Bake at 475°F until lightly browned, 15 minutes. Brush with the melted butter.

CRANBERRY-APPLE BREAKFAST CRUMBLE ▶

MAKES **10 CUPS** // HANDS-ON **15 MINUTES** // TOTAL **1 HOUR, 5 MINUTES**

EXTRA POINT

This also makes a yummy dessert! Serve with a scoop of vanilla ice cream, or top with a dollop of whipped cream, if you'd like.

This sweet, satisfying crumble couldn't be easier to throw together.

FILLING
3½ to 4 cups peeled and chopped Honeycrisp or Granny Smith apples (about 2 large)
1½ cups fresh or frozen, thawed cranberries
½ cup packed light brown sugar
½ cup granulated sugar
2 tablespoons all-purpose flour
1 teaspoon lemon zest plus 2 teaspoons fresh juice (from 1 lemon)
1 teaspoon vanilla extract
¼ teaspoon kosher salt

TOPPING
1½ cups uncooked old-fashioned regular rolled oats
½ cup chopped pecans
½ cup packed light brown sugar
½ cup (about 2⅛ ounces) all-purpose flour
1 teaspoon ground cinnamon
½ teaspoon kosher salt
½ cup (4 ounces) unsalted butter, melted

1 Make the Filling: Preheat the oven to 350°F. Stir together the apples, cranberries, sugars, flour, zest, juice, vanilla, and salt in a large bowl. Spoon the mixture into a greased 2-quart oval baking dish.
2 Make the Topping: Combine the oats, pecans, brown sugar, flour, cinnamon, and salt in a medium bowl. Drizzle the melted butter over the oats mixture. Using your fingertips, mix until crumbly.
3 Sprinkle the oat mixture over the fruit mixture, and bake at 350°F until golden and bubbly, 50 minutes to 1 hour.

SNICKERDOODLE DOUGHNUT HOLE MUFFINS

MAKES **2 DOZEN** // HANDS-ON **25 MINUTES** // TOTAL **55 MINUTES**

These little muffins are dangerously good, combining the spice of snickerdoodles and the richness of doughnuts. They're easy to transport and the perfect size for tailgaters to grab on the go.

TENT
TALK

True or False: In the NFL, jersey numbers correspond to certain positions. There is no such rule in the college game.

MUFFINS
½ cup sour cream
¼ cup vegetable oil
1 large egg, at room temperature
1 teaspoon vanilla extract
½ cup granulated sugar
1 cup (about 4 ounces) all-purpose flour
½ teaspoon baking soda
¼ teaspoon kosher salt
½ teaspoon ground cinnamon
¼ teaspoon freshly grated nutmeg

COATING
½ cup (4 ounces) salted butter, melted
1 cup granulated sugar
1½ teaspoons ground cinnamon
½ teaspoon freshly grated nutmeg

1 Make the Muffins: Preheat the oven to 350°F. Lightly grease a 24-cup miniature muffin pan with cooking spray. Stir together the sour cream, oil, egg, vanilla, and ½ cup sugar in a small bowl. Whisk together the flour, baking soda, salt, ½ teaspoon cinnamon, and ¼ teaspoon nutmeg in a medium bowl. Whisk the sour cream mixture into the flour mixture. (The batter will be very thick.) Spoon 1 tablespoon of the batter into each prepared muffin cup, keeping the batter rounded on top.

2 Bake at 350°F until golden and springy when touched lightly on top, 10 to 12 minutes. Cool in the pan 5 minutes. Remove from the pan to a wire rack; cool completely, about 15 minutes.

3 Meanwhile, make the Coating: Place the melted butter in a small bowl. Whisk together 1 cup sugar, 1½ teaspoons cinnamon, and ½ teaspoon nutmeg in another small bowl.

4 Dip 1 muffin in the butter; immediately dredge in the sugar mixture, and place on a serving platter. Repeat with the remaining muffins, butter, and sugar mixture.

BANANAS FOSTER COFFEE CAKE
WITH VANILLA SAUCE

SERVES **8 TO 10** // HANDS-ON **20 MINUTES** // TOTAL **1 HOUR, 15 MINUTES**

This rum-less riff on the classic sweet breakfast cake, with its crunchy pecan–cinnamon–brown sugar topping and warm, creamy glaze, will be the rave at your next tailgate.

1½ cups mashed ripe bananas
2½ cups heavy cream
2 cups packed brown sugar
1½ cups (12 ounces) butter, softened
2 teaspoons vanilla extract
1 (8-ounce) package cream cheese, softened
2 large eggs

3¼ cups plus 3 tablespoons all-purpose flour
⅝ teaspoon table salt
½ teaspoon baking powder
½ teaspoon baking soda
1½ cups chopped pecans
1 teaspoon ground cinnamon
1 cup granulated sugar

EXTRA
POINT

To make ahead, bake the coffee cake and make the sauce a day in advance. Cool both, and cover. Chill the sauce, and reheat it just before serving.

1 Preheat the oven to 350°F. Cook the bananas, ¼ cup of the cream, ½ cup of the brown sugar, and ¼ cup of the butter in a skillet until the mixture is bubbly. Cool; stir in 1 teaspoon of the vanilla.

2 Beat the cream cheese and ½ cup of the butter at medium speed with an electric mixer until creamy. Add 1 cup of the brown sugar; beat until fluffy. Beat in the eggs 1 at a time.

3 Stir together 3 cups of the flour, ½ teaspoon of the salt, baking powder, and baking soda; add to the cream cheese mixture. Beat at low speed to blend. Stir in the banana mixture. Spoon into a greased and floured 13- x 9-inch baking pan.

4 Combine the pecans, cinnamon, remaining ½ cup brown sugar, and ¼ cup of the flour. Melt ¼ cup of the butter; stir into the pecan mixture. Sprinkle over the batter. Bake at 350°F until a wooden pick inserted in the center comes out clean, about 45 minutes. Cool in the pan on a wire rack 10 minutes.

5 Combine the granulated sugar, remaining 3 tablespoons flour, and remaining ⅛ teaspoon salt in a saucepan over medium. Add the remaining 2 cups of the cream and the remaining ½ cup butter; bring to a boil. Boil, whisking constantly, until slightly thickened, about 2 minutes. Remove from the heat; stir in the remaining ¼ cup cream and 1 teaspoon vanilla. Drizzle the glaze over the cake.

LIBATIONS

A STEAMING MUG OF SOMETHING SWEET AND HOT, AN ICE-COLD COOLER TOPPED WITH CITRUS—BEVERAGES CAN BE THE REAL GAME CHANGER ON DAYS SPENT BY THE STADIUM. WITH FRUITY WASSAIL, CLASSIC HOT COCOA, LEMONY-GINGER PUNCH, SWEET TEA SPIN-OFFS, AND MORE, THERE'S A RECIPE HERE YOU'LL RAISE YOUR GLASS TO IN FOOTBALL SEASON AND BEYOND.

WAR EAGLE!

It's hello. It's goodbye. It's "Give 'em hell!"
and "We're in this together!" It's definitely one
of the best traditions in college sports. And it's
definitely not the school's official mascot...

An Auburn fan's tendency to shout "War Eagle" at every opportunity has caused more than a little confusion over the years. Opposing teams, and even a few uninformed sportscasters, have mistakenly assumed that the school's mascot is a bald or golden eagle.

Not so! Auburn's official mascot for every sport, men's and women's, is the tiger. War Eagle—or War Damn Eagle—is the school's battle cry.

There are lots of stories about how this tradition took hold, most of them untrue. What's safe to say is that these words are etched on the heart of every Auburn fan.

An eagle majestically flies over Jordan-Hare Stadium to thunderous cheers below before home games, circling the stadium before landing at midfield. The bells in the tower at Samford Hall play the school's fight song, "War Eagle," every day at noon. When the game is on the line, the faithful chant, "Warrrrrrrrrr . . . Eagle!"

Utter the phrase to an Auburn fan anywhere in the world, and you'll form an instant bond.

"For me, living far away from my home state, it means connection," says a wistful Texas-based Auburn alum. "On the rare occasion when I meet someone wearing an AU shirt, I know that this person knows something of Auburn and its orange and blue sunsets, of Foy Union and Hey Day, of the Tiger traditions."

"When I," she says with a smile, "meet this person's eyes and say, 'War Eagle!' we're transported for a second to the prettiest little town on the Plains."

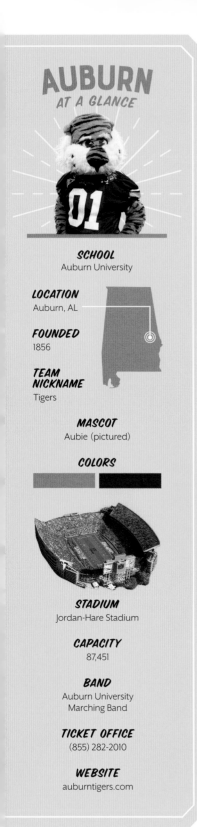

AUBURN
AT A GLANCE

SCHOOL
Auburn University

LOCATION
Auburn, AL

FOUNDED
1856

TEAM NICKNAME
Tigers

MASCOT
Aubie (pictured)

COLORS

STADIUM
Jordan-Hare Stadium

CAPACITY
87,451

BAND
Auburn University
Marching Band

TICKET OFFICE
(855) 282-2010

WEBSITE
auburntigers.com

// LOVELIEST VILLAGE OF THE PLAIN

As the sun sinks low on the horizon, the green in front of Auburn's historic Samford Hall fills with people. Some exercise their canine companions, others gather for study groups or an early picnic dinner.

"Isn't it beautiful?" asks Mary Witte Crump, surveying the park before turning to toss a stick for her energetic English Lab, Cabela.

"I didn't come here my freshman year," the Auburn senior confesses. "I was supposed to be the 33rd person in my family to attend Auburn, but I wanted something different."

The Huntsville native attended another SEC school for a year. But when her grandfather became ill, he asked a favor. "He said, 'Try it for me. Just one year, that's all I ask.'" She smiles as she remembers. "I fell in love with Auburn. I think it's one of the prettiest places on earth."

// 'NEATH THE SUN-KISSED SKY

Sweet Auburn—it's poetry to students, fans, and residents.

There was a time when this Alabama town was considered so remote and inaccessible that opposing teams refused to play here. But that was then. The town and the school that share a name have grown up together.

The two Auburns merge at the intersection of College Street and Magnolia Avenue. Known as Toomer's Corner, it's named for former State Senator Sheldon Toomer, the businessman who founded Toomer's Drugs in 1896. Though it no longer claims a functioning pharmacy, guests can still order sandwiches, banana splits, and hand-squeezed lemonade from the soda fountain and lunch counter.

Boutiques, eateries, and bookstores line College Street and cater to the student population. The town salutes the school's greatest with a downtown Tiger Trail—more than 100 granite plaques

bearing the names of athletes, coaches, and administrators embedded in the sidewalks of downtown Auburn.

// EYE OF THE TIGER

From College Street and Samford Hall, the campus fans out across the fertile plains. At its heart sits Auburn's Jordan-Hare Stadium, a soaring structure carrying the names of those who helped build the school's football program into a powerhouse.

When it was dedicated in 1939, the structure was simply Auburn Stadium. In 1949, it was renamed in honor of Cliff Hare, a member of Auburn's first football team who went on to serve as dean of the School of Chemistry and the first president of the Southern Athletic Conference (which would later become the SEC).

The name Jordan (pronounced JURD-en) was added to the stadium in 1973 to honor coach Ralph "Shug" Jordan. The move was unprecedented, as Auburn became the first to name a stadium for a man still coaching. In his 25 seasons at Auburn, from 1951 to 1975, Jordan amassed a record of 176-83-6, and his undefeated 1957 team brought home a national championship.

// WAR DAMN EAGLE

Another name on the football complex was added in 2005. The field itself bears the name of legendary Auburn coach and athletic director Pat Dye, who holds a record of 99-39-4 from 1981-1992. The official name of the school's facility: Pat Dye Field at Jordan-Hare Stadium.

Crowds converge on the stadium two-and-a-half hours before game time for the often imitated but never duplicated Tiger Walk, when players stroll from the Athletics Complex down Donahue Drive to Jordan-Hare amid a sea of orange and blue. These days, a fierce tiger statue stands guard at the redbrick Tiger Walk Plaza, which serves as the official entrance to Jordan-Hare. Ten murals gracing the east side of the stadium tell the story of Auburn's greatest players and teams and their triumphs.

Heisman Drive circles the stadium. It's a nod to both the trophy's namesake, John Heisman, who coached at Auburn from 1895 to 1899, and the school's three Heisman winners—Pat Sullivan, Bo Jackson, and Cam Newton.

// EVER TO CONQUER, NEVER TO YIELD

And every Auburn win brings Tiger fans back to Toomer's Corner. For years, they made it "snow toilet paper" as they rolled the live oak trees that flanked the entrance columns. Then the unthinkable happened. After a particularly bitter loss, a fan from a rival school announced on a radio call-in show that he'd poisoned the famous trees.

Efforts to save them failed, and the once-mighty live oaks have been felled. They were replaced with saplings, but a deliberately set fire damaged one of them so badly that they had to be replaced again in early 2017.

Ask fans if they're still angry, and most will shrug and look away. "It still hurts," admits one Auburn grad, "but it's better now that the new trees have been planted."

Even on a warm day, when the deep redbrick of Samford Hall glows in the afternoon light and Toomer's Corner is full of people, bits of toilet paper are still visible from the previous week's victory.

"Killing those trees didn't change who we are," the alum continues. "It didn't change our traditions. People still celebrate here. Like our creed says, 'I believe in Auburn and love it.' You can't kill that."

FUN FACT

Coach Ralph "Shug" Jordan's childhood nickname is derived from his love of the sweet sorghum syrup produced across the South and in his boyhood home of Selma, Alabama.

DISPLAY VASES OF THISTLES, GERBERA DAISIES, AND WHITE WILDFLOWERS FOR A TOUCH OF FESTIVE COLOR.

THOUGH SMALL, "TURF" COASTERS AND STRIPED STRAWS AND DISPOSABLE CUTLERY CREATE BIG IMPACT.

WinCraft Made in the U.S.A.

AUBURN
TIGERS

Watermelon-Mint Lemonade	Smoked War Eagle Wings with White Sauce	Sweet-Hot Potato Salad	Peach Cobbler Bread Pudding
P. 55	P. 148	P. 210	P. 235

SERVES 10

A BOLD PENNANT AND THICK ORANGE AND BLUE RIBBONS POP OFF A WHITE SURFACE FOR A SIGNATURE LOOK.

KENTUCKY LEMON-MINT PUNCH

SERVES 8 // HANDS-ON 15 MINUTES // TOTAL 15 MINUTES

Ale-8-One soda, or simply Ale-8 if you hail from the Bluegrass State, is a true Kentucky classic, created in Winchester, Kentucky, over 90 years ago. It tastes like ginger ale with a burst of citrus. If it's not available at a store near you, order it online or substitute ginger beer or ginger ale. Don't assemble this punch until ready to serve—transporting everything in a cooler to your tailgate site—so that it's fizzy and ice cold upon pouring.

2 lemons, thinly sliced
1 cup loosely packed mint leaves
2 pints lemon sorbet (such as Häagen-Dazs), softened

4 (12-ounce) bottles chilled ginger and citrus-flavored soft drink (such as Ale-8-One) (or 1½ quarts ginger ale or ginger beer)

Muddle 1 lemon slice and ½ cup of the mint leaves in a large pitcher until the juices release and the mint is fragrant. Add the sorbet and soft drink, stirring until the sorbet is melted and the mixture is combined. Discard the solids. Serve with the remaining lemon slices and mint leaves.

WATERMELON-MINT LEMONADE

SERVES 10 // HANDS-ON 10 MINUTES // TOTAL 1 HOUR, 25 MINUTES

Think Toomer's Lemonade but reimagined with a watermelon twist. War Eagle to that! For even easier prep, use prechopped watermelon; just remove the seeds before blending.

8 cups 2-inch-cubed seedless watermelon (from 1 [5-pound] watermelon)
1½ cups granulated sugar
1 bunch fresh mint

4 cups water
2 cups fresh lemon juice (from 12 to 14 lemons)
Garnishes: mint sprigs, lemon slices

1 Process the watermelon, in 2 batches, in a blender until smooth, about 30 seconds. Pour through a fine mesh strainer into a large pitcher to equal 5 cups juice; discard the solids.
2 Combine the sugar, mint, and 1 cup of the water in a saucepan, and cook over high, stirring until the sugar dissolves, about 5 minutes. Remove from the heat, and let stand 15 minutes. Discard the mint. Stir the mint simple syrup, lemon juice, and remaining 3 cups water into the watermelon juice in the pitcher. Refrigerate until chilled, about 1 hour. Serve over ice. Garnish, if desired.

TENT TALK

How many players must a team have on the line of scrimmage to avoid an illegal formation penalty?

A. 5
B. 6
C. 7
D. 11

SWEET TEA LEMONADE

SERVES **8** // HANDS-ON **20 MINUTES**
TOTAL **4 HOURS, 20 MINUTES, INCLUDES 4 HOURS CHILLING**

A mix of two classic warm-weather beverages, you'll crave this smooth sipper.

3 cups granulated sugar
10 cups water
1 lemon, sliced, plus more slices for garnish (optional)
4 large mint sprigs, plus more for garnish (optional)

8 black tea bags
1 cup fresh lemon juice (from about 4 large lemons)

1   Mix the sugar and 3 cups of the water in a saucepan, and bring to a boil over medium-low, stirring until the sugar dissolves. Turn off the heat; stir in the lemon slices and mint. Allow to cool, then pour through a fine wire-mesh strainer into a large pitcher; discard the lemon slices and mint.
2   Bring 4 cups of the water to a boil. Place the tea bags in a bowl; pour the water over the tea bags, and let steep 10 minutes. Remove and discard the bags. Let the tea cool.
3   In another bowl, mix the lemon juice with the remaining 3 cups water.
4   Add the tea and lemon juice mixture to the syrup in the pitcher. Cover and chill for at least 4 hours. Serve over ice; garnish with additional lemon slices and mint sprigs, if desired.

PEACH-ROSEMARY TEA ▶

SERVES **10** // HANDS-ON **30 MINUTES** // TOTAL **1 HOUR**

This drink was made with Gamecock and Georgia Bulldog fans in mind. Georgia is the "Peach State," and South Carolina harvests the most peaches in the South.

ROSEMARY SYRUP
1 cup granulated sugar
1 cup water
2 fresh rosemary sprigs

TEA
8 cups water
3 family-size black tea bags (such as Lipton)

3 cups ice cubes, plus more for serving
1 cup Rosemary Syrup
2 (11.5-ounce) cans peach nectar, chilled (such as Kern's)
3 cups frozen sliced peaches
Fresh rosemary sprigs

1   Make the Rosemary Syrup: Combine the sugar, 1 cup water, and 2 rosemary sprigs in a small saucepan; bring to a boil over medium, stirring often. Reduce the heat to medium-low, and simmer until the sugar dissolves, about 5 minutes. Remove from the heat, and cool to room temperature, about 30 minutes. Refrigerate in an airtight container up to 2 weeks.
2   Make the Tea: Bring the 8 cups water to a boil in a large stockpot. Remove from the heat, and add the tea bags. Let steep until the desired strength, about 5 minutes. Discard the tea bags. Stir in the ice cubes, Rosemary Syrup, peach nectar, and frozen peach slices. Serve over the additional ice, and garnish with the fresh rosemary sprigs.

SWEET PINK

SERVES 10 // HANDS-ON 5 MINUTES // TOTAL 40 MINUTES

Easy fall Saturdays and pink lemonade go together like placekickers and holders. All tailgate guests will love this tart pink lemonade mixed with tea and mint simple syrup. It can also be served over a scoop of vanilla ice cream for an ice-cream float—a sure score for any mini fans at your tent. Pink lemonade powder can be substituted for pink lemonade concentrate, if desired. This can be refrigerated for up to 3 days. Garnish with additional mint sprigs, if desired.

8 cups cold water
3 family-size tea bags
¼ cup granulated sugar
8 mint sprigs
1 (12-ounce) can frozen pink lemonade
**   concentrate, thawed**

1 medium lemon, sliced (about 4 ounces)
1 cup strawberries, hulled and halved
**   (about 7 ounces)**

1 Bring 4 cups of the cold water to a boil in a saucepan over medium-high. Add the tea bags; remove from the heat, and steep 5 minutes. Pour into a pitcher; discard the tea bags. Add 3 cups of the cold water. Cool completely, about 30 minutes.

2 Meanwhile, combine the sugar, 4 of the mint sprigs, and the remaining 1 cup cold water in the saucepan. Bring to a boil over medium-high, stirring until the sugar dissolves. Remove from the heat, and cool completely, about 20 minutes. Discard the mint.

3 Stir the mint syrup and pink lemonade concentrate into the tea in the pitcher. Add the lemon slices, strawberries, and remaining 4 mint sprigs. Serve over ice.

SWEET MAGNOLIA

SERVES 8 // HANDS-ON 10 MINUTES // TOTAL 10 MINUTES

This bright beverage has a floral hint from the strawberries, orange blossom water, and bitters, making it an ideal spritzer for The Grove at Ole Miss. It can be made in advance, but be sure to stir well before serving because the ingredients will separate. For a festive touch, use duct tape to make "football laces" on the sides of drinking cups or jars.

1 (10-ounce) package frozen strawberries
**   in syrup, thawed**
3 cups limeade

3 cups ginger ale
1 teaspoon orange blossom water
¼ teaspoon nonalcoholic bitters

Process the strawberries and 1 cup of the limeade in a blender until smooth; pour into a pitcher. Stir in the ginger ale, orange blossom water, bitters, and remaining 2 cups limeade. Serve over ice.

TENT TALK

How many schools made up the original list of founding SEC members?

A. 8
B. 10
C. 12
D. 13

DO THE GATOR CHOMP

Florida's famous Gator Chomp starts with arms extended straight forward, right hand over left. The palm of the left hand is up; the palm of the right is down. Now, spread your palms and then slap them together.

Chomp! Chomp! Chomp! ChompChompChomp!

Slow at first, then faster and faster. Add a menacing two-note musical motif, and the effect is complete.

Terrifying creatures, alligators are capable of swallowing their prey in a single bite. If dinner is too big to gulp whole, a gator will execute a death roll, keeping a tight grip on its prey and spinning until the meat shreds.

On game day, Ben Hill Griffin Stadium in Gainesville becomes The Swamp, infested with legions of hungry alligators. One chomping gator is enough to make the faint of heart swoon. Just imagine the feeling of thousands of chomping Gators trying to gobble you whole. It'll make you shiver.

The Gator Chomp was brought to Florida in 1981 by bandmates who noticed another SEC school's cheerleaders clapping their hands together while tubas played the theme from *Jaws*. At the next game, the duo coordinated with the band and cheerleaders, and the gesture became school tradition.

These days, Florida fans chomp before every kickoff and after big plays and every win. Gators often greet each other with the Chomp. Some famous Florida alums have even chomped on national television. It shows that no matter where they go, Florida's Gators are ready to take a bite out of the world.

rives us.

FUN FACT

Catholics who abstain from eating meat on Fridays during Lent may count alligator meat as fish, according to a 2010 ruling by the Archbishop of New Orleans.

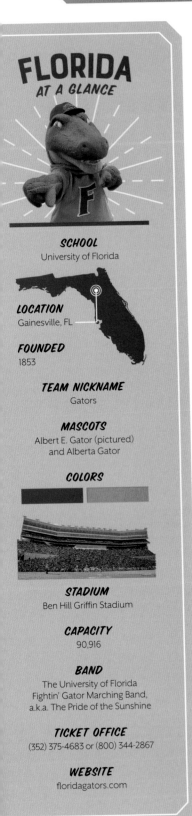

FLORIDA
AT A GLANCE

SCHOOL
University of Florida

LOCATION
Gainesville, FL

FOUNDED
1853

TEAM NICKNAME
Gators

MASCOTS
Albert E. Gator (pictured)
and Alberta Gator

COLORS

STADIUM
Ben Hill Griffin Stadium

CAPACITY
90,916

BAND
The University of Florida
Fightin' Gator Marching Band,
a.k.a. The Pride of the Sunshine

TICKET OFFICE
(352) 375-4683 or (800) 344-2867

WEBSITE
floridagators.com

// PRIDE OF OLD FLORIDA

A runner in orange and blue stretches before beginning her morning jog around the shadowy interior of Ben Hill Griffin Stadium in Gainesville, Florida. She joins dozens of other exercising Gators, many of whom run the stadium's steps or lap the mezzanine in pursuit of physical fitness.

On days like this, the stadium is quiet—an oasis where visitors find peace and solace in the workaday world. "Usually there's no one here but me and the joggers at this time of day," says a student worker at the stadium's apparel shop outside the south end zone.

But on game days, when it fills with more than 90,000 fans, Ben Hill Griffin Stadium becomes "The Swamp," one of the most intense and hostile environments in all of college football.

// DOWN WHERE THE GATORS PLAY

For many years, this was simply Florida Field. Then the university added the name of a generous citrus magnate—and in 2016, paid tribute to its most famous former quarterback and head football coach. Today, the facility's official name is Steve Spurrier-Florida Field at Ben Hill Griffin Stadium.

That's a mouthful, but no one calls it that. Even the walls say something different: "This is . . . The Swamp." It's painted right there on the corner of the south end zone. Spurrier himself named it that in '92.

"A swamp is where Gators live," he is quoted as saying. "We feel comfortable there, but we hope our opponents feel tentative. A swamp is hot and sticky and can be dangerous. We feel like it's an appropriate nickname for our stadium."

Even late into the fall, Gainesville can be blazing hot and miserably humid. The stadium itself sits in a sinkhole, erasing any hope of a breeze. The playing surface and first 32 rows of seats actually sit below ground level. Miserable? Sure—unless you're a Gator.

// REPTILE RHAPSODY

Not surprisingly, there are alligators all over campus. A menacing, life-sized Bull Gator lies in wait in front of The Swamp, a tribute to Florida's 2006 national championship team. Football players are often put on pedestals in these parts, and none more so than Florida's three Heisman winners. Tim Tebow ('07), Steve Spurrier ('66), and Danny Wuerffel ('96)—all winning Gator quarterbacks—stand memorialized in bronze on the western side of the stadium.

Albert E. Gator and his gal-pal Alberta pose hand-in-hand at the UF Gator Club Plaza in front of the Emerson Alumni Hall, their index fingers raised to declare their school No. 1.

Outside Heavener Hall, an 8-foot-tall, 6-foot-wide bronze statue features an alligator sitting on top of the world. Called Gator Ubiquity, it symbolizes the depth and breadth of the school's reach. As they say in these parts, the Gator Nation is everywhere.

To see actual alligators in the wild, one only has to head over to Lake Alice, a small freshwater lake in the midst of the rambling Gainesville campus. A boardwalk bridges the wetlands and circles the man-made body of water, where alligators often bask in the sun.

// WHERE PALM AND PINE ARE BLOWING

Though natural areas abound on Florida's campus, few places are more beautiful or more beloved than the Plaza of the Americas, the campus green at the historic heart of the campus. Landscape architect Frederick Law Olmsted, Jr., and his brother John Charles Olmsted drew the plans in 1925, and the oldest buildings here are listed on the National Register of Historic Places.

Today, this is a place to hang out, relax, and nap beneath live oaks that drip with Spanish moss. It's also one of the best spots to listen to the concerts that rain down from the Gothic-style

Century Tower, built to celebrate the 100th anniversary of the university and honor students who died in the two World Wars.

The bells mark the time for Florida students, chiming on the quarter hours from 8 a.m. to 8 p.m. and playing "Florida Chimes" on the hour. Each weekday during the academic year at 12:35 p.m. and 4:55 p.m., and often on Sundays, the school's carillonneurs climb the tower steps to play the bells, their repertoire ranging from Mozart to Metallica.

// ALL HAIL, FLORIDA

If you had to sum up Florida's attitude, though, it might be this: Work hard, play hard. After all, this is one of the country's top-ranked public universities.

You certainly don't become football champions over and over again without putting in the reps either. And if practice makes perfect, there's no wonder UF consistently makes the list of best party schools.

On game days, the areas surrounding Ben Hill Griffin Stadium are infested with tail-"gators." Tent cities go up on every patch of green and in every puddle of shade. And all those Gator statues? They're perfect spots for snapping selfies and Christmas card photos.

When the UF players arrive before the game, thousands gather to greet them—and the party moves inside the stadium. After chomping their way through three quarters of football, fans stand, lock arms, and sway in unison, singing "We Are the Boys of Old Florida." When the team wins—as they so often do—Gators fans slide out of The Swamp to take a bite out of the local party scene.

GO BOLD: USE A DEEP BLUE TABLECLOTH AND CONTRAST WITH BRIGHT ORANGE AND WHITE DISHES AND DETAILS.

HAND-PAINTED PADDLE FANS ADD CHEER AND OFFER TAILGATERS RELIEF FROM THE HEAT.

FLORIDA
GATORS

Cuban Black Bean Salsa with Avocado-Lime Dressing	Florida Citrus Seafood Chowder	Grilled Gator Kebab Banh Mi	Key Lime-White Chocolate Cookies
P. 88	P. 118	P. 184	P. 255

SERVES 8

SEW OR IRON ON
EMBROIDERED GATOR
PATCHES TO LINEN NAPKINS
FOR A SPECIAL TOUCH.

SPARKLING CHERRY LIMEADE

MAKES **ABOUT 8 CUPS** // HANDS-ON **10 MINUTES** // TOTAL **10 MINUTES**

Make a festive tailgate sipper by adding maraschino cherries and sparkling water to frozen limeade concentrate. The salted rims of the glasses add a special touch but can easily be left out to save time. This recipe can be doubled to serve a crowd. For a pretty presentation, serve it from a glass pitcher or glass beverage dispenser.

1 lime, cut into wedges (optional)
Margarita salt (optional)
1 (12-ounce) can frozen limeade
    concentrate, thawed
3½ cups cold water

½ cup liquid from jarred red maraschino
    cherries
2 cups sparkling water
Garnishes: lime slices, maraschino cherries

1   Rub the rims of 8 chilled glasses with the lime wedges, and dip the rims in the salt to coat, if desired.

2   Stir together the limeade concentrate and cold water in a pitcher; add the liquid from the maraschino cherries.

3   Fill the prepared glasses with ice. Pour the limeade mixture into the glasses, filling each two-thirds full; add the sparkling water to fill. Garnish with the lime slices and cherries, if desired.

NOTE: We tested with San Pellegrino Sparkling Natural Mineral Water.

RED GRAPEFRUIT PUNCH ▶

SERVES **10** // HANDS-ON **5 MINUTES** // TOTAL **5 MINUTES**

Cold and revitalizing, this is the drink you'll crave at a noon tailgate, especially one under the hot Texas sun. We call for Ruby Red grapefruit since it's the official state fruit of Texas. Place all the ingredients in the refrigerator for 24 hours (and keep chilled in a cooler) so this punch can be mixed and served immediately.

1 (59-ounce) bottle chilled grapefruit juice
    (such as Simply Grapefruit)
1 (25.3-ounce) bottle chilled sparkling
    blood orange fruit beverage (such as
    San Pellegrino)

2 (12-ounce) bottles chilled cream soda
1 (12-ounce) bottle chilled ginger ale
1 Ruby Red grapefruit, thinly sliced

Stir together the grapefruit juice, blood orange beverage, cream soda, and ginger ale in a large punch bowl or pitcher. Add the grapefruit slices. Serve chilled.

TENT TALK

A football playing field—the area between the two goals—is 100 yards long. How wide is it?

A. 50 yards
B. 50⅓ yards
C. 53 yards
D. 53⅓ yards

ARKANCIDER-HONEYBEE GRAPE CIDER

MAKES **16 CUPS** // HANDS-ON **5 MINUTES** // TOTAL **35 MINUTES**

This new take on mulled cider couldn't be better for a chilly game-day tailgate. The sweetness of the grape juice is rounded out by the spices and cut with the orange. It's fuel for Arkansas fans before they storm Donald W. Reynolds Razorback Stadium and "Call the Hogs."

8 cups water
4 regular-size orange pekoe tea bags
8 cups 100% grape juice
¼ cup honey
2 teaspoons whole black peppercorns

2 whole star anise
1 cinnamon stick
1 orange, quartered
Orange slices (optional)
Cinnamon sticks (optional)

1 Bring the water to a boil in a large saucepan over high. Remove the pan from the heat, and add the tea bags. Let steep 5 to 8 minutes. Discard the tea bags.
2 Stir in the grape juice, honey, peppercorns, star anise, cinnamon stick, and orange quarters; return the pan to the heat, and bring the mixture to a boil over medium-high. Reduce the heat to medium, and simmer 20 minutes.
3 Pour the mixture through a fine mesh strainer, discarding the solids. Serve the cider with the orange slices and cinnamon sticks, if desired.

EXTRA
POINT

This can be made a day ahead and reheated before serving. It also can be enjoyed cold. Swap out the spices and tea for other varieties, if desired.

PINEAPPLE-CRANBERRY WASSAIL

MAKES **5½ CUPS** // HANDS-ON **15 MINUTES** // TOTAL **25 MINUTES**

Wassail is a traditional mulled beverage best enjoyed during the fall and winter. This version with pineapple, orange juice, cranberries, and spices takes the trophy and has an aroma to match. Serve from a thermal carafe to keep it warm.

4 cups cubed fresh pineapple
1 cup fresh orange juice
1 cup fresh or frozen cranberries
½ cup packed light brown sugar
1 navel orange, sliced

2 (3-inch) cinnamon sticks, plus more for garnish
4 whole cloves
4 cups water
1 tablespoon fresh lemon juice

1 Bring the pineapple, orange juice, cranberries, brown sugar, orange slices, 2 cinnamon sticks, cloves, and water to a boil in a 4-quart saucepan over medium-high. Reduce the heat to medium-low, and simmer, stirring occasionally, 5 minutes.
2 Remove from the heat, and pour through a fine mesh strainer into a pitcher, discarding the solids. Stir in the lemon juice. Serve immediately; garnish individual servings with additional cinnamon sticks, if desired.

TENT *TALK*

True or False: A touchdown has always been worth 6 points.

RAMMER JAMMER COFFEE PUNCH

SERVES 8 // HANDS-ON **10 MINUTES** // TOTAL **10 MINUTES**

This rich and creamy cold-brew coffee punch is exactly what you need to get your game face on for a morning scrimmage at Alabama's Bryant-Denny Stadium—or, for that matter, anywhere. The coffee provides a solid caffeine kick that's softened by the sweet half-and-half and gelato. Serve from a punch bowl, or place a scoop of the gelato in individual cups and pour the punch on top.

¼ cup granulated sugar
¼ cup water
1 quart cold-brew black coffee concentrate (such as CoolBrew)
1 cup half-and-half
¼ teaspoon ground cinnamon, plus extra for garnish

1 pint vanilla bean gelato (such as Talenti)
1 pint double dark chocolate gelato (such as Talenti)
Whipped cream

1 Combine the sugar and water in a small microwavable bowl; microwave on HIGH until the sugar dissolves, about 45 seconds. Pour into a 2-quart punch bowl or container, and stir in the coffee, half-and-half, and cinnamon. Cover and chill until ready to serve.

2 Just before serving, add scoops of the gelato to the punch. Serve cups of the punch garnished with a dollop of the whipped cream and a sprinkle of the cinnamon.

HOT CHOCOLATE

MAKES **4½ CUPS** // HANDS-ON **15 MINUTES** // TOTAL **15 MINUTES**

Kids and adults alike adore hot chocolate. Serve it to tailgate guests to keep their hands warm on cold days. Like your hot cocoa extra rich? Increase the heavy cream to 3 cups, and decrease the milk to 1 cup. Serve with marshmallows for an extra-special touch.

2 cups milk
½ cup granulated sugar
½ cup unsweetened cocoa

Pinch of table salt
2 cups heavy cream
2 teaspoons vanilla extract

Mix the milk, sugar, cocoa, and salt in a saucepan, and bring to a low boil over medium, whisking often. Whisk in the cream, and cook, whisking often, until bubbles begin to form around the edges of the pan, 3 to 5 minutes. Remove from the heat, and stir in the vanilla. Serve immediately.

TENT TALK

True or False: In college football, the crew manning the first down measuring chain and the down indicator box are placed on the home side of the field.

SEC TEAM SPRITZERS

Toast your team in style with these festive beverages.
If you choose to make them—let's say—more spirited,
your secret's safe with us. Cheers!

CRIMSON TIDAL WAVE

Muddle ¼ cup blackberries, 2 lime wedges, and 1 Tbsp. raw sugar in a 10-oz. glass. Fill glass with crushed ice. Add ¼ cup cherry juice, and top with a splash of sparkling water or club soda. Stir gently; garnish with blackberries and a maraschino cherry, if desired.

ARKANSAS GRAPEBACK

Muddle ¼ cup raspberries, 3 mint leaves, and 2 Tbsp. simple syrup in a 10-oz. glass; stir in 2 Tbsp. fresh lime juice. Fill glass with crushed ice. Top with grape soft drink (such as Grapette); garnish with a twist of lime, Concord grapes, and mint leaves, if desired.

PLAINSMAN

Stir together ½ cup tomato juice; 1 Tbsp. pickle juice (preferably Wickles Pickles); 1 tsp. each Worcestershire sauce, fresh lemon juice, and prepared horseradish; and ¼ tsp. black pepper in a 10-oz. glass. Fill glass with crushed ice. Top with a splash of sparkling water or club soda; garnish with celery leaves, a cucumber spear, and a lemon slice, if desired.

═ SET UP A SPRITZER STATION ═

Equip tailgaters to make their own drinks. Designate a drink-making spot, and stock it with supplies guests will need, such as a muddler, jigger, cocktail shaker, glasses, toothpicks, and, of course, the ingredients. Use two coolers—one for crushed ice for the drinks and another for chilling ingredients that should be kept cool, such as soda, sparkling water, fruit, and herbs. Don't forget to display the recipe! Consider ordering coasters printed with the recipe from a source such as vistaprint.com. They will creatively convey the recipe and double as party favors.

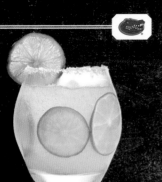

LIMEAID GATOR-AID

Salt rim of a 10-oz. glass with kosher salt, and fill glass with crushed ice. Add ½ cup limeade and 4 round lime slices. Top with ¼ cup coconut water; stir gently. Garnish with a lime slice, if desired.

BULLDOG BLITZ

Muddle ½ cup chopped peeled peaches, 3 basil leaves, and 1 Tbsp. raw sugar in a 10-oz. glass. Fill glass with crushed ice, and top with ½ cup ginger ale. Garnish with 3 small basil leaves and a peach slice, if desired.

BIG BLUE QUENCHER

Gently muddle ½ cup blueberries, 1 thyme sprig, and 2 Tbsp. simple syrup in a cocktail shaker. Add 2 Tbsp. fresh lemon juice and ½ cup crushed ice; shake vigorously for 10 seconds. Strain into a 10-oz. glass filled with crushed ice. Top with a splash of sparkling water or club soda; stir gently. Garnish with blueberries threaded onto a toothpick and a thyme sprig, if desired.

ROARIN' REBEL

Muddle 2 lemon wedges, 2 Tbsp. honey, and 1 tsp. balsamic vinegar in a 10-oz. glass. Fill glass with crushed ice, and top with ½ cup cherry soft drink; stir gently. Garnish with black cherries, if desired.

BIG SPUR SPLASH

Muddle ½ peeled peach, 4 sliced strawberries, and 2 Tbsp. simple syrup in a 10-oz. glass. Add crushed ice, and stir in ½ cup pineapple juice. Top with a splash of grapefruit juice. (Do not stir.) Garnish with strawberry slices and blackberries, if desired.

BIG ORANGE CRUSH

Muddle 2 orange slices, 1 lemon slice, and 1 Tbsp. raw sugar in a 10-oz. glass. Fill glass with crushed ice, and stir in ¼ cup each mango juice and orange juice. Top with a splash of sparkling water or club soda. Garnish with a cinnamon stick and an orange slice, if desired.

VICTORY GOLD

Muddle ¼ cup chopped pineapple,
¼ cup fresh raspberries, and 1 Tbsp.
raw sugar in the bottom of a 10-oz.
glass. Fill glass with crushed ice. Top
with ¼ cup grapefruit juice and ½ cup
lemonade. (Do not stir.) Add sparkling
water or club soda; garnish with
pineapple and raspberries, if desired.

COWBELL CREAMER

Line the rim of a chilled 12-oz. glass
with unsweetened cocoa; drizzle
1 Tbsp. chocolate syrup around the
inside of the glass. Add 1 cup whole
milk, 2 Tbsp. chocolate syrup, 1 Tbsp.
cold-brew coffee concentrate, and
½ tsp. ground cinnamon to a cocktail
shaker filled with ice. Shake vigorously
for 15 seconds, and strain into
prepared glass, being careful not to stir
in the chocolate sauce. Garnish with
1 Tbsp. chocolate shavings, if desired.

MIZZOU FIZZOU

Muddle 2 orange wedges in a 10-oz.
glass. Stir in 1 Tbsp. grenadine, and
fill glass with crushed ice. Top with
½ cup ginger ale, and stir gently.
Garnish with a lemon twist, if desired.

GIG 'EM COOLER

Muddle 4 mint leaves, 2 lime wedges,
and 1 Tbsp. raw sugar in a 10-oz. glass.
Fill glass with crushed ice, and stir
in ½ cup apple juice. Gently stir in
2 Tbsp. pomegranate juice, and top
with a splash of sparkling water or
club soda. Garnish with mint leaves
and a lime slice, if desired.

DYNAMITE TEA

Muddle 3 thin jalapeño chile slices,
2 lime wedges, 1 Tbsp. cilantro leaves,
2 Tbsp. simple syrup, and 1 Tbsp. fresh
lime juice in a 10-oz. glass. Fill the
glass with crushed ice, and top with
½ cup sweetened iced tea; stir gently.
Garnish with a pickled jalapeño chile
and a cilantro sprig, if desired.

DINK & DUNK

WHAT'S A TAILGATE WITHOUT SMALL BITES TO GRAZE ON? HAVE THESE DIPS, SALSAS, SNACK MIXES, AND MORE AT THE READY FOR TAILGATERS TO MUNCH ON BETWEEN PLAYS, AT HALFTIME, AND ANYTIME THEY NEED A PICK-ME-UP. WITH SWEET HEAT PIMIENTO CHEESE, LOADED POTATO SKINS, SUGAR-AND-SPICE CARAMEL POPCORN, AND OTHER NIBBLES, THERE'S SOMETHING HERE FOR ALL.

FUN FACT

Newspapers report that, prior to a bulldog, Georgia teams were accompanied by a billy goat dressed with black and red ribbons during the 1892 inaugural season.

DAMN GOOD DAWG

Tough. Tenacious. Testy. What Georgia's bulldog mascot lacks in stature, he makes up for with attitude. His characteristic underbite and droopy jowls give him a perpetual pout. He swaggers like a muscle-bound general as he patrols between the hedges. And then there's the name, Uga. It's a play on the abbreviation for the University of Georgia, but sounds like *Ugh-uh*!

The stocky mascot made his first appearance in 1956, when UGA alum Sonny Seiler attended a football game accompanied by the white English bulldog pup he and his new wife received as a wedding present. Today, few college mascots claim the fame that Georgia's top dog enjoys.

In 1982, Uga traveled to New York to witness running back Herschel Walker's Heisman Trophy triumph. He has appeared on the cover of *Sports Illustrated* magazine as the nation's No. 1 mascot. Both Uga and Seiler had cameos in the Clint Eastwood-directed movie *Midnight in the Garden of Good and Evil.*

Uga spends game days in an air-conditioned doghouse, lounging on bags of ice. And every player in the SEC knows it's best to let sleeping dogs lie. UGA fans still celebrate the day Uga tried to take a bite out of Auburn wide receiver Robert Baker during the '96 playing of the Deep South's Oldest Rivalry.

Only ten bulldogs have been privileged to carry the name Uga. Former mascots find their final resting place in a tomb at the southwest corner of Sanford Stadium. When an infrequent passing of the collar ceremony occurs, the retiring Uga receives the thanks of a grateful Dawg nation. "Damn good dog!" they shout.

GEORGIA
AT A GLANCE

SCHOOL
University of Georgia

LOCATION
Athens, GA

FOUNDED
1785

TEAM NICKNAME
Bulldogs

MASCOT
English bulldog named Uga

COLORS

STADIUM
Sanford Stadium

CAPACITY
92,746

BAND
Georgia Redcoat Marching Band

TICKET OFFICE
(877) 542-1231 or (706) 542-1231

WEBSITE
georgiadogs.com

// 'NEATH THE PINE TREE'S STATELY SHADOW

The chapel bell rings sharply, its sudden clang echoing across the campus at the University of Georgia in Athens. Passersby look on with interest as the small crowd gathered at the base of the tower sends up a joyful shout. After a few moments, the onlookers smile and move on, knowing a fellow Bulldog has claimed a triumph today.

For generations, the bell occupied a cupola atop the chapel and called students for religious services, signaled mealtimes, and announced emergencies. Safety and aesthetic concerns caused it to be dethroned and moved to a wooden trestle behind the building in 1913. Today, any member of the Georgia family may ring that bell.

"The Chapel bell is our victory bell," says one UGA senior. "We ring it for athletic victories and for personal victories. People will stand in line for hours to ring the bell after a big win on the football field. The first time I rang it, I waited until 1 o'clock in the morning to get a turn."

// HAIL TO GEORGIA

The chapel sits near the historic heart of North Campus, a few steps from the modest cast-iron arch that has marked the school's entrance since 1858. When first installed, the gateway and attached fence served a more plebian purpose—to keep cattle from grazing on campus. But even then, the Arch meant much more.

Founded in 1785, Georgia is the oldest state-chartered university in the nation and is widely considered the birthplace of public higher education. The UGA Arch is modeled after the one pictured on the Great Seal of Georgia, with three pillars representing the words of the state motto. These ideals—wisdom, justice, and moderation—are impressed upon students from their first day on campus.

Generations of UGA students have walked beneath the Arch—or not,

if they harken to tradition. Visit on a busy day, and you'll notice that many students studiously skirt the landmark, even during the rush to get to class. The reason?

Student Daniel H. Redfearn, Class of 1910, was so awed by the Arch and all it represented that he refused to walk under it, as a sign of respect. Students today still follow his lead and eschew passing beneath the hallowed Arch until they walk into the world, diploma in hand.

// HOW 'BOUT THEM DAWGS

From its official entrance at the Arch, the campus cascades across the rolling hills of the Georgia Piedmont, following the contours of the West Oconee River. Campus buildings old and new sit amid lush green lawns, hidden gardens, and magnificent old-growth trees.

The North Campus lawn has been part of the plan since 1801, when architects laid out Old College, the school's first permanent building. Few places on campus are more hallowed than Herty Field, the school's original gridiron, named for the chemistry professor who coached the first Georgia football team.

Thousands walk through, and linger in, the UGA Memorial Garden on their way to and from the Miller Learning Center. The Founders Memorial Garden, just off Lumpkin Street, honors the Athens ladies who founded the country's first garden club. Farther afield sit the Butts-Mehre Heritage Hall and Dooley Sculpture Garden, named for three of the school's most prolific coaches—Wally Butts, Harry Mehre, and Vince Dooley.

These blankets of green serve as the perfect place to set up a tailgate and celebrate the Dawgs. Sanford Stadium sits in the belly of a natural ravine, with the UGA campus hugging its very edges. Fans invade the campus quads on game days, though tailgating is forbidden before 7 a.m.

"Our leaders figured out a long time ago that students would rather stand around and visit with alumni than attend classes," says one undergraduate with a guilty smile.

// BETWEEN THE HEDGES

The greatest garden spot of them all—Sanford Stadium—grew from seeds of rivalry.

In the 1920s, Georgia's field could not accommodate large crowds, causing the Bulldogs to travel to Atlanta each year to play nemesis Georgia Tech. When the undefeated 1927 Dawgs team suffered a stinging loss to the Yellow Jackets, Dr. Steadman Vincent Sanford, longtime chairman of athletics, vowed to build a bigger stadium.

Sanford paid for the project by giving lifetime seats to boosters who cosigned the bank loan for the construction. When it opened in 1929, the playing field was completely surrounded by privet hedges. Many Georgia greats have donned silver britches and played their hearts out here, Heisman winners Frank Sinkwich and Herschel Walker among them.

NFL quarterback Fran Tarkenton, who played high school and college football in Athens, best sums up the feelings of the Bulldog Nation: "I have played in many stadiums, but to me there are only two special stadiums—Yankee Stadium in New York and Sanford Stadium in Athens—and there is no comparison between the two. There is no place in the world precisely like the grass that grows between the hedges in Athens, Georgia."

RED ANEMONES WITH THEIR BLACK EYES ARE A PERFECT FLORAL PICK FOR A TAILGATE AT SANFORD STADIUM.

A PLAID BLANKET OR LINEN— IN ONLY RED, BLACK, AND WHITE—SCREAMS UGA AND CREATES A COZY FALL FEEL.

GEORGIA
BULLDOGS

**Chicken and
Smoked Sausage
Brunswick Stew**
P. 122

**Cornmeal Biscuit-
Smoked Pork
Sandwiches with
Peach Jam**
P. 177

**Georgian
Cabbage Slaw**
P. 196

**Peanut Brittle
Puppy Chow**
P. 253

SERVES 10

USE PLANTERS OF ARTIFICIAL
GRASS IN HONOR OF THE
ICONIC HEDGES THAT LINE
THE DAWGS' HOME FIELD.

RALLY BEADS AND MINI
FOOTBALLS AND NAPKINS
EMBLAZONED WITH THE UGA
LOGO COMPLETE THE LOOK.

CRAB *AND* CORN DIP

SERVES **8** // HANDS-ON **10 MINUTES** // TOTAL **25 MINUTES**

Any creamy corn dip is a super-Southern classic, and this dip is no exception. The buttery, crunchy panko crust is the perfect complement to the sweet corn and crabmeat. You can also serve it with tortilla chips.

1½ (8-ounce) packages cream cheese, softened
½ cup sour cream
¼ cup mayonnaise
2 teaspoons Dijon mustard
1 teaspoon lemon zest plus 1 tablespoon fresh juice (from 1 lemon)
1 teaspoon kosher salt
½ teaspoon black pepper
1 pound fresh jumbo lump crabmeat, drained and picked over

1 cup fresh corn kernels (from 2 ears)
2 tablespoons chopped fresh chives, plus more for garnish (optional)
2 tablespoons chopped fresh flat-leaf parsley
1 tablespoon chopped fresh tarragon
1 cup panko (Japanese-style breadcrumbs)
¼ cup (2 ounces) unsalted butter, melted
Buttery crackers (such as Captain's Wafers)

1 Preheat the oven to 425°F. Stir together the cream cheese, sour cream, mayonnaise, Dijon, lemon zest and juice, salt, and pepper in a large bowl until combined. Fold the crabmeat, corn, chives, parsley, and tarragon into the cream cheese mixture; transfer to a 2-quart baking dish.

2 Stir together the panko and butter in a small bowl until coated, and sprinkle over the crab and corn dip. Bake at 425°F until bubbly and golden, about 15 minutes. Garnish with the additional chives, if desired. Serve with the crackers.

EXTRA POINT

Make the dip without the panko mixture up to a day in advance; store it, covered in plastic wrap, in the refrigerator, and top with the panko mixture before baking.

HOT BROWN FONDUE

MAKES **5 CUPS** // HANDS-ON **15 MINUTES** // TOTAL **15 MINUTES**

Making a game-day snack doesn't get easier than this savory 15-minute dip that can be made with leftover roasted turkey or chicken. Garnish with additional diced pimientos and scallions, if desired. (Pictured on page 2, bottom right)

2 tablespoons butter
2 tablespoons all-purpose flour
2 cups milk
¾ teaspoon paprika
¼ teaspoon table salt
8 ounces white American cheese, chopped (about 2 cups)

8 ounces Swiss cheese, shredded (about 2 cups)
1 (4-ounce) jar diced pimiento, drained
1 pound deli-roasted turkey, minced
6 bacon slices, cooked and crumbled
3 scallions, coarsely chopped
Toast points

1 Melt the butter in a medium saucepan over medium; whisk in the flour until smooth. Cook, whisking constantly, 1 minute. Gradually whisk in the milk; bring to a boil, whisking constantly.

2 Reduce the heat to low; whisk in the paprika and salt. Gradually add the cheeses, whisking until smooth after each addition. Remove from the heat; whisk in the pimiento, turkey, bacon, and scallions. Transfer to a fondue pot or slow cooker on WARM. Serve with the toast points.

TENT TALK

When the defense returns a blocked extra point or a failed two-point try, how many points is the team awarded?

A. 1 point
B. 2 points
C. 3 points
D. 6 points

SAUSAGE-CHEESE DIP

SERVES 10 // HANDS-ON 15 MINUTES // TOTAL 1 HOUR, 5 MINUTES

Conecuh is a hickory-smoked sausage produced in sweet home Alabama. You can sub andouille sausage for Conecuh, if desired, but if you're tailgating on The Plains at Auburn or at The Capstone at Alabama, we recommend sticking with Conecuh—when in Rome, y'all.

1 pound hickory-smoked sausage (such as Conecuh), chopped
½ cup thinly sliced scallions (about 6 scallions)
24 ounces processed cheese (such as Velveeta)

1 (10-ounce) can diced tomatoes and green chiles (such as Ro-Tel)
Corn chips (such as Fritos)

1 Cook the sausage in a skillet over medium-high, stirring often, until browned, 8 to 10 minutes. Add the scallions; cook, stirring often, until wilted, about 2 minutes. Drain the mixture.

2 Place the sausage mixture, processed cheese, and diced tomatoes and chiles in a slow cooker. Cover and cook on HIGH until the cheese is melted and bubbly, 45 to 50 minutes. Serve with the corn chips.

SLOPPY JOE DIP ▶

SERVES 12 // HANDS-ON 30 MINUTES // TOTAL 45 MINUTES

Sweet, meaty, and slightly saucy, this dip truly tastes like a sloppy Joe! You can skip Step 3, if desired, and instead place the dip in a slow cooker on the WARM setting at your tailgate site.

2 teaspoons vegetable oil
1½ pounds lean ground beef
½ cup chopped yellow onion (from 1 onion)
2 garlic cloves, minced (about 1 tablespoon)
1 (15-ounce) can fire-roasted diced tomatoes
¼ cup ketchup
2 tablespoons Dijon mustard

2 tablespoons dark brown sugar
2 tablespoons tomato paste
1 tablespoon Worcestershire sauce
1 tablespoon white vinegar
1 teaspoon paprika
1 teaspoon crushed red pepper
½ teaspoon kosher salt
1 (8-ounce) package pre-shredded Cheddar cheese (about 2 cups)
Corn chips (such as Fritos Scoops)

1 Heat the oil in a large skillet over medium-high. Add the beef, and cook, stirring often, until the meat crumbles and is no longer pink, 5 to 7 minutes. Add the onion and garlic, and cook until softened, about 3 minutes. Stir in the tomatoes, ketchup, Dijon, brown sugar, tomato paste, Worcestershire, vinegar, paprika, red pepper, and salt.

2 Reduce the heat to low, and simmer, stirring occasionally, until the sauce is slightly thickened, about 15 minutes. Stir in 1 cup of the shredded cheese.

3 Preheat the oven to 400°F. Transfer the mixture to a 2-quart baking dish. Sprinkle with the remaining 1 cup cheese, and bake at 400°F until the cheese is melted, about 15 minutes. Serve with the corn chips.

EXTRA POINT

The sloppy Joe sauce can be made up to 2 days in advance, chilled, and reheated. If you have any dip left over, it saves well and reheats easily.

SLOW-COOKER VIDALIA ONION DIP

MAKES **6 CUPS** // HANDS-ON **10 MINUTES** // TOTAL **6 HOURS, 30 MINUTES**

This Vidalia onion dip is a breeze to throw together and is comfort food for cold game days. The onions are caramelized overnight in the slow cooker before being mixed with the cheeses, which lets their sweet flavor come alive. Serve with kettle-cooked chips, pretzels, or crudités, or even spread on a sandwich for a creamy, oniony surprise. Garnish with additional chopped chives, if desired.

TENT TALK

Which school claims the most Super Bowl MVPs?

A. Alabama
B. Georgia
C. Florida
D. Texas A&M

8 cups chopped sweet onions (such as Vidalia) (about 4 large onions)
2 tablespoons apple cider vinegar
2 tablespoons unsalted butter
¾ teaspoon kosher salt
½ teaspoon black pepper
1 (8-ounce) package cream cheese, cut into cubes
4 ounces Gruyère cheese, shredded (about 1 cup)
4 ounces white Cheddar cheese, shredded (about 1 cup)
2 tablespoons finely chopped fresh chives

1   Combine the onions, vinegar, butter, salt, and pepper in a 3- to 4-quart slow cooker coated with cooking spray. Cover and cook on LOW until the onions are golden and soft, about 6 hours. Drain and discard the liquid from the onions; return to the slow cooker.
2   Stir in the cream cheese, Gruyère, Cheddar, and chives; cook, covered, on LOW until melted, stirring occasionally, about 20 minutes. Serve warm.

BROCCOLI SALAD DIP

MAKES **2½ CUPS** // HANDS-ON **20 MINUTES** // TOTAL **20 MINUTES**

Spin the classic salad into a crowd-pleasing dip, and pair it with everything from crudités to pretzel rods. Garnish with additional shredded Cheddar for prettiest presentation, if desired. (Pictured on page 2, top left)

½ pound fresh broccoli
6 ounces cream cheese, softened
⅔ cup plain low-fat Greek yogurt
¼ cup apple cider vinegar
2 teaspoons granulated sugar
¼ teaspoon kosher salt
4 thick-cut bacon slices, cooked and chopped
½ cup coarsely chopped cashews
2 ounces sharp Cheddar cheese, shredded (about ½ cup)
⅓ cup minced red onion

1   Remove and discard the large leaves and tough ends of the stalks from the broccoli. Peel and coarsely chop the stems; coarsely chop the florets.
2   Process the cream cheese, Greek yogurt, apple cider vinegar, sugar, and salt in a food processor until smooth. Add the broccoli; pulse 12 to 15 times or until finely chopped. Fold the bacon, cashews, cheese, and red onion into the cream cheese mixture. Serve immediately, or chill up to 3 days.

CUBAN BLACK BEAN SALSA
WITH AVOCADO-LIME DRESSING

SERVES 8 // HANDS-ON 25 MINUTES // TOTAL 25 MINUTES

EXTRA
POINT

The longer this salsa sits, the better the flavor. It's also a delicious next-day addition to salads or topping for grilled chicken or meats.

This salsa is loaded with bright flavors from the bell pepper, grape tomatoes, and lime, as well as varied textures from soft black beans to crunchy pumpkin seeds. You can make this salsa up to a day in advance and refrigerate until tailgate time; it will be fine served at room temperature at your tailgate site. Top with the pumpkin seeds right before serving to keep them crispy.

1 ripe avocado

3 tablespoons fresh lime juice (from 2 limes)

2 tablespoons avocado oil

¾ teaspoon kosher salt

⅓ teaspoon ground cumin

⅛ teaspoon cayenne pepper

⅓ cup chopped fresh cilantro

½ cup water

1½ (15-ounce) cans black beans, drained and rinsed

1 cup halved grape tomatoes (from 1 pint)

1 cup fresh or frozen yellow corn kernels (from 1 ear corn)

¾ cup chopped red bell pepper (from 1 bell pepper)

¾ cup chopped yellow bell pepper (from 1 bell pepper)

⅓ cup finely chopped red onion (from 1 small onion)

⅓ cup roasted salted pepitas (shelled pumpkin seeds)

Tortilla chips

1   Combine the avocado, lime juice, oil, salt, cumin, cayenne, and 3 tablespoons of the cilantro in a food processor. Process until smooth, adding up to ½ cup water, ¼ cup at a time, if necessary to thin the dressing.

2   Combine the beans, tomatoes, corn, bell peppers, onion, and 3 tablespoons of the pepitas in a large bowl. Toss with half of the dressing. Top with the remaining pepitas, dressing, and cilantro. Serve with the tortilla chips.

BOILED PEANUT HUMMUS
with PORK RINDS

SERVES 10 // HANDS-ON 15 MINUTES // TOTAL 3 HOURS, 15 MINUTES

Food doesn't get more Southern than boiled peanuts. Here, we reinvent them as a spicy and satisfying hummus served alongside another Southern classic—pork rinds. The combination of their creamy-crunchy texture is perfect. If your crowd doesn't love pork rinds, serve the hummus with toasted pita chips or crudités.

2 quarts water
1¼ cups blanched raw peanuts
2 tablespoons kosher salt
1 tablespoon ground cumin
1 tablespoon smoked paprika
½ teaspoon cayenne pepper
2 tablespoons roasted tahini (sesame paste)
1 small garlic clove

1 tablespoon fresh lemon juice (from 1 lemon)
¼ cup extra-virgin olive oil
½ cup warm water, plus more for desired consistency
2 tablespoons finely chopped fresh chives (optional)
8 ounces pork rinds or chicharrones

TENT TALK

What were the first footballs made of?

A. Pigskin
B. Pig bladders
C. Cowhide
D. Naugahyde

1   Bring the water, peanuts, salt, cumin, paprika, and cayenne pepper to a boil in a large stockpot over medium-high. Reduce the heat to low, and simmer until the peanuts are tender, 3 to 4 hours.

2   Drain the peanuts, discarding the liquid. Let the peanuts stand until cool enough to handle, 15 to 20 minutes. Combine the peanuts, tahini, garlic, lemon juice, and oil in a blender. Add the ½ cup warm water, and process until completely smooth, stopping to scrape down the sides as needed, about 3 minutes. Slowly add up to ½ cup more warm water, 1 tablespoon at a time, if needed to reach the desired consistency. Transfer to a bowl, and, if desired, sprinkle with the chives. Serve with the pork rinds.

GRILLED JALAPEÑO POPPERS

SERVES 12 // HANDS-ON 20 MINUTES // TOTAL 30 MINUTES

Kick off the game with a fun appetizer that gets everyone in the spirit. These little bites are loaded with cheese, and the best part—you can customize them to reflect your favorite SEC team. See pages 106-107 for school-specific variations.

1 (8-ounce) package cream cheese, softened
4 ounces sharp Cheddar cheese, grated (about 1 cup)
2 tablespoons finely chopped scallions
2 teaspoons Worcestershire sauce

1 garlic clove, grated
¼ teaspoon kosher salt
⅛ teaspoon black pepper
12 green jalapeño chiles or mini sweet peppers, halved lengthwise and seeded

Preheat the grill to medium-high (about 450°F). Stir together the cream cheese, Cheddar, scallions, Worcestershire, garlic, salt, and black pepper. Spoon 1 to 2 tablespoons of the cheese mixture into each jalapeño half. Place the jalapeño halves, cut sides up, on lightly greased grill grates. Grill, covered, until the jalapeños are charred and the cheese is melted, about 8 minutes.

SWEET HEAT PIMIENTO CHEESE

SERVES 8 // HANDS-ON 15 MINUTES
TOTAL 24 HOURS, 15 MINUTES, INCLUDES 24 HOURS CHILLING

EXTRA
POINT

The candied jalapeño slices are delicious served over cream cheese with crackers. Also, chop them and stir into potato salad, chicken salad, or deviled egg filling.

The texture of this pimiento cheese, made with two types of cheeses grated on different sides of the grater, is what makes this slightly spicy pimiento cheese unforgettable. You can make this dish up to 2 days in advance—you'll want to start at least a day ahead to get the candied jalapeños just right—and transport it in a cooler to your tailgate site.

1 (12-ounce) jar pickled jalapeño chile slices, drained
1 tablespoon lime zest (about 2 limes)
¾ cup granulated sugar
1 cup mayonnaise
1 (4-ounce) jar diced pimientos, drained

⅛ teaspoon cayenne pepper
1 (8-ounce) block sharp Cheddar cheese
1 (8-ounce) block extra-sharp white Cheddar cheese
Assorted crackers, corn chips, breadsticks

1   Drain the jalapeño slices, reserving the slices in the jar. Add the lime zest and ¼ cup of the sugar to the drained jalapeño slices in the jar; secure the lid, and shake to coat the slices. Remove the lid; add ¼ cup of the sugar. Secure the lid, and shake to coat. Repeat the process with the remaining ¼ cup sugar. Chill 24 hours or up to 1 week, shaking the jar several times a day to disperse any sugar that may have settled.

2   Finely chop the drained, candied jalapeño slices to equal ¼ cup, and place in a large bowl. Stir in the mayonnaise, diced pimientos, and cayenne.

3   Shred the sharp Cheddar cheese using the large holes of a box grater. Shred the extra-sharp white Cheddar cheese using the small holes of a box grater. Gradually stir the shredded cheeses into the mayonnaise mixture until blended. Cover and chill until ready to use. Serve with the assorted crackers, corn chips, and breadsticks.

COWBOY CAVIAR

SERVES 10 // HANDS-ON 20 MINUTES // TOTAL 35 MINUTES

Chock-full of black beans, peas, and vegetables with some heat from smoky paprika and jalapeño chile, this dip is top notch—even "Good Bull" for an Aggie fan. Kick up the heat by leaving in the jalapeño seeds, or take them out for a milder dip. This also makes a nice relish for grilled meats or topping for baked potatoes.

3 tablespoons olive oil

2 tablespoons fresh lime juice (from 1 lime)

1½ teaspoons red wine vinegar

1 teaspoon ground cumin

1 teaspoon kosher salt

½ teaspoon smoked paprika

½ teaspoon honey

1 (15-ounce) can black beans, drained and rinsed

1 (15-ounce) can black-eyed peas, drained and rinsed

1 cup fresh corn kernels (from 2 ears)

1 cup chopped yellow bell pepper (from 1 bell pepper)

1 cup chopped plum tomato (from 2 tomatoes)

½ cup finely chopped red onion (from 1 small onion)

½ cup chopped fresh cilantro

2 tablespoons finely chopped jalapeño chile or serrano chile

Tortilla chips

Whisk together the oil, lime juice, vinegar, cumin, salt, paprika, and honey in a large bowl. Add the beans, peas, corn, bell pepper, tomatoes, onion, cilantro, and jalapeño; stir to coat well. Let stand 15 minutes, stirring occasionally. Serve with the tortilla chips.

LOADED POTATO SKINS

SERVES 8 // HANDS-ON 45 MINUTES // TOTAL 1 HOUR, 45 MINUTES

EXTRA
POINT

You can bake the potatoes and scoop the flesh in advance and then proceed with Step 2 at your tailgate site, using a baking sheet on the grill rather than in the oven.

A crowd-pleaser at any gathering, potato skins are an especially welcome finger food at tailgates where guests eat while standing and mingling. Leave off the tomato, sour cream, sauce, and chives until ready to serve to keep them cold and fresh.

8 medium-size russet potatoes

1 tablespoon canola oil

6 tablespoons (3 ounces) salted butter, melted

1¼ teaspoons kosher salt

1 teaspoon black pepper

1 cup finely chopped country ham (about 4 ounces)

½ cup finely chopped red onion (from 1 small onion)

8 ounces white Cheddar cheese, shredded (about 2 cups)

1 cup diced tomato (from 2 medium plum tomatoes)

½ cup sour cream

1 cup barbecue sauce of choice

3 tablespoons chopped fresh chives

1 Preheat the oven to 400°F. Pierce the potatoes all over with a fork; rub all over with the oil. Place on an aluminum foil-lined baking sheet, and bake at 400°F until tender when pierced with a fork, about 1 hour. Let cool on the baking sheet about 10 minutes. Place an oven rack in the center of the oven; increase the oven temperature to broil.

2 Cut the potatoes in quarters lengthwise, and scoop out the flesh, leaving a ¼-inch layer of potato next to the skin. (Reserve the removed potato flesh for another use, if desired.) Brush the potato quarters all over with the melted butter; sprinkle with the salt and pepper, and place on the baking sheet, skin side up.

3 Broil until browned and crisp, about 5 minutes. Remove from the oven, and turn the potato skins over. Top evenly with the ham, red onion, and cheese. Broil until the cheese melts and browns, 3 to 4 minutes. Top with the tomato, sour cream, barbecue sauce, and chives, and serve hot.

TIGER TASSO SKEWERS

SERVES **10** // HANDS-ON **15 MINUTES** // TOTAL **15 MINUTES**

These ingredients scream Louisiana, and the combination of their spicy, smoky, tangy, and sweet flavors will have tailgaters screaming "Geaux Tigers!" Pork tasso is a cured, spice-rubbed cut of pork shoulder and a classic south Louisiana commodity. Mayhaw is the apple-like fruit of a plant found around bayous.

20 (4-inch) wooden skewers
8 ounces very thinly sliced pork tasso, cut into 20 (1-inch-wide) strips
16 ounces smoked Gouda cheese, cut into 40 (½-inch) cubes
1 (12-ounce) jar Cajun-style or other spicy pickle chips

⅔ cup mayhaw jelly (or other jelly such as apple)
¼ cup rice vinegar
1 tablespoon Louisiana hot sauce

1   Soak the skewers in water 30 minutes. Cut each tasso strip in half crosswise. Wrap 1 tasso half strip around 1 cheese cube, covering 3 sides, and thread onto a skewer. Add 1 pickle chip. Repeat the procedure with another tasso half strip and 1 cheese cube, threading onto the skewer on top of the pickle chip. Repeat the process with the remaining skewers, tasso half strips, cheese cubes, and pickle chips. Store in an airtight container in the refrigerator up to 1 day.

2   Stir together the mayhaw jelly, rice vinegar, and hot sauce in a small saucepan over medium. Bring to a boil, and cook, stirring occasionally, until the mixture is reduced by one-third, about 8 minutes. Remove from the heat, and let cool completely. Store in an airtight container in the refrigerator up to 2 days. To serve, place the skewers on a serving platter, and drizzle with the mayhaw sauce.

EXTRA POINT

If you can't find thinly sliced tasso, ask your butcher to cut it into prosciutto-style slices. You can order tasso from your butcher, or substitute a salty ham, such as prosciutto.

HOME IS WHERE THE HEART IS

"The sun shines bright," they sing as one, "in my old Kentucky home." Tears well in the eyes of some alumni. Others hug loved ones a little closer. It's a defining moment before every football game—and often right after.

At the University of Kentucky, to galvanize the crowds, they don't sing their alma mater. They sing their state song.

Longing for home was a prominent theme for Stephen Foster. It's said he composed this anti-slavery ballad in 1852 after visiting Kentucky and witnessing slaves toiling on a plantation. "My Old Kentucky Home, Good-Night!" sold thousands of copies and became the state song in 1928. Today, this song is woven into the very fabric of the state—and that of its flagship university.

Many people recognize it as a preamble to the Kentucky Derby. Fans sing "My Old Kentucky Home" as the horses parade before the annual Run for the Roses.

Federal Hill, a mansion Foster visited, is now a state park. That structure, the phrase "My Old Kentucky Home," and a thoroughbred appear on Kentucky's state quarter.

Though Kentucky and Louisville are fierce rivals on the gridiron, their bands take the field during the annual Governor's Cup game and play the state song together. These traditions just underscore what everyone in the Bluegrass State already knows. Kentuckians sing their state song whenever and wherever they gather.

"This song doesn't belong to one school or the other. It belongs to the entire state," says one alumnus. "We feel a lot of pride about being from Kentucky."

FUN FACT

The Governor's Cup game between Kentucky and their in-state archrival Louisville will continue through November 2022.

BIG BLUE U

Two rambunctious imps dressed in Kentucky blue smile ear-to-ear from their perch astride the statue at Wildcat Alumni Plaza on the University of Kentucky campus in Lexington.

"Chee-e-e-se!" they sing in unison, as Mom snaps photos. Dad watches patiently, ready to spring into action if a kid loses his footing.

The antics of these young Kentucky fans draw indulgent smiles from others waiting to chronicle their own memories before their beloved Cats take the field. These sprouts are UK's future—and everyone knows nurturing seeds takes patience and time.

C-A-T-S! CATS, CATS, CATS!

Few people are lucky enough to see a real wildcat. They're cagey and shy, avoiding human contact whenever possible. But Bowman, a large bronze wildcat sculpture, stands watch over Kentucky's famous Avenue of Champions on the northern edge of campus.

Though the football stadium was moved in 1973, many of the finest moments in Kentucky football—and basketball—history happened right here. The region's pigskin infatuation took root at Stoll Field, adjacent to the plaza, during the South's first intercollegiate football game on April 9, 1880. In that game, Kentucky University, now called Transylvania University, beat Centre College by a score of 13¾ to 0.

It would be another year before the A&M College of Kentucky, forerunner of today's UK, played their first game. But it didn't take long for the Cats to master the finer points. Many consider the Kentucky squad of 1898 one of the greatest teams in Wildcats history. Simply known as The Immortals, the team is the only University of Kentucky squad to remain undefeated, untied, and unscored upon.

FUN FACT

Blue, the university's live wildcat mascot, lives at the Salato Wildlife Education Center near Frankfort. He never goes to games. Like most of his kin, Blue is shy.

While UK has never had a consensus national champion, the single-loss 1950 team captured a share of the prize. The head coach in those years was none other than the young Paul "Bear" Bryant, who led the Cats for eight seasons, from 1946-1953.

// KENTUCKY'S SEC TRAILBLAZERS

Many admirable young men have suited up at Kentucky, yet few have changed the game like Nate Northington, Greg Page, Wilbur Hackett, and Houston Hogg. Page and Northington were the first African-American players to sign with an SEC school. Hackett and Hogg joined the team a year later.

Northington officially broke the SEC's color barrier during UK's home game against Ole Miss on Sept. 30, 1967. But it was a bittersweet achievement. His teammate, roommate, and friend, Greg Page, had died the day before of a neck injury sustained during a practice 38 days earlier.

It's been more than 50 years since they played football, but these trailblazers still stand tall on the UK campus. A larger-than-life statue of the four is located between the football training facility and Kroger Field, a reminder of the courage and sacrifice that transformed the face of college football.

// TO THE BLUE AND WHITE BE TRUE

While football had a hand in building the Big Blue Nation, the school's success on the hardwood is what really solidified Kentucky's brand worldwide.

Memorial Coliseum, once called the Cathedral of College Basketball, stands just across the street from Stoll Field and Wildcat Alumni Plaza. Even on football days, fans stop to gaze at this building, their minds replaying highlight reels of their favorite memories.

This massive building covers almost an entire city block and was built to

honor the more than 10,000 Kentuckians who were killed in World War II and Korea. UK was almost unbeatable here. In 26 seasons, the Cats posted an incredible home record of 307–38.

The Coliseum still hosts women's basketball, gymnastics, and volleyball, but the men have played at Rupp Arena in downtown Lexington since 1976.

// ON, ON, U OF K!

Many of the football festivities unfold due south of the Avenue of Champions, near Kroger Field. Because it was sited on a former UK experimental farm, the stadium is surrounded by acres of wide-open parking lots.

"We begin tailgating before daylight some days, depending on when the game starts," says one Kentucky booster. "We'll sometimes have 40 or 50 people join us. Many times, we'll stay there until midnight—or after. Tailgating creates a camaraderie you just don't have with other sports."

While the tailgating scene is lively, what you witness around the stadium is just the tip of the iceberg. Lexington is also the epicenter of the country's thoroughbred racing industry. Television schedules often dictate when games are played. But in October, UK fans can sometimes go to the thoroughbred races at Keeneland Racecourse during the day, take in a Kentucky football game in the evening, and then make the rounds at the establishments on Limestone Street.

"In Kentucky," says one UK fan with a wink, "we call this a trifecta."

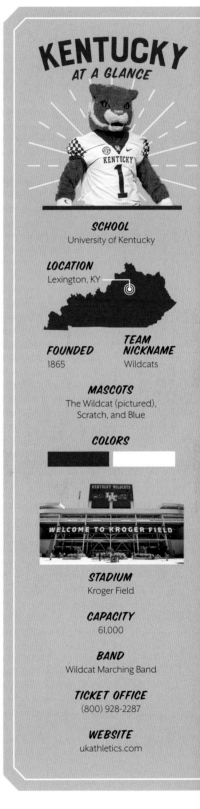

KENTUCKY
AT A GLANCE

SCHOOL
University of Kentucky

LOCATION
Lexington, KY

FOUNDED
1865

TEAM NICKNAME
Wildcats

MASCOTS
The Wildcat (pictured), Scratch, and Blue

COLORS

STADIUM
Kroger Field

CAPACITY
61,000

BAND
Wildcat Marching Band

TICKET OFFICE
(800) 928-2287

WEBSITE
ukathletics.com

POM-POMS AND PENNANTS ARE GO-TO ITEMS WITH WHICH TO THEME A TABLE, AND THEY DOUBLE AS CHEERING TOOLS.

MIX THE PATTERNS IN COCKTAIL NAPKINS, LINEN NAPKINS, AND THE TABLE RUNNER TO ADD INTEREST.

KENTUCKY
WILDCATS

UK

Kentucky
Lemon-Mint Punch
P. 55

Loaded
Potato Skins
P. 94

Game-Day
Hot Brown
Turkey Sliders
P. 165

Green Bean
Benedictine Salad
P. 200

SERVES 8

JULEP CUPS ARE A NOD TO
A KENTUCKY CLASSIC. A
SILVER TIERED FOOD STAND
ADDS HEIGHT TO THE TABLE.

CREATE A TALKING PIECE BY
FILLING A SMALL TIN BUCKET
LABELED "PENALTY FLAGS"
WITH YELLOW NAPKINS.

SAUSAGE *AND* CHEDDAR DEVILED EGGS

SERVES 8 // HANDS-ON 25 MINUTES // TOTAL 1 HOUR

TENT
TALK

True or False: In college football, a pass is ruled complete only if both of the player's feet are in bounds.

Sausage, egg, and cheese biscuits deliciously transformed into deviled eggs? No foul here! Any brand of breakfast sausage will work, but we recommend that Vandy fans use Jimmy Dean since it's located near Nashville.

8 large eggs
½ (1-pound) package ground pork breakfast sausage, cooked and crumbled (such as Jimmy Dean)
2 ounces Cheddar cheese, shredded (about ½ cup)
¼ cup mayonnaise
1½ tablespoons pickle relish
1 tablespoon apple cider vinegar

2 teaspoons yellow mustard
1 teaspoon paprika
¾ teaspoon kosher salt
¼ teaspoon cayenne pepper
¼ cup thinly sliced fresh scallions (green parts only) (from 2 scallions)
2 tablespoons hot sauce (such as Crystal) (optional)

1   Bring a large pot of water to a boil over high. Add the eggs with a slotted spoon, and boil 12 minutes. Immediately plunge the cooked eggs into a bowl of ice water. Cool completely. Peel the eggs; discard the shells.

2   Halve the eggs lengthwise. Carefully remove the yolks, leaving the whites intact. Place the yolks in a medium bowl, and mash with a fork until crumbled. Reserve 2 tablespoons each of the sausage and cheese. Add the mayonnaise, relish, vinegar, mustard, paprika, salt, cayenne, and remaining sausage and cheese to the yolks; stir until combined.

3   Spoon the mixture into the egg white halves; place on a platter. Sprinkle each with the reserved sausage and cheese; top with the scallions and, if desired, hot sauce.

GRAHAM NUT CLUSTERS ▸

SERVES 12 // HANDS-ON 10 MINUTES // TOTAL 30 MINUTES

EXTRA
POINT

Make this up to 5 days in advance, and store in an airtight container. To customize this snack for your team, use only chocolate pieces in the colors of your team.

Sweet cereal, nuts, pretzels, and chocolate pieces make a memorable munchy for adults and kids alike. Serve the snack from a large bowl, small bucket, or even a decorative (new and unworn) football helmet with a stack of small plastic cups so guests can serve themselves as they come back for more.

6 cups honey graham cereal
1 cup honey-roasted peanuts
1 cup coarsely chopped pecans
½ cup (4 ounces) butter

1 cup firmly packed light brown sugar
¼ cup light corn syrup
2 cups pretzel sticks
1 cup candy-coated chocolate pieces

1   Preheat the oven to 350°F. Combine the cereal, peanuts, and pecans in a large bowl.

2   Melt the butter in a 3-quart saucepan over medium-low; stir in the sugar and corn syrup. Bring to a boil over medium; boil 2 minutes.

3   Pour the butter mixture over the cereal mixture, and stir quickly to coat. Spread in a single layer on a lightly greased aluminum foil-lined jelly-roll pan.

4   Bake at 350°F for 10 minutes. Transfer to wax paper, and cool completely, about 10 minutes. Break into pieces, and toss with the pretzel sticks and chocolate pieces.

SUGAR-AND-SPICE CARAMEL POPCORN

MAKES 12 CUPS // HANDS-ON 15 MINUTES // TOTAL 50 MINUTES

Old Bay seasoning is our secret ingredient in this popcorn. It's the perfect savory balance to the sweet caramel.

3 (3.5-ounce) bags microwave popcorn, popped
Vegetable cooking spray
4 teaspoons Old Bay seasoning
½ cup (4 ounces) butter
1 cup granulated sugar
⅓ cup apple cider vinegar

1   Place the popcorn in a large bowl; lightly coat with the cooking spray. Sprinkle with the Old Bay seasoning, and toss to coat.
2   Melt the butter in a 2-quart heavy saucepan over medium. Stir in the sugar and vinegar, and bring to a boil. Boil, without stirring, 8 to 10 minutes or until a candy thermometer registers 300°F. Immediately pour the butter mixture over the popcorn mixture, and stir to coat. Spread the popcorn on wax paper, and cool completely, about 25 minutes. Break into pieces, and serve.

◄ CARAMEL-WALNUT SNACK MIX

SERVES 8 // HANDS-ON 15 MINUTES // TOTAL 1 HOUR

You won't be able to get enough of this crunchy-sweet snack. The corn cereal and black walnuts are nods to Missouri's native foods, and using only yellow M&M's makes this recipe an even more appropriate dish for Mizzou.

5 cups popped popcorn
3 cups corn cereal squares (such as Corn Chex)
2 cups pretzel squares (such as Snyder's of Hanover Snaps Pretzels)
1 cup walnut pieces (black walnut if possible)
¾ cup packed light brown sugar
6 tablespoons (3 ounces) salted butter, softened
3 tablespoons light corn syrup
1 teaspoon vanilla extract
½ teaspoon baking soda
1 cup yellow candy-coated chocolate-covered peanuts (such as Peanut M&M's)

1   Preheat the oven to 300°F. Combine the popcorn, cereal squares, pretzel squares, and walnut pieces in a large bowl.
2   Place the sugar, butter, and syrup in a small saucepan over medium. Cook, stirring occasionally, until the mixture comes to a boil, 3 to 4 minutes. Reduce the heat to medium-low, and cook, stirring often, until the sugar is completely dissolved, 1 to 2 minutes. Remove from the heat, and add the vanilla and baking soda, stirring constantly. Pour the syrup mixture over the popcorn mixture, stirring gently until well combined and evenly coated.
3   Spread the popcorn mixture in a single layer on a parchment paper-lined rimmed baking sheet. Bake at 300°F until golden and caramelized, 25 to 30 minutes, stirring after 15 minutes. Remove from the oven, and let cool completely, about 15 minutes. Transfer to a serving bowl, and stir in the candies.

SEC TEAM GRILLED JALAPEÑO POPPERS

Personalize grilled pepper poppers to suit your favorite team, or make two batches—one themed for your team and one themed for the opponent. See page 91 for the base Grilled Jalapeño Poppers recipe.

BAMA BLITZ

Substitute 12 red jalapeños for green jalapeños. Prepare recipe as directed, adding ½ cup pulled smoked chicken to cheese mixture. Drizzle poppers evenly with ¼ cup white barbecue sauce, and garnish with chives.

WHOLE HOG

Substitute 12 mini red sweet peppers for jalapeños. Prepare recipe as directed, adding ½ cup chopped country ham to cheese mixture. Top each popper with about 1 tsp. bacon jam.

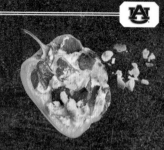

DIXIELAND

Substitute 12 mini orange sweet peppers for jalapeños. Prepare recipe as directed, adding ¼ cup each drained diced pimientos and crumbled bacon to cheese mixture: sprinkle with ¼ cup crushed Ritz crackers before grilling.

CUBAN GATOR

Substitute 12 mini orange sweet peppers for jalapeños. Substitute 3¾ oz. Swiss cheese for Cheddar. Prepare recipe as directed, adding ½ cup chopped deli ham and 2 tsp. Dijon mustard to cheese mixture. Top each with a dill pickle slice.

BULLDOG BITE

Substitute 12 mini red sweet peppers for jalapeños. Prepare recipe as directed, adding ¼ cup sweet onion relish to cheese mixture. Top each popper with about 1 tsp. hot pepper jelly.

WILDCAT BLUES

Substitute 2 oz. crumbled blue cheese and 2 oz. shredded Monterey Jack cheese for Cheddar. Prepare recipe as directed. Top poppers evenly with ½ cup glazed walnuts.

DEATH VALLEY LURE

Substitute 12 mini yellow sweet peppers for jalapeños. Prepare recipe as directed, adding ½ cup cooked crawfish tail meat, 1 tsp. Cajun seasoning, and 1 tsp. Tabasco hot sauce to cheese mixture.

DAWG POUND

Substitute 3½ oz. Edam cheese for Cheddar. Substitute 12 red jalapeños for green jalapeños. Prepare recipe as directed, adding ½ cup chopped cooked shrimp to cheese mixture. Garnish with chowchow relish.

TIGER'S LAIR

Substitute 12 mini yellow sweet peppers for jalapeños. Prepare recipe as directed, adding ½ cup pulled pork to cheese mixture. Drizzle each popper with about 1 tsp. sweet barbecue sauce before serving.

COME-BACK REBELS

Substitute 12 mini red sweet peppers for jalapeños. Prepare recipe as directed, adding 2 Tbsp. each mayo and chili sauce, ¼ tsp. dry mustard, and ¼ tsp. onion powder to cheese mixture. Top with ⅓ cup crispy fried onions before grilling.

ROOSTER'S CROW

Substitute 12 red jalapeños for green jalapeños. Prepare recipe as directed, adding ½ cup cooked black-eyed peas, ¼ cup cooked Carolina Gold rice, and 1 tsp. hot sauce to cheese mixture. Garnish with shaved celery.

BIG ORANGE SMOKEY

Substitute 12 mini orange sweet peppers for jalapeños. Substitute 4½ oz. smoked mozzarella cheese for Cheddar. Prepare recipe as directed, adding ¼ cup chopped smoked almonds and ½ tsp. smoked paprika to cheese mixture.

AGGIE SPIRIT

Substitute 12 red jalapeños for green jalapeños. Substitute 3 oz. Manchego cheese for Cheddar. Prepare recipe as directed, adding ½ cup crumbled fresh Mexican chorizo to cheese mixture. Garnish with cilantro.

MR. C'S REVENGE

Substitute 12 mini yellow sweet peppers for jalapeños. Prepare recipe as directed, adding ¾ tsp. each cayenne pepper, paprika, and chili powder, and ¼ tsp. garlic powder to cheese mixture. Top with a pickled okra slice.

BOWL ELIGIBLE

A LARGE POT OF SIMMERING SOUP, STEW, OR CHILI IS A WARM WELCOME ON GAME DAY. SERVE FRIENDS AND FAMILY THESE BOWLS LOADED WITH BEEF, PORK, CHICKEN, OR SEAFOOD—THERE ARE EVEN MEATLESS OPTIONS. DON'T FORGET TO BRING TOPPINGS AND CRACKERS OR BREAD FOR DIPPING.

WELCOME TO DEATH VALLEY

FUN FACT

LSU still uses the old-fashioned H-style, or offset, goalposts. Before each game, the team takes the field by running through the north end zone goalpost.

WELCOME TO DEATH VALLEY

These menacing words are etched on the video display board at the north end zone in Tiger Stadium at LSU and repeated on the upper deck of the south end zone. The greeting sounds cordial enough, friendly even. But it might as well read: "Abandon all hope, ye who enter here."

Tiger Stadium is massive, a goliath among the moss-draped live oaks and red-tiled roofs of the LSU campus. When stuffed to capacity, it becomes the fifth-largest city in the state, a real "Louisiana gumbo of humanity," you might call it. Even in the fall, it can be extremely hot and sticky in Baton Rouge.

The stadium is quiet as a church most days, peaceful and serene. But when a ball game is being played, you can barely hear yourself think. Noise levels have been recorded at 130 decibels—and higher. In 1988, when LSU beat Auburn with a touchdown in the final seconds of the game, the roar from Tiger Stadium registered as an actual earthquake on the Richter Scale. Some say "Deaf Valley" might be a more appropriate name.

After dark, Tiger Stadium is even more terrifying. As tough as it is to walk away with a W during the daylight hours, it's doubly difficult on a Saturday night in Death Valley. LSU has won almost 75% of all night games since they lighted the stadium in 1931.

Yes, this is a miserable place to play football—unless you're a Tiger, of course. Then the stadium is a jungle and you're a king. Lesser creatures stand little chance when the mighty Tigers are on the prowl. Welcome to Death Valley, indeed.

// GEAUX TIGERS!

The rat-a-tat-tat of the drum line echoes through the live oaks at Louisiana State University as the Golden Band from Tigerland begins its march down Victory Hill.

Thousands line North Stadium Drive in Baton Rouge for the procession to Tiger Stadium before every home football game. First the LSU football team parades through, game faces set as they make their way to the playing field. Then comes the carefully choreographed band.

The drum cadence continues until the entire unit has reached the edge of the stadium. When the band stops, the crowd grows quiet—until the brass takes over, blasting out the first four notes of LSU's thrilling "Pregame Salute."

"It's hard to explain to an outsider, but all Tiger fans know those four notes," says one excited alum. "It's a tradition that stirs the blood of every true LSU fan."

// EAT 'EM UP, TIGERS

Hours, sometimes days, before kickoff, fanatic followers of the purple and gold flood Louisiana's capital city and settle in for a fabulous fete. LSU's campus of red-tiled Italian Renaissance buildings provides the perfect setting. What you'll find here is a microcosm of Louisiana culture—part Mardi Gras, part frat party, part family reunion.

Huge motor homes crank up booming sound systems. Tents go up on every available patch of grass. Serious tailgaters bring crews of like-minded cooks and revelers. When fans of the opposing team walk by, the taunts begin. But those who respond with good humor will likely be invited to partake in the feast.

"Food is a huge part of Louisiana culture, and you will see all of the favorites here on game day," says a hungry Tiger fan. "There's gumbo, red

FUN FACT

Despite LSU's affection for Mike the Tiger, the school's nickname is actually a nod to Civil War history. Louisiana's troops in Lee's Army of Northern Virginia were known as Tigers.

beans and rice, jambalaya, boudin, cochon de lait, a dozen different kinds of étouffée—and that's just to name a few." He wolfishly smiles. "This year, we made rotisserie alligator for the Florida game."

LSU fans even have a cheer that incorporates spicy Creole sausage and a cornmeal-based Cajun breakfast cereal. It goes like this: "Hot boudin, cold coush-coush, come on Tigers, push, push, push!" (In this case, push sounds like "poosh.").

// GLORY OF THE PURPLE AND GOLD

For all of the pregame celebrating that goes on around Baton Rouge, it's just the appetizer for the main course that waits inside Tiger Stadium.

Longtime fans point to Billy Cannon's 89-yard punt return that gave the No. 1 ranked Tigers a 7-3 win over No. 3 Ole Miss in 1959; without that "Halloween Run," Cannon might not be a Heisman winner today. Others say Bert Jones' last-second touchdown pass in 1972 definitely makes the Tigers' all-time highlight reel. Even now, no one can explain how a single second remained on the clock, but they do know it was enough time for LSU to score and beat Ole Miss.

And then there are the three national championships. The undefeated Tigers team of '58 featured Coach Paul Dietzel's three-platoon system with All-SEC

runners Billy Cannon, Warren Rabb, and Johnny Robinson in the backfield. The Bowl Championship Series computer algorithm favored the Tigers in 2003, causing them to edge the USC Trojans to get to the championship matchup against Oklahoma. And in 2007, the team overcame triple-overtime losses to both Kentucky and Arkansas to get to the title game against Ohio State.

Recent Tiger teams have been so loaded with talent that LSU has sent more players to the NFL than any other team in the nation. Today, LSU's finest are remembered at National Championship Plaza on the west side of the stadium. In addition to the title teams, the school's All-Americans and members of the College Football Hall of Fame are honored here.

// I LIKE MIKE

There's a fiercely snarling statue of Mike the Tiger, but most fans prefer to visit the frisky feline at his home outside Tiger Stadium. LSU is one of only two schools with a live tiger mascot (the other is Memphis) and the only one with a real tiger living on campus. Mike the Tiger always enjoys a steady stream of visitors. But on game day, his 15,000-square-foot home between Tiger Stadium and the Pete Maravich Assembly Center is a mob scene.

Both live and costumed mascots are named Mike in honor of Mike Chambers, the Tigers' athletic trainer when the first mascot was purchased in 1936. These days, the school refuses to buy animals bred in captivity, but they do take rescues in need of a home.

Mike VII, the current reigning feline mascot, came to campus in the fall of 2017. Though they still mourn Mike VI, who succumbed to cancer, LSU fans have fallen head over tail in love with their new cat. Mike VII has thousands of followers on both Facebook and Twitter. Fans can even spy on his enclosure via Tiger Cam at mikethetiger.com

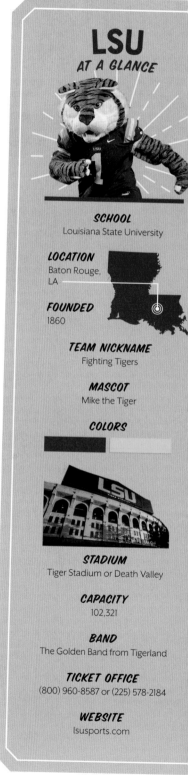

LSU
AT A GLANCE

SCHOOL
Louisiana State University

LOCATION
Baton Rouge, LA

FOUNDED
1860

TEAM NICKNAME
Fighting Tigers

MASCOT
Mike the Tiger

COLORS

STADIUM
Tiger Stadium or Death Valley

CAPACITY
102,321

BAND
The Golden Band from Tigerland

TICKET OFFICE
(800) 960-8587 or (225) 578-2184

WEBSITE
lsusports.com

CHOOSE PLASTIC CUTLERY IN BRIGHT YELLOW AND PURPLE. CORRAL THE PIECES IN WIRE BASKETS AND GLASS CUPS.

LSU
FIGHTING TIGERS

LSU

Tiger Tasso Skewers	Creole Gumbo	Fried Oyster Po'Boy Sliders	Mike's Maque Choux Salad
P. 95	P. 117	P. 178	P. 213

SERVES 10

LAY A PURPLE FABRIC SQUARE OVER A YELLOW-GOLD TABLECLOTH. ADD PATTERN WITH TIGER-STRIPE ACCENTS.

BILLOWING TRI-COLORED POM-POMS AND A RALLY HAT ANCHOR THIS LOOK IN LSU SCHOOL SPIRIT.

CREOLE GUMBO

SERVES **10** // HANDS-ON **55 MINUTES** // TOTAL **3 HOURS, 55 MINUTES**

With deep, rich flavors—including smokiness and a hint of spice from the poblano chile—and just thick enough with its chunky sausage, shrimp, and okra, this dish is everything you want in a gumbo and a guaranteed success for game days at LSU's Death Valley. You can make this gumbo up to 2 days in advance and reheat in a slow cooker at your tailgate site.

1 pound andouille sausage, cut into ½-inch-thick slices

⅓ cup (about 2½ ounces) salted butter

2 tablespoons bacon drippings

½ cup (about 2⅛ ounces) all-purpose flour

3 large celery stalks, chopped (about 1 cup)

2 medium-size yellow onions, chopped (about 3 cups)

1 large poblano chile, chopped (about 1 cup)

3 garlic cloves, minced (about 1 tablespoon)

8 to 10 cups unsalted chicken stock

1 pound fresh okra, trimmed and cut into ½-inch pieces (about 4½ cups)

1 (14.5-ounce) can petite diced tomatoes, undrained

2 bay leaves

1 tablespoon Worcestershire sauce

1 tablespoon Louisiana hot sauce

1 tablespoon kosher salt

1 teaspoon black pepper

1 pound peeled and deveined raw medium shrimp

½ pound fresh lump crabmeat, drained and picked over

1½ tablespoons filé powder

Hot cooked white rice

⅔ cup thinly sliced scallions (about 5 to 6 scallions)

1 Place the sausage in a large Dutch oven over medium; cook, stirring often, until browned on both sides, about 10 minutes. Using a slotted spoon, remove the sausage to drain on paper towels, reserving the drippings in the Dutch oven.

2 Add the butter and bacon drippings to the hot drippings in the Dutch oven, stirring until melted. Gradually whisk in the flour; cook, whisking constantly, until the mixture is a deep golden brown and thickened, being careful not to burn, 10 to 15 minutes.

3 Add the celery, onions, and poblano, and cook, stirring often, until the vegetables are almost tender, 12 to 15 minutes. Add the garlic, and cook, stirring often, until the vegetables are very tender and the garlic is aromatic, about 3 minutes. Gradually stir in 8 cups of the stock. Stir in the sausage, okra, tomatoes, bay leaves, Worcestershire, hot sauce, salt, and black pepper. Increase the heat to medium-high, and bring the mixture to a boil.

4 Reduce the heat to low, and simmer, partially covered, stirring occasionally, until thickened, about 3 hours. If the gumbo is too thick, add the remaining 2 cups stock, ½ cup at a time, until the desired consistency. Remove and discard the bay leaves. Stir in the shrimp and crabmeat, and cook until the shrimp turn pink, about 5 minutes. Stir in the filé powder, and remove from the heat. Serve the gumbo over the hot cooked rice, and garnish with the sliced scallions.

FLORIDA CITRUS SEAFOOD CHOWDER

SERVES 8 // HANDS-ON **25 MINUTES** // TOTAL **35 MINUTES**

EXTRA
POINT

This stew reheats well. Make it a day ahead, and rewarm it over low heat at your tailgate. Or, prepare through Step 3, and add the seafood, cream, and herbs on-site.

This shrimp and crabmeat seafood stew is light and bright enough for those warm early autumn football games—and, let's be honest, most days at The Swamp at The University of Florida—while rich and creamy enough for cooler weather later in the season. Serve it in mugs to tailgate companions to help keep their hands warm on cold days. For the freshest flavor, nothing beats fresh crab; however, previously frozen easy-peel shrimp will still taste excellent when you can't get the fresh variety.

4 cups seafood stock

1½ teaspoons orange zest plus 2 cups fresh juice (from 8 oranges)

6 tablespoons (3 ounces) unsalted butter

2 cups chopped leek (from 1 leek)

1 tablespoon chopped fresh thyme

2½ teaspoons kosher salt

½ teaspoon cayenne pepper

6 garlic cloves, chopped (about 2 tablespoons)

½ cup dry white wine or dry sherry

6 tablespoons all-purpose flour

3 cups diced red potatoes (about 1 pound potatoes)

1 pound peeled, deveined raw medium-size shrimp, cut into bite-size pieces

1 pound fresh jumbo lump crabmeat, drained and picked over

1 cup fresh yellow corn kernels (from 1 ear)

1 cup heavy cream

1 tablespoon fresh lime juice (from 1 lime)

2 tablespoons thinly sliced fresh chives

2 tablespoons chopped fresh dill

Saltine crackers

1 Stir together the stock, orange zest, and orange juice. Reserve ½ cup of the stock mixture.

2 Heat the butter in a large Dutch oven over medium-high until foamy, 2 to 3 minutes. Add the leek, thyme, salt, cayenne, and garlic; cook, stirring often, until translucent, 6 to 8 minutes. Add the wine; cook until almost evaporated, 2 to 3 minutes.

3 Whisk together the flour and reserved ½ cup stock mixture until smooth. Add the flour mixture, potatoes, and remaining stock mixture to the Dutch oven; bring to a boil. Reduce the heat to medium, and simmer, stirring often, until the potatoes are just tender, 10 minutes.

4 Add the shrimp, crabmeat, and corn; simmer until the shrimp are just cooked, 2 to 3 minutes. Remove from the heat. Stir in the cream, lime juice, and half each of the chives and dill. Divide the chowder among 8 bowls. Garnish with the remaining chives and dill, and serve with the saltines.

SLOW-COOKER CHICKEN SOUP

MAKES **11 CUPS** // HANDS-ON **20 MINUTES** // TOTAL **6 HOURS, 30 MINUTES**

Toss in the ingredients, switch on the slow cooker, and enjoy time with friends before the game. Dice the meat and cook the noodles right at the end.

2 pounds bone-in chicken thighs, skinned and trimmed (about 5 thighs)

3 medium carrots, cut into ½-inch pieces (1¼ cups)

1 celery root, cut into ½-inch pieces (2 cups)

1 medium leek, white and light green parts only, cleaned, chopped

2 garlic cloves, peeled and smashed

2 fresh thyme sprigs

2 fresh sage sprigs

1 fresh rosemary sprig

1 bay leaf

1½ teaspoons table salt

1 teaspoon freshly ground black pepper

8 cups chicken broth

2 cups wide egg noodles

3 tablespoons finely chopped fresh parsley, plus more for garnish

1 tablespoon fresh lemon juice

EXTRA POINT

To make sure the egg noodles aren't mushy and overcooked, don't leave them in the slow cooker any longer than 10 to 15 minutes.

1 Place the chicken, carrots, celery root, leek, garlic, thyme, sage, rosemary, bay leaf, salt, pepper, and chicken broth in a 6-quart slow cooker. Cover and cook on LOW 6 hours or until the chicken and vegetables are tender and the chicken separates from the bone.

2 Remove the chicken from the slow cooker. Dice the meat, discarding the bones. Return the meat to the slow cooker. Stir in the noodles and parsley. Cover and cook on HIGH until the noodles are tender, 10 to 15 minutes. Stir in the lemon juice. Serve immediately, and garnish with additional chopped fresh parsley, if desired.

CHICKEN CHILI

SERVES **8** // HANDS-ON **15 MINUTES** // TOTAL **50 MINUTES**

Using a rotisserie chicken for this crowd-pleaser saves you time and hassle.

1 (2-pound) whole rotisserie chicken

2 (28-ounce) cans whole peeled plum tomatoes, undrained

2 tablespoons olive oil

2 cups chopped yellow onions

4 garlic cloves, minced

2 green bell peppers, chopped

2 yellow bell peppers, chopped

2½ teaspoons kosher salt

2½ teaspoons chili powder

2 teaspoons ground cumin

1 teaspoon paprika

½ teaspoon cayenne pepper

½ cup chopped fresh cilantro, plus more for topping

Sour cream, for topping

1 Remove the skin from the chicken, and discard; shred the meat to measure about 4 cups, and set aside.

2 Pulse the tomatoes in a food processor until slightly crushed.

3 Heat the oil in a large Dutch oven over medium. Add the onions and garlic, and cook, stirring occasionally, until tender, about 8 minutes. Add the bell peppers, salt, chili powder, cumin, paprika, and cayenne, and cook, stirring, 2 minutes.

4 Increase the heat to high; stir in the crushed tomatoes, and bring to a boil. Reduce the heat to medium, and stir in the chicken. Cover and simmer, stirring occasionally, until heated through, about 30 minutes. Stir in the cilantro. Serve with the additional cilantro and the sour cream.

CHICKEN *AND* SMOKED SAUSAGE BRUNSWICK STEW

SERVES 10 // HANDS-ON 40 MINUTES // TOTAL 1 HOUR

EXTRA POINT

This stew can be made up to 3 days in advance and reheated on-site. Use your favorite brand of andouille.

A play on classic Georgia-style Brunswick stew, which contains pulled pork instead of chicken, this recipe calls for both chicken and smoked pork sausage. Comprised of creamy beans, sweet-tangy broth, spicy sausage, and tender chicken, the result is a thick, sweet, and slightly mustardy stew that's great anytime but just right on a chilly autumn game day.

2 tablespoons olive oil

1 pound andouille sausage, cut into half-moons

3 pounds bone-in, skinless chicken thighs (about 8 thighs)

1 tablespoon unsalted butter

1¼ pounds Yukon Gold potatoes, cut into 1-inch cubes (about 2 large potatoes)

2 cups chopped sweet onion (such as Vidalia) (from 1 onion)

1 cup chopped celery (from 3 celery stalks)

1 cup chopped carrots (from 3 large carrots)

1 tablespoon tomato paste

1 (28-ounce) can diced tomatoes

1 cup chicken broth

¼ cup packed light brown sugar

¼ cup apple cider vinegar

¼ cup Dijon mustard

2 tablespoons chopped fresh thyme

1 tablespoon kosher salt

2 teaspoons unsweetened cocoa

1 (15-ounce) can baby lima beans, drained and rinsed

2 cups fresh or frozen corn kernels

¾ teaspoon black pepper

1   Heat 1 tablespoon of the oil in a large Dutch oven over medium-high. Add the sausage, and cook, stirring often, until browned, about 10 minutes. Using a slotted spoon, transfer the sausage to a plate lined with paper towels. Add the remaining 1 tablespoon oil to the Dutch oven. Cook the chicken, in batches, until browned, about 5 minutes. Flip and cook until browned on the other side, about 2 minutes. Place the chicken on a plate; set aside.

2   Add the butter to the Dutch oven, and swirl to melt. Add the potatoes, onion, celery, and carrots; cook over medium-high, stirring occasionally, until the vegetables soften, about 4 minutes. Add the tomato paste, and cook until darkened, stirring constantly, about 1 minute. Stir in the diced tomatoes, broth, brown sugar, vinegar, Dijon, thyme, salt, and cocoa. Bring to a boil, and return the chicken to the Dutch oven; reduce the heat to medium-low to maintain a simmer, and cook, uncovered, until the chicken is very tender, 20 to 30 minutes.

3   Remove the chicken, and let cool slightly. Shred into bite-size pieces. Add the shredded chicken, sausage, lima beans, corn, and pepper to the Dutch oven, and simmer, stirring often, until warmed through, about 5 minutes. Serve hot.

MEMPHIS-STYLE BBQ CHILI

SERVES **8** // HANDS-ON **30 MINUTES** // TOTAL **2 HOURS, 30 MINUTES**

Give classic cool-weather chili a makeover with a touch of sweetness from barbecue sauce and baked beans. Once the heat from the paprika, chili powder, and cayenne hits, you'll be thankful for the sour cream topping.

TENT
TALK

True or False: When a punter buries the opposition deep in its own territory without letting the ball cross the goal line, he is aiming for the Coffee Corner.

2 tablespoons canola oil

1 (2-pound) boneless pork shoulder roast (Boston butt), cut into 1-inch cubes

2 cups chopped yellow onion (from 1 large onion)

1 tablespoon paprika

1 tablespoon chili powder

2 teaspoons garlic powder

2 teaspoons dried oregano

2 teaspoons dry mustard

1 teaspoon celery salt

½ teaspoon cayenne pepper

3 cups chicken stock

2 cups barbecue sauce (such as Stubb's Original)

2 (15-ounce) cans navy beans, drained and rinsed

1 (15-ounce) can baked beans

Toppings: sliced cabbage, sour cream, shredded Cheddar cheese

Corn chips (such as Fritos)

1. Heat 1 tablespoon of the oil in a large Dutch oven over medium-high. Add half of the cubed pork roast, and cook until browned on all sides, 7 to 9 minutes. Transfer to a plate. Drain the oil from the Dutch oven. Repeat with the remaining oil and pork.

2. Add the onion to the Dutch oven. Cook until slightly caramelized, stirring occasionally, 8 to 10 minutes. Add the browned pork, paprika, chili powder, garlic powder, oregano, mustard, celery salt, and cayenne, and cook, stirring constantly, until fragrant, about 1 minute. Add the stock, barbecue sauce, navy beans, and baked beans, and bring to a boil.

3. Reduce the heat to medium-low; cover and simmer until the meat is very tender, about 1 hour and 30 minutes. Increase the heat to medium-high, and simmer uncovered, stirring occasionally until slightly thickened, about 20 minutes. Top as desired, and serve with the corn chips.

WHITE BEAN-AND-PORK CHILI

SERVES 8 // HANDS-ON 15 MINUTES // TOTAL 55 MINUTES

This chili gets spice from chiles, tang from lime juice, and texture from cheese.

4 tablespoons olive oil
2 pounds ground pork
1 medium-size white onion, chopped (about 2 cups)
1 poblano chile, seeded, chopped
3 garlic cloves, minced
2 (4.5-ounce) cans chopped green chiles, undrained
1 tablespoon ground cumin

1 tablespoon kosher salt
2 (15.5-ounce) cans white beans (such as cannellini or Great Northern), drained and rinsed
3⅓ cups reduced-sodium chicken broth
6 ounces Monterey Jack cheese, shredded (about 1½ cups)
2 tablespoons fresh lime juice

1 Heat 2 tablespoons of the oil in a Dutch oven over medium-high. Add the pork, and cook, stirring until crumbled and no longer pink, 6 to 8 minutes. Drain the pork, and set aside. Wipe the Dutch oven clean.

2 Heat the remaining 2 tablespoons oil in the Dutch oven over medium. Add the onion, poblano, garlic, green chiles, cumin, and salt, and cook, stirring often, until the vegetables are tender, 3 to 4 minutes.

3 Increase the heat to high. Stir in the beans, broth, and pork, and bring to a boil. Reduce the heat to medium-low, and simmer, stirring occasionally, until heated through, about 40 minutes. Add the cheese and lime juice, and stir until the cheese is melted. Serve immediately.

SLOW-COOKER BRISKET CHILI ▶

SERVES 10 // HANDS-ON 20 MINUTES // TOTAL 9 HOURS, 20 MINUTES

Black beans, brisket, spices, and quick hands-on prep take this to the next level.

3 tablespoons all-purpose flour
2 tablespoons ancho chile powder
1 tablespoon ground cumin
1 tablespoon kosher salt
1 teaspoon dried oregano
2 pounds beef brisket, trimmed and cut into 1-inch cubes
2 (15-ounce) cans black beans

1 (14.5-ounce) can fire-roasted diced tomatoes, drained
1 red bell pepper, chopped
1 medium-size red onion, chopped
3 garlic cloves, minced
¾ cup beef broth
4 tablespoons olive oil
Jalapeño slices (optional)

1 Stir together the flour, ancho chile powder, cumin, salt, and oregano in a small bowl. Sprinkle the spice mixture evenly on each side of the beef brisket cubes, and set aside.

2 Combine the black beans, tomatoes, bell pepper, onion, garlic, and beef broth in a 6- to 7-quart slow cooker.

3 Heat 2 tablespoons of the oil in a large skillet over medium-high. Add half of the brisket cubes; cook, stirring often, until browned on all sides, 5 to 7 minutes. Transfer the beef to the slow cooker. Repeat the procedure with the remaining oil and brisket.

4 Cover and cook on LOW 8 hours. Uncover; cook until slightly thickened, about 1 hour. Garnish with the jalapeño slices, if desired.

HAIL, STATE! MORE COWBELL!

Clang-a, clang-a, clang-a, clang-a, clang-a.

The sound of cowbells is music to a Mississippi State fan's ears—and pure torture to opponents.

The genesis of this tradition is difficult to trace, but the favored story involves State's nemesis and an off-course cow. During a hard-fought contest with Ole Miss, it's said a lone Jersey, apparently seeking greener pastures, wandered onto the playing field wearing a bell. The cow was sent back to the barn, while State went on to trounce its opponent.

Soon the cow was considered the school's good luck charm. But cows aren't the most genial travelers, which students quickly discovered, so they settled for bringing her bell to games instead. Today, cowbells are firmly woven into Mississippi State lore, a time-honored symbol of school spirit and school pride.

In some families, babies get cowbells at birth. Others inherit them when a friend or family member passes on to

their final reward. Cowbells are hidden under Christmas trees, presented with birthday cakes, and wrapped as graduation presents. As it turns out, that's just part of the tradition. You never purchase your first ringer. It should be a gift.

Some cowbells are fitted with handles and heavy-duty grips. They're painted, monogrammed, and plastered with stickers. Some fans have vast collections that they display at tailgate parties. There's even a cowbell app for those who prefer a virtual ring. Just download and shake your phone.

The conference banned all artificial noisemakers in 1974, but the decision was revisited in 2010. MSU fans can ring their bells only at "appropriate times"; otherwise, the school will be fined. For now, at least, Bulldog fans can keep raising bell.

FUN FACT

Built in 1914, Davis Wade Stadium at Scott Field is the oldest stadium in the Southeastern Conference. A 2014 expansion brought capacity to 61,337.

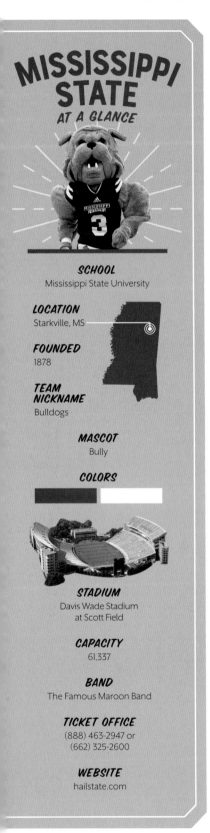

MISSISSIPPI STATE

AT A GLANCE

SCHOOL
Mississippi State University

LOCATION
Starkville, MS

FOUNDED
1878

TEAM NICKNAME
Bulldogs

MASCOT
Bully

COLORS

STADIUM
Davis Wade Stadium
at Scott Field

CAPACITY
61,337

BAND
The Famous Maroon Band

TICKET OFFICE
(888) 463-2947 or
(662) 325-2600

WEBSITE
hailstate.com

// HAIL, DEAR OL' STATE!

Small but mighty. These are the words that come to mind when you face Mississippi State's bulldog. He's no more than knee high. He doesn't snarl like a crazed canine. He's just Bully. And you have to get past him to get to Davis Wade Stadium in Starkville.

The bulldog moniker is one that Mississippi State has earned over the years, not a cute little nickname they chose. Early MSU football teams were called the Aggies, a nod to the school's land-grant roots, and then the Maroons, the color of their uniforms. But spectators often commented on the teams' bulldoggish style of play. Student-athletes who suit up for State have always had to be tenacious and tough.

The school's first Bully, a scrawny English bulldog, joined the team in 1935, but his reign was cut short in 1939 after an encounter with a campus bus. He's buried on the 50-yard line at Davis Wade Stadium beneath the team bench. The bulldog didn't become the school's official mascot until Mississippi State College was granted university status in 1961.

// ROON! WHITE!

Small but mighty could also describe the school itself. With just under 22,000 students, Mississippi State is one of the more modest schools in the Southeastern Conference. The population of the entire county is barely double the student population. Davis Wade Stadium, though seemingly huge when you stand beside it, holds only 61,337 people. That's nearly 50,000 fewer than the largest stadium in the SEC.

But Mississippi State has a proud tradition. The school has educated many of the state's legislators, farmers, accountants, meteorologists, engineers, and others.

MSU's cutting-edge Mitchell Memorial Library is home to the Ulysses S. Grant Presidential Library. Letters and photographs from Grant's presidency,

from 1869 to 1877, are part of the collection, as are his family Bible and family scrapbooks. There's no small irony in Grant's return to the Deep South. As the leader of the Union army, he masterminded the defeat of the Confederate forces at Vicksburg.

Author John Grisham's papers are also among the prominent collections here. Though many know the writer attended law school at Ole Miss and had his practice in Oxford, few realize he received his undergraduate degree in accounting from Mississippi State. An avid baseball fan, Grisham penned the introduction to the book *Inside Dudy Noble: A Celebration of MSU Baseball.*

// YELL LIKE H-E-L-L

When it comes to football, Mississippi State fans are as passionate as any in the country.

Alumni love the Drill Field, the original campus green with its twin buildings on the north and south ends. Many visit the Chapel of Memories, constructed with bricks salvaged from the original campus building that burned in 1959.

Yet on game day all eyes are on The Junction, where tents go up on Friday and the festivities really start ringing on Saturday morning. A more convivial bunch you won't find anywhere. "MSU fans are known for their Southern hospitality," says one proud Dawg. "It's more than a football game for us. We enjoy getting here early, hanging out with friends and family, and preparing to support our Bulldogs."

It may be all sweet tea and barbecue before the game, but it's hell's bells by the time the Dawgs make their walk through The Junction to the stadium. Mississippi State fans have cowbells, and they know how to use them. The atmosphere inside Davis Wade is deafening.

A sign inside one tailgate tent sums it up. "Love us or fear us. Either way, you're going to hear us."

// LOYAL SONS, WE'LL ALWAYS BE

It's true Mississippi State has never won a national championship in football. But they have fielded some fine teams, and these underdogs have been known to take down the conference giants—while also making their mark on the SEC in other ways.

The new Dowsing-Bell Plaza, located on the north side of Davis Wade Stadium, honors the legacy of the school's first African-American student-athletes, Frank Dowsing, Jr., and Robert Bell, who broke the color barrier at MSU in 1969. Dowsing was a two-time All-SEC defensive back, while Bell earned three letters as a defensive back.

Mississippi State also hired the first African-American head coach in SEC history. Sylvester Croom, Jr., led the Bulldogs from 2004 to 2008, paving the way for other coaches of color.

State fans still have a place in their hearts for star quarterback Dak Prescott. Redshirted as a freshman, Prescott played backup quarterback in 2012 and 2013 until a concussion sidelined the starter. He played 11 games that season and ended the year as MVP of the Liberty Bowl. In 2014, Prescott led State to a 10-2 record and its first No. 1 ranking in school history. In 2015, he seemingly reached new heights each week, until he owned every quarterback record at the school. Prescott was drafted by the Dallas Cowboys and was named NFL Offensive Rookie of the Year in 2016. Fans adore Prescott, and the feeling's mutual.

"At Mississippi State, we don't have fans," Prescott has said. "We have family."

FUN FACT

Davis Wade Stadium in Starkville is named for booster Floyd Davis Wade, Sr., co-founder of Aflac.

MAROON AND WHITE
BUTTER COOKIES

MISSISSIPPI
STATE

BULLDOGS

HAILS

CHOOSE MAROON BLOOMS AND
MAROON-AND-WHITE GINGHAM
LINENS AND LINERS FOR
SCHOOL-SPIRITED COLOR.

THE ULTIMATE
BULLY BURGER

MISSISSIPPI STATE
BULLDOGS

Sweet Heat
Pimiento Cheese
P. 92

The Ultimate
Bully Burger with
Dill Pickle Sauce
P. 169

Saucy Cola
Baked Beans
P. 203

Maroon-and-White
Butter Cookies
P. 254

SERVES 8

PAINT A PORTABLE WOODEN
TABLE (OR A PICNIC
TABLE AT HOME) MAROON
FOR A RUSTIC-CHIC LOOK.

PUT COWBELLS TO USE AS
DECOR BEFORE THE GAME.
WOODEN DOG BONE CUTOUTS
DOUBLE AS FOOD LABELS.

SWEET HEAT PIMIENTO
CHEESE

TE™

CARAMELIZED ONION-POTATO SOUP

SERVES 8 // HANDS-ON 55 MINUTES // TOTAL 2 HOURS, 25 MINUTES

This comforting soup has all the classic flavors of an old-fashioned onion soup. The addition of golden potatoes and rich Edam cheese gives it a smooth, creamy texture. If you can't find Edam, substitute with similar Gouda. And if you find yourself tailgating on Mississippi State's campus, whether visiting or at home, definitely use the Edam sold at the Mississippi State Cheese Store.

2 tablespoons salted butter

1 tablespoon olive oil

5 cups chopped sweet onions (about 4 large onions)

1 teaspoon granulated sugar

3 tablespoons all-purpose flour

1 (32-ounce) container chicken broth

2½ pounds Yukon Gold potatoes, peeled and cut into ½-inch cubes

2 cups water

1 teaspoon chopped fresh thyme

1 teaspoon table salt

½ teaspoon black pepper

1 bay leaf

4 ounces Edam cheese, grated (about 1 cup)

1 cup half-and-half

Toppings: chopped fresh chives, crumbled cooked bacon, sour cream, black pepper

EXTRA POINT

You can take this soup to your tailgate site in a slow cooker without the cheese and half-and-half. When you arrive, heat it up, and then stir in the cheese and half-and-half.

1 Melt the butter with the oil in a large Dutch oven over medium. Add the onions and sugar, and cook, stirring often, until the onions are caramel colored, 45 to 50 minutes.

2 Sprinkle the onions with the flour, and cook, stirring constantly, 1 minute. Gradually add the chicken broth, stirring constantly, until well blended and slightly thickened. Stir in the potatoes, water, thyme, salt, pepper, and bay leaf; bring to a boil. Reduce the heat to low, and simmer, stirring occasionally, until the potatoes are tender, 30 to 35 minutes. Remove and discard the bay leaf.

3 Place half of the soup in a food processor or blender. (If using a blender, remove the center piece of the blender lid [to allow steam to escape]; secure the lid on the blender, and place a clean towel over the opening in the lid.) Process until smooth. Return the mixture to the Dutch oven over low; stir well. Stir in the cheese and half-and-half; cook until the cheese is melted and the mixture is thoroughly heated, about 2 minutes. Add the desired toppings.

COACH'S FAVORITE MEATY CHILI ▶

SERVES **8** // HANDS-ON **20 MINUTES** // TOTAL **1 HOUR, 50 MINUTES**

Tender black beans, corn kernels, and shredded Cheddar give this smoky chili plenty of heartiness to help you stay on your A-game all day long. It's great served alone or over rice or corn chips. Serve with cornbread, if desired.

TENT
TALK

Which Southeastern Conference school has the largest stadium?

A. Tennessee
B. Texas A&M
C. LSU
D. Alabama

1 tablespoon canola oil
1½ pounds beef stew meat
1 cup chopped red bell pepper (about 1 bell pepper)
1 cup chopped yellow onion (about 1 onion)
2 tablespoons finely chopped garlic (about 5 garlic cloves)
1 tablespoon chipotle chile powder
2 teaspoons kosher salt
1 teaspoon black pepper

1 cup chicken stock
1½ cups frozen corn kernels
½ cup sweet-and-smoky barbecue sauce
2 (15.5-ounce) cans black beans, drained and rinsed
2 (15-ounce) cans diced fire-roasted tomatoes
4 ounces Cheddar cheese, shredded (about 1 cup)
½ cup sour cream
¼ cup sliced scallions (about 2 scallions)

1 Heat the oil in a Dutch oven over medium-high. Pat the beef dry with a paper towel. Add the beef to the Dutch oven; cook, stirring occasionally, until browned on all sides, about 8 minutes. Add the bell pepper, onion, and garlic; cook, stirring occasionally, until starting to soften, about 3 minutes. Add the chile powder, salt, and pepper; cook, stirring often, 1 minute.

2 Add ½ cup of the stock to the Dutch oven, and bring to a boil. Cook, stirring from the bottom of the pan to loosen the browned bits, 1 minute. Add the corn, barbecue sauce, beans, and tomatoes; bring to a boil. Reduce the heat to medium-low; cover and cook, stirring occasionally, until the beef is tender, about 1 hour to 1 hour and 30 minutes. Stir in the remaining ½ cup stock, if needed, for the desired consistency. Serve the chili with the cheese, sour cream, and scallions.

TOMATO-RED PEPPER SOUP

SERVES **4 TO 6** // HANDS-ON **15 MINUTES** // TOTAL **15 MINUTES**

Amp up classic tomato soup with tangy roasted red peppers. Pair this simple soup with basic grilled cheese sandwiches for a double crowd-pleaser. Moreover, this soup can be easily doubled to feed more guests.

1 (28-ounce) can whole tomatoes
1 (12-ounce) jar roasted red peppers, drained
¼ cup half-and-half
1½ teaspoons kosher salt

1 teaspoon granulated sugar
½ teaspoon freshly ground black pepper
2 garlic cloves
¼ cup water

Process the tomatoes, red peppers, half-and-half, salt, sugar, pepper, garlic, and water in a food processor until smooth, stopping to scrape down the sides as needed. Transfer the mixture to a medium saucepan, and cook over medium-high, stirring often, until hot, about 8 minutes. Serve immediately.

HOT OFF THE GRIDIRON

FROM SAUCY CHICKEN WINGS AND HEARTY SLIDERS TO SHRIMP AND GRITS AND LOADED NACHOS, AND BEYOND—INCLUDING DISHES TO GRILL, SMOKE, FRY, AND SLOW-COOK—THESE RECIPES OFFER FULL COVER FOR ALL YOUR MAIN-DISH TAILGATING WANTS AND NEEDS.

DRUM ROLL, PLEASE!

Meet Big MO. He stands 9 feet tall, measures 4½ feet wide, weighs 800 pounds, and is the biggest force in the Southeastern Conference. In fact, no other drum anywhere in the U.S. compares size-wise.

A proud member of the Marching Mizzou Band, Big MO has guardians that come from the school's national honorary band service fraternity and sorority, Kappa Kappa Psi and Tau Beta Sigma. A crew of five rolls him to the games, dances with him during "The Missouri Waltz," and beats him mightily after each Tiger score. They also take the lead on the school's famous M-I-Z-Z-O-U chant.

In 1981, fans from the Tiger Quarterback Club of St. Louis paid $5,000 for a big red drum with gold flecks, strapped it to the bed of a pickup, and raced the instrument to Columbia, Missouri. After painting it black and gold, they introduced Big MO to the Mizzou family at the Tiger Fall Rally, held the week of the first football game.

Over time, Big MO took a beating and began to look a little worse for wear. In 2011, the Big MO Foundation raised the money to build a bigger and better drum. The job was accepted by a custom drum maker in Barnesville, Georgia, named Neil Boumpani, a music professor and percussionist in his own right.

The new and improved Big MO, the largest bass drum in the country, was christened at the university's Homecoming in 2012, the same year Mizzou joined the Southeastern Conference. The original Big MO now has a place of honor in the Missouri Student Union.

FUN FACT

MO is the standard postal abbreviation for Missouri.

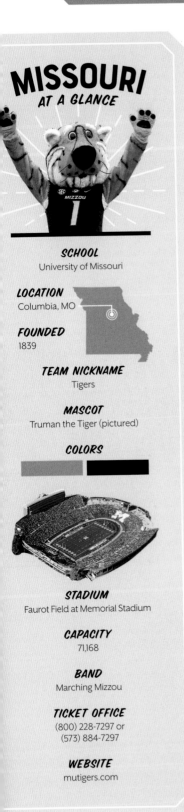

MISSOURI
AT A GLANCE

SCHOOL
University of Missouri

LOCATION
Columbia, MO

FOUNDED
1839

TEAM NICKNAME
Tigers

MASCOT
Truman the Tiger (pictured)

COLORS

STADIUM
Faurot Field at Memorial Stadium

CAPACITY
71,168

BAND
Marching Mizzou

TICKET OFFICE
(800) 228-7297 or
(573) 884-7297

WEBSITE
mutigers.com

// A BULLY FOR OL' MIZZOU

The dome of Jesse Hall rises majestically behind the six soaring limestone columns that sit on the Francis Quadrangle at the University of Missouri in Columbia. Pressed against a blue autumn sky, the columns are stately, beautiful—and intriguing.

On a snowy Saturday in January 1892, a fire started by faulty wiring engulfed Academic Hall. When the smoke had cleared, the columns were all that was left of the school's original building.

To a visitor or a prospective student, these orphaned columns might seem out of place on a manicured lawn. But to alumni, they represent the cherished ideals upon which the university was built: excellence, discovery, responsibility, and respect.

The Columns provide the perfect backdrop for all kinds of university gatherings—parties, picnics, and yes, even protests. Thousands of freshmen enter Mizzou through The Columns in the fall Tiger Walk ceremony, and graduating seniors exit the same way in the spring at Tiger Prowl.

// TIGER TOWN!

Founding fathers always planned to have a university in Columbia, and they set aside land in the town's original plans.

The oldest public institution west of the Mississippi, the University of Missouri is on par academically with the likes of Duke, Johns Hopkins, and Vanderbilt. It's quite beautiful, too. The entire campus is a botanical garden, cultivated and maintained for the enjoyment and education of the Mizzou community.

In fact, the university is so integrated into the town that the mascot was plucked from the pages of Columbia's history. Three SEC schools claim a tiger as their mascot—Auburn, LSU, and Missouri. But MU's mascot is not named for an animal.

Though teams have worn the black and gold of a Bengal tiger since 1890, Mizzou takes its team name from the band of armed residents—the "Missouri Tigers"—whose swift and fierce defense repelled marauding Confederate guerillas during the Civil War. Truman the Tiger, the school's costumed mascot, is named for native son and 33rd U.S. President Harry S. Truman.

// WELCOME TO THE ZOU!

Mizzou's Memorial Stadium—a.k.a. The Zou—sits in a natural valley south of the original campus. Though completed in 1926, an uncharacteristically wet autumn kept sod from being laid before the first game against Tulane. Rain marred the contest, too, resulting in what sportswriter Bob Broeg called "a scoreless mudpie tie."

Even today, the feature that most defines the stadium is the 90-foot-wide by 95-foot-tall whitewashed "M" that sits on a grassy hill behind the north end zone. Freshmen fashioned the monument from rocks left over from the original stadium construction just in time for the Oct. 1, 1927, game against archrival Kansas.

New students still maintain the giant "M," giving the rocks a coat of white paint each year before the first home game. At the end of the season, senior football players each take a rock from the pile as a personal keepsake.

// EVERY TRUE SON

Though Memorial Stadium honors those lost in World War I, the playing field pays tribute to longtime coach Don Faurot. The mastermind behind the Split-T offense, Faurot amassed a record of 101-80-10 at Mizzou, a record that stood until Gary Pinkel came along in 2001.

In 15 seasons under Pinkel's direction, MU claimed 10 winning seasons with 10 bowl appearances. His best came in 2007, when the Tigers ended the regular season ranked No. 1 in the AP Poll. Missouri ultimately lost to Oklahoma in the Big 12 championship, but they prevailed against Arkansas in the Cotton Bowl to finish the year 12-2 and No. 4 in the country.

Pinkel also oversaw Mizzou's transition from Big 12 play to the Southeastern Conference in 2012, when his team was invited to become the SEC's 14th team. By the time he retired in 2015, the coach had amassed a record of 118-73 and had sent dozens of players to the NFL, many as first-round draft picks.

// COME HOME TO MIZZOU-RAH!

Traditions run deep at Ol' Mizzou. Tailgates feature Kansas City- or St. Louis-style barbecue, and thousands greet the Fighting Tigers as they make their way to the stadium before a game. Truman the Tiger roars into the football stadium aboard a vintage Boone County fire truck known as "Truman's Taxi."

Fans are drilled on how to do their part, including locking arms and swaying during the playing of "Old Missouri," the school's alma mater. Freshman learn the important lessons on day one: Come Early, Stay Late, Be Loud, Wear Gold, Hate Kansas.

In fact, disdain for their archrival helped give birth to one of football's most endearing traditions. In 1911, Athletic Director Chester Brewer invited alumni to "come home" for the Tigers' game against (who else?) Kansas. More than 10,000 answered his call, and the modern homecoming day celebration was born.

These days, Homecoming at Mizzou is a two-week party, with intramural competitions, a Friday night pep rally, and a hometown parade. Missouri fans even bleed for their school—a three-day blood drive extracts nearly 5,000 pints from MU's sturdiest stock.

FUN FACT

The Columns at Mizzou are one of the most photographed spots in the state of Missouri, surpassed only by the Gateway Arch in St. Louis.

DISPOSABLE WOODEN CUTLERY LOOKS SPECIAL WHEN BUNDLED WITH REFEREE-STRIPED NAPKINS.

A STARK BLACK TABLECLOTH ALLOWS THE BOLD GOLD DECOR AND BEAUTIFUL FOOD TO TAKE CENTER STAGE

MISSOURI
TIGERS

Caramel-Walnut
Snack Mix
P. 105

Sweet and Spicy
Mizzou Ribs
P. 172

Loaded Golden
Ravioli Nachos
P. 217

Tiger Stripes
Frozen Custard
P. 240

SERVES 8

SET OUT SMALL BOXES OR
CUPS FOR THE SNACK MIX.
RANUNCULUS AND CRASPEDIA
ARE IDEAL GOLDEN BLOOMS.

TOUCHDOWN!

BBQ CHICKEN DRUMSTICKS

SERVES **8** // HANDS-ON **30 MINUTES** // TOTAL **1 HOUR, 10 MINUTES**

This simple recipe should become a staple of your game-day table. The apple cider vinegar and paprika lend the barbecue sauce a bright, smoky flavor. If your tailgate site doesn't allow grills, prepare these drumsticks at home and reheat them on-site. This pairs particulary well with Wedge Salad on a Stick (pictured at left); see page 199 for the recipe.

see page 199 for the recipe.

1 tablespoon vegetable oil

1 cup finely chopped white onion (8 ounces)

4 garlic cloves, minced (about 1 tablespoon)

2 cups ketchup

½ cup packed dark brown sugar

3 tablespoons Worcestershire sauce

3 tablespoons apple cider vinegar

1 teaspoon smoked paprika

½ teaspoon cayenne pepper

1 tablespoon kosher salt

1 tablespoon black pepper

16 chicken drumsticks (about 4 pounds)

TENT TALK

What is a gridiron?

A. An iron used to brand cattle

B. An old-fashioned iron used to press clothing

C. A metal grate used for grilling

D. None of the above

1 Heat the oil in a large heavy-bottomed saucepan over medium. Add the onion, and cook, stirring often, until tender, about 5 minutes. Add the garlic, and cook until fragrant, about 1 minute. Stir in the ketchup, brown sugar, Worcestershire, vinegar, paprika, cayenne, and 1 teaspoon each of the salt and black pepper; bring to a boil. Remove from the heat. Process with an immersion blender until smooth, and reserve ½ cup.

2 Preheat 1 side of a grill to medium-low (300°F to 350°F), leaving the other side unlit. Sprinkle the drumsticks with the remaining 2 teaspoons each salt and pepper. Place the drumsticks over the unlit side of the grill, and grill, covered, 20 minutes. Turn the drumsticks, brush with ½ cup barbecue sauce, and grill, covered, 20 minutes. Turn the drumsticks, brush with another ½ cup barbecue sauce, and grill, covered, until cooked through, 30 to 40 minutes. Transfer the drumsticks to the lit side of the grill, and grill until the skin is crispy, 2 to 3 minutes. Serve with the reserved ½ cup sauce.

SMOKED WAR EAGLE WINGS
WITH WHITE SAUCE

SERVES **10** // HANDS-ON **25 MINUTES**
TOTAL **10 HOURS, 15 MINUTES, INCLUDES 8 HOURS CHILLING**

EXTRA POINT

This recipe utilizes two classic Alabama sauces: white sauce and Alabama-style BBQ sauce, which has a consistency similar to vinegar or hot sauce.

Smoky, tangy, tender, tempting—make these your go-to smoked wings when tailgating near Auburn's Jordan-Hare Stadium or following the Tigers on the road. The brine gives the meat a sweet flavor and keeps it tender. The wings will change to an amber color when the smoke has thoroughly penetrated the meat. After smoking the wings, while they're still hot, toss them in the hot sauce and Alabama-style barbecue sauce. Serve the wings with the White Sauce drizzled on top or on the side for dunking.

WINGS
4 cups sweet brewed iced tea (such as Milo's)
½ cup water
5 tablespoons kosher salt
4 pounds chicken drumettes and flats

WHITE SAUCE
1 cup mayonnaise
¼ cup apple cider vinegar

1 tablespoon black pepper
2 teaspoons Worcestershire sauce
1½ teaspoons granulated sugar
1 teaspoon kosher salt

ADDITIONAL INGREDIENTS
¼ cup hot sauce (such as Frank's RedHot Original)
¼ cup Alabama-style red barbecue sauce (such as Golden Rule or Dreamland)

1   Make the Wings: Place the tea in a 4- to 6-quart food-safe container. Heat the water and salt in a small saucepan over high, stirring constantly, until the salt is dissolved, about 5 minutes. Add to the tea. Add the chicken, and cover and chill 8 hours or up to overnight.

2   Prepare the smoker according to the manufacturer's instructions for indirect heat. Bring the internal temperature to 250°F. Maintain the temperature. Drain the chicken, discarding the brine; pat the chicken dry with paper towels. Place the chicken on the grate over indirect heat, and smoke, until cooked through, 1½ to 2 hours, maintaining the temperature inside the smoker around 250°F. Move to direct heat, and smoke, covered, until charred, about 5 minutes. Remove from the smoker.

3   Make the White Sauce: Whisk together all the White Sauce ingredients. (The sauce will keep in the refrigerator for up to 3 days.)

4   Stir together the hot sauce and barbecue sauce in a large bowl. Add the chicken, and toss to coat. Transfer to a platter, and serve with the White Sauce.

WONDER WINGS

SERVES **6 TO 8** // HANDS-ON **25 MINUTES** // TOTAL **1 HOUR, NOT INCLUDING SAUCES**

Our easy, indirect-to-direct-heat grilling technique turns out tender wings with crisp skin. Pair them with either of the two sauces below. Serve with Street Corn Salad (pictured at left); see page 203 for the recipe.

3 pounds chicken wings
2 teaspoons vegetable oil
1 teaspoon kosher salt

½ teaspoon freshly ground black pepper
Classic White Sauce or Buttery Hot Sauce
   (recipes follow)

1   Light 1 side of the grill, heating to medium-high (350°F to 400°F); leave the other side unlit. Dry each wing well with paper towels. Toss together the wings and oil in a large bowl. Sprinkle with the salt and pepper, and toss to coat.

2   Place the chicken over the unlit side of the grill, and grill, covered, 15 minutes on each side. Transfer the chicken to the lit side of the grill, and grill, uncovered, 10 to 12 minutes or until the skin is crispy and lightly charred, turning every 2 to 3 minutes. Toss the wings immediately with the desired sauce. Let stand, tossing occasionally, 5 minutes before serving.

TENT *TALK*

The line of scrimmage—also known as the neutral zone—is an imaginary line that separates the offensive team from the defensive team. Approximately how wide is the line of scrimmage?

A. 10 inches
B. 11 inches
C. 12 inches
D. 18 inches

CLASSIC WHITE SAUCE

MAKES **ABOUT ²/₃ CUP** // HANDS-ON **10 MINUTES** // TOTAL **10 MINUTES**

This tangy sauce is so addictively good that you might find yourself pairing it with all sorts of meats, from pork tenderloin to cuts of beef to lamb shanks.

⅓ cup mayonnaise
3 tablespoons chopped fresh chives, plus
   more for garnish
1 tablespoon prepared horseradish
4 teaspoons apple cider vinegar

2 teaspoons Creole mustard
1 teaspoon coarsely ground black pepper
¼ teaspoon granulated sugar
1 finely grated garlic clove

Whisk together all the ingredients. Garnish with the additional chives, if desired.

BUTTERY HOT SAUCE

MAKES **ABOUT ¹/₃ CUP** // HANDS-ON **5 MINUTES** // TOTAL **5 MINUTES**

Pairing rich butter with spicy cayenne pepper and paprika and the molasses from the brown sugar is a match made in heaven. It's oh-so-good with the wings.

¼ cup (2 ounces) butter, melted
3 to 4 teaspoons cayenne pepper
2 teaspoons dark brown sugar
¾ teaspoon kosher salt

½ teaspoon smoked paprika
½ teaspoon garlic powder
1 tablespoon apple cider vinegar

Cook the melted butter, cayenne, sugar, salt, paprika, and garlic powder in a small saucepan over medium, stirring constantly, 1 minute or until fragrant. Remove from the heat, and stir in the apple cider vinegar.

CHICKEN, WHITE BEAN, *AND* SPINACH SALAD

SERVES 6 // HANDS-ON 30 MINUTES // TOTAL 8 HOURS, 30 MINUTES

EXTRA POINT

Slow-cook the beans and chicken, and shred the chicken the day before. Assemble the salad at your tailgate.

When it comes to a salad that's worthy of a trip to the tailgate, you won't find a better one than this. White beans and chicken breasts are slow-cooked in savory stock and then mixed with fresh spinach, orange segments, almonds, goat cheese, and a tangy dressing for a hearty main dish.

1 pound dried white beans
4 cups unsalted chicken stock
1 tablespoon chopped garlic
½ teaspoon smoked paprika
1½ teaspoons kosher salt
1¼ teaspoons black pepper
4 skinless, bone-in chicken breasts
½ cup plus 1 tablespoon olive oil

3 oranges
¼ cup Champagne vinegar
2 tablespoons finely chopped shallots
4 ounces fresh baby spinach
¼ cup slivered almonds, toasted
4 ounces goat cheese, crumbled (about 1 cup)

1. Combine the white beans, chicken stock, garlic, paprika, and ½ teaspoon each of the salt and pepper in a 5- to 6-quart slow cooker. Cover and cook on LOW 6 hours.

2. Sprinkle the chicken with ½ teaspoon each of the salt and pepper. Heat 1 tablespoon of the oil in a large skillet over medium-high; add the chicken, and cook until golden, 2 minutes per side. Nestle the chicken into the beans in the slow cooker at the end of the 6-hour bean cook time. Cover; cook on LOW until the chicken and beans are tender and done, about 2 hours. Transfer the chicken to a cutting board; remove the meat from the bones and shred. Discard the bones. Remove 3 cups of beans; drain. (Save the remaining beans for another use.) Let the chicken and beans cool.

3. Squeeze the juice from 1 orange to equal ¼ cup. Peel the remaining 2 oranges; cut into segments. Whisk together the orange juice, vinegar, shallots, and remaining ½ teaspoon salt and ¼ teaspoon pepper in a large bowl. Add the remaining ½ cup oil in a steady stream, whisking until incorporated. Add the spinach, shredded chicken, beans, orange segments, almonds, and cheese, and toss with the dressing.

BUFFALO CHICKEN MEATBALL SLIDERS

SERVES **32** // HANDS-ON **30 MINUTES**
TOTAL **1 HOUR, 45 MINUTES, INCLUDES 1 HOUR CHILLING**

This recipe makes enough sliders for an army. If you're tailgating with your child on game day at the university he or she attends, tell them to invite all their friends, and feed them this hearty dish. (Pictured on page 2, bottom left)

1 tablespoon kosher salt
2 teaspoons fennel seeds
1 teaspoon black peppercorns
2 pounds ground chicken
½ cup firmly packed fresh flat-leaf parsley leaves, chopped
½ cup finely grated Parmesan cheese
½ small sweet onion, grated
2 large eggs, lightly beaten
2 garlic cloves, minced
1 tablespoon extra-virgin olive oil
1 (5-ounce) bottle Buffalo-style hot sauce
32 small rolls or buns, split
Garnishes: thinly sliced celery, fresh flat-leaf parsley leaves, dill pickle slices

BLUE CHEESE SAUCE
4 ounces blue cheese, crumbled (about 1 cup)
½ cup heavy cream
¼ cup sour cream
½ shallot, minced
½ teaspoon firmly packed lemon zest
2 tablespoons fresh lemon juice
Kosher salt
Freshly ground black pepper

TENT TALK

On what yard line is the ball placed for an extra point attempt or a two-point conversion try in college football?

A. 10-yard line
B. 5-yard line
C. 3-yard line
D. 2-yard line

1 Place the salt, fennel seeds, and black peppercorns in a mortar bowl or spice grinder; grind to a fine powder, using a pestle or spice grinder. Place the chicken, parsley, Parmesan, onion, eggs, garlic, olive oil, and crushed spices in a large bowl. Combine the mixture with your hands until blended and smooth, 2 minutes. Cover; chill 1 hour.

2 Meanwhile, make the Blue Cheese Sauce: Process the blue cheese, heavy cream, sour cream, shallot, lemon zest, and lemon juice in a food processor or blender until smooth and creamy. Season with the salt and pepper to taste.

3 Preheat the oven to 400°F. Drop the chicken mixture by rounded spoonfuls 1½ inches apart onto an aluminum foil-lined jelly-roll pan lightly coated with cooking spray, using a medium-size cookie scoop (about 1½ inches).

4 Bake at 400°F for 10 to 12 minutes or until done. Toss the meatballs with the hot sauce. Serve on the split rolls with the Blue Cheese Sauce. Garnish, if desired.

NASHVILLE HOT CHICKEN SLIDERS

SERVES 8 // HANDS-ON 40 MINUTES
TOTAL 1 HOUR, 40 MINUTES, INCLUDES 1 HOUR CHILLING

EXTRA
POINT

You don't have to
toast the buns, but we
recommend doing
so to keep them from
becoming soggy from
the sauce.

Crispy, spicy-sweet chicken tenders topped with a crunchy pickle and sandwiched between toasted slider buns? We say "yes and please!" to this iconic Nashville food. Tailgaters who don't love spice will need to stay wide.

3 cups whole buttermilk
3 tablespoons cayenne pepper
3 tablespoons kosher salt
2 tablespoons black pepper
16 chicken breast tenders (about 2 pounds)
2 tablespoons light brown sugar

6 cups peanut oil
3 cups (about 12 ounces) self-rising flour
1 tablespoon cornstarch
1 teaspoon garlic powder
2 tablespoons unsalted butter, softened
16 slider buns
16 dill pickle slices (or more, if desired)

1 Combine the buttermilk, 1½ tablespoons of the cayenne, and 1 tablespoon each of the salt and pepper in a large bowl. Add the chicken; toss to coat. Chill 1 hour.

2 Combine the brown sugar and remaining 1½ tablespoons cayenne in a bowl. Heat the oil in a large Dutch oven over medium to 200°F. Whisk 1 cup of the hot oil into the brown sugar mixture; set aside. Continue heating the remaining oil in the Dutch oven to 350°F over medium.

3 Combine the flour, cornstarch, garlic powder, and remaining 2 tablespoons salt and 1 tablespoon pepper in a shallow baking dish. Remove the chicken from the buttermilk, and let the excess drip off. Dredge in the flour mixture; shake off the excess.

4 Fry the chicken in the hot oil until golden brown and cooked through, 5 to 6 minutes.

5 Preheat the broiler on low with the rack 6 inches from the heat. Spread the butter on the cut side of each bun slice, and place on a rimmed baking sheet. Broil until lightly toasted, about 4 minutes. Remove from the oven.

6 Toss the hot chicken in the reserved brown sugar-oil mixture. Place 1 chicken tender and 1 pickle (or more) on the bottom half of each slider bun. Top each with the other half of the bun.

FUN FACT

Ole Miss battles Mississippi State for the Golden Egg Trophy each year. The name derives from the more egg-like shape of footballs used in the early 1900s, when the rivalry began.

HOTTY TODDY, GOSH ALMIGHTY

The most famous Ole Miss cheer
starts with a simple question. "Are you ready?"
And there is only one acceptable answer.
"Hell, yes!"

The Hotty Toddy. Some of the words that make up this cheer are nonsensical but sound oddly musical in a fun and fabulous way. And some of them are a little naughty, too, as the cheer is peppered with colorful swear words. But the Hotty Toddy chant is to Ole Miss what Faulkner is to Mississippi. Irreplaceable.

"Damn right!"

The roots of this cheer are hard to trace. The first reliable reference can be found in a 1926 issue of *The Mississippian*, the school's student newspaper. But the cheer was written then as "Heighty, Tighty," a phrase associated with Virginia Tech's military band.

How the words morphed into Hotty Toddy is anybody's guess. All you really need to know is that the Hotty Toddy is now synonymous with Ole Miss and Oxford. It's the first thing new students learn and the last thing they shout at graduation. It's ubiquitous at tailgate parties, football games, and get-togethers all over the world.

And, if you listen closely, the Hotty Toddy answers the question, "Who the hell are we?" By nature, Ole Miss fans are spirited, hospitable, and fun-loving. If you're not clear on this, stop by The Grove on a football Saturday. This grassy 10-acre expanse is a microcosm of Mississippi culture. Tents are outfitted with fresh flowers amid heirloom silver and china. Students wear sky-high stilettos and party dresses, bow ties and seersucker. When pundits ponder the best tailgating school in the country, the answer is easy: "Ole Miss, by damn!"

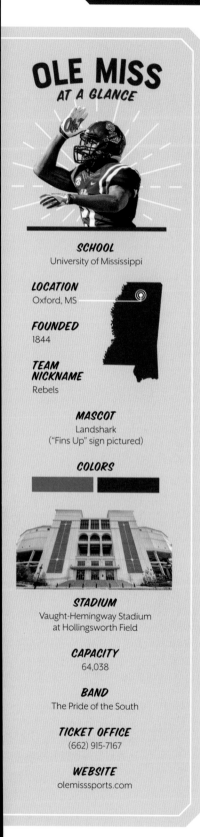

OLE MISS
AT A GLANCE

SCHOOL
University of Mississippi

LOCATION
Oxford, MS

FOUNDED
1844

TEAM NICKNAME
Rebels

MASCOT
Landshark
("Fins Up" sign pictured)

COLORS

STADIUM
Vaught-Hemingway Stadium
at Hollingsworth Field

CAPACITY
64,038

BAND
The Pride of the South

TICKET OFFICE
(662) 915-7167

WEBSITE
olemisssports.com

// HODDY TODDY COCKTAIL PARTY

The Grove may be peaceful and quiet on any given weekday or Sunday, but on a fall Saturday when the Rebels play at home, this tree-shaded area at the heart of Ole Miss becomes the epicenter of the school's famous tailgating scene.

The Grove is off limits until Friday evening, when there's a mad dash to grab the best spots. In recent years, tailgating has spread to the nearby Circle and the grounds of the Lyceum. By morning, a sea of cardinal red, navy blue, and bright white tents fills with rejoicing fans. What unfolds throughout the day is a Southern garden party gone wild.

Elaborate flowers, heirloom silver, and fine china grace linen-draped tables. In some tents, chandeliers hang, while others feature bubbling drink fountains worthy of a country club wedding. Fare ranges from simple hors d'oeuvres to elaborate catered buffets.

In the open spaces, kids toss footballs and coeds prance about in heels and sundresses, escorted by young men in jackets and loafers. More than one lovestruck swain has proposed to his sweetheart in the cardinal-red and navy-blue Grove on game day.

The party reaches a fever pitch two-and-a-half hours before game time when the players and coaching staff stroll through the crowd on their way to Vaught-Hemingway Stadium.

// THE BALLAD OF ARCHIE WHO

Football is more than a game here at Ole Miss. It's a way of life. One has to look no further than the local speed limit to find this truth. Cars may go no faster than 18 mph. Why? That's the number favorite son Archie Manning wore when he quarterbacked the Rebels.

Manning came to Ole Miss in 1968 but didn't start until his sophomore year. In a rare nationally televised prime-time game against Alabama in 1969, he threw for 436 yards and three touchdowns and rushed for 104 yards in a 33-32 loss. By the end of his junior year and an 8-3 season, fans were wearing "Archie's Army" buttons, and the kid from Drew, Mississippi, was featured on the September 1970 issue of *Sports Illustrated*.

The fervor drove opponents crazy. Tennessee fans even wore "Archie Who?" buttons—until Manning's Rebels eviscerated the Vols 38-0. After that game, a postal clerk from Magnolia penned a song titled "The Ballad of Archie Who," set to the tune of Johnny Cash's "Folsom Prison Blues." Archie Fever gripped the nation.

During his senior year, Archie married homecoming queen Olivia Williams and was drafted by the New Orleans Saints. The couple went on to have three long, lean sons. As the boys developed into superb athletes, Ole Miss fans began to hope. Oldest son Cooper signed with Ole Miss, but a latent spinal condition left him unable to play. Middle son Peyton chose his own path and put together a remarkable career at Tennessee.

// ELI'S COMIN'

Then came Eli. Euphoria ensued when Archie's youngest announced that he would play at Ole Miss. The song "Eli's Coming" was played all over campus before the youngest Manning had even graduated from high school.

While at Ole Miss, Eli set or tied 45 Ole Miss records. He passed for 10,119 yards and 81 touchdowns, still among the best in the SEC, and brought home a house full of hardware, including the Maxwell Award as the nation's best all-around player, the Johnny Unitas Golden Arm Award, and SEC MVP honors.

Today, a wide brick wall marks the entrance to Manning Way, the street that curves around Vaught-Hemingway. Though it was named for Archie, the speed limit here was changed to 10 mph to honor Eli's number in 2012 after he led the Giants to a win in Super Bowl XLVI.

// NEVER QUIT

Other players have made an impact on Ole Miss, too. On Oct. 28, 1989, during a game against Vanderbilt, defensive back Roy Lee "Chucky" Mullins broke up a pass near the goal line. When the play was over, Mullins lay on the field, unmoving. He had shattered four vertebrae and was paralyzed from the neck down.

Though he ultimately returned to campus as a student, Mullins died on May 6, 1991, of a blood clot. Several movies and documentaries have been made about his life and legacy. In 2014, Coliseum Drive on campus was renamed Chucky Mullins Drive in his honor. Today, Rebel players touch a statue with Mullins' likeness before taking the field.

While Mullins' No. 38 jersey was retired, one defensive player each year—whoever most embodies Chucky Mullins' "never quit" attitude—receives the Chucky Mullins Courage Award and earns the right to wear his number.

// A NEW MASCOT IN TOWN

Beginning in the 2018 football season, a new mascot will walk the Ole Miss sidelines. Though the school will continue to be known as the Rebels, the Landshark will replace Rebel the Bear as the university's mascot. The term "Landshark" originated from Tony Fein, a senior linebacker and Iraq War army veteran, during the 2008 season when the Rebels ended a four-year losing streak by finishing their regular season with a 9-4 record. Since then, to celebrate big plays, fans and players cry "Fins Up!" and form a "shark fin" by touching their thumbs to their foreheads.

Roy Lee Mullins, left, takes the field during a game on September 24, 1988 at Vaught-Hemingway Stadium in Oxford, Mississippi.

FUN FACT

Tailgating at The Grove began in 1991. Too much rain turned the area into a marsh. It was closed to all vehicles, and fans had to abandon their cars for tent-style feasting.

SCATTERED MINI BOW TIES
AND TINY PENNANTS ARE
DETAILS ALL WILL LOVE. USE
THEM AS TAILGATE FAVORS.

OleMiss®

OUTLINE THE TABLE, OR
SNAKE THROUGH IT, USING
A BRIGHT RED-AND-BLUE
TASSEL BANNER.

OLE MISS
REBELS

Ole Miss

Sweet Magnolia **P. 59**	Fried Catfish Fingers with Comeback Sauce **P. 183**	Pimiento Cheese Hush Puppies with Dilly Tartar Sauce **P. 214**	Mississippi Mud Pie Trifle **P. 228**

SERVES 8

Ole Miss

TRAYS AREN'T JUST FOR TRANSPORTING FOOD. USE THEM AS SERVEWARE TO CONTAIN AND HIGHLIGHT.

CAROLINA CHICKEN BURGERS *WITH* CREAMY ANCHO SLAW

SERVES **6** // HANDS-ON **20 MINUTES**
TOTAL **1 HOUR, 5 MINUTES, INCLUDES SAUCE AND SLAW**

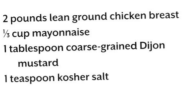

The secret ingredient in our chicken burgers? Mayo. It gives lean meat moisture.

2 pounds lean ground chicken breast
⅓ cup mayonnaise
1 tablespoon coarse-grained Dijon mustard
1 teaspoon kosher salt

½ teaspoon freshly ground black pepper
6 sesame seed hamburger buns
Carolina Burger Sauce (recipe follows)
Creamy Ancho Slaw (recipe follows)
Dill pickle slices

1 Preheat the grill to medium-high (350°F to 400°F). Gently combine the chicken, mayonnaise, mustard, salt, and pepper in a bowl. Shape the mixture into 6 patties.
2 Grill the patties, covered, 5 to 6 minutes on each side or until a meat thermometer inserted into the thickest portion registers 165°F. Grill the buns 1 minute on each side or until toasted. Spread the Carolina Burger Sauce on the bottom half of each bun. Top with the patties, Creamy Ancho Slaw, pickles, and the top half of each bun.

CAROLINA BURGER SAUCE

MAKES **ABOUT 1 CUP** // HANDS-ON **20 MINUTES** // TOTAL **20 MINUTES**

Shallots, ketchup, mustard, and crushed red pepper give this sauce sweet-hot flavor.

¾ cup ketchup
⅓ cup apple cider vinegar
¼ cup coarse-grained Dijon mustard
1 large shallot, minced

1 tablespoon dark brown sugar
¼ teaspoon crushed red pepper
Kosher salt
Freshly ground black pepper

Stir together the ketchup, apple cider vinegar, mustard, shallot, sugar, and red pepper in a medium saucepan. Bring to a boil over medium; reduce the heat to low, and simmer, stirring occasionally, 8 to 10 minutes or until thickened. Season with the salt and black pepper to taste. Refrigerate in an airtight container up to 2 weeks.

CREAMY ANCHO SLAW

SERVES **6** // HANDS-ON **10 MINUTES** // TOTAL **25 MINUTES**

Cabbage tossed in a creamy, sweet, and slightly spicy mayonnaise is perfection.

½ cup mayonnaise
2 tablespoons apple cider vinegar
1¼ teaspoons ancho chile powder
1 teaspoon granulated sugar
½ small head savoy cabbage, shredded

1 large celery stalk, chopped
½ cup grated carrot
Kosher salt
Freshly ground black pepper

Whisk together the mayonnaise, apple cider vinegar, ancho chile powder, and sugar in a large bowl. Add the cabbage, celery, and carrot. Toss to coat, and add the salt and black pepper to taste. Let stand 15 minutes before serving, tossing occasionally.

RANCH TURKEY BURGERS

SERVES **4** // HANDS-ON **15 MINUTES** // TOTAL **20 MINUTES**

Take a break from beef and gobble up these turkey burgers. Swap the ground turkey for ground chicken if you prefer. A mix of sour cream, mayonnaise, and buttermilk keeps the patties moist, while a few spice-rack staples add the ranch flavor everyone loves.

1¼ pounds ground turkey
½ teaspoon garlic powder
½ teaspoon onion powder
½ teaspoon dried dill
¼ cup sour cream
¼ cup mayonnaise
3 tablespoons buttermilk

¾ teaspoon kosher salt
¾ teaspoon black pepper
1 tablespoon olive oil
1 teaspoon apple cider vinegar
4 (1.5-ounce) hamburger buns, toasted
Romaine lettuce heart leaves, thin tomato slices, and red onion slices for topping

1 Combine the turkey, garlic powder, onion powder, dill, and 1 tablespoon each of the sour cream, mayonnaise, and buttermilk in a medium bowl. Divide the turkey mixture into 4 (5-ounce) portions; shape into 1-inch-thick patties. Sprinkle the patties with ½ teaspoon each of the salt and pepper.

2 Heat the oil in a large nonstick skillet over medium-high. Add the burgers to the skillet; cover and cook until the bottoms are browned, about 4 minutes. Turn the burgers; cover and cook until browned and a meat thermometer inserted in the thickest portion registers 165°F, about 3 minutes.

3 Stir together the apple cider vinegar and remaining 3 tablespoons each sour cream and mayonnaise, 2 tablespoons buttermilk, and ¼ teaspoon each salt and pepper in a small bowl. Spread about 1 tablespoon of the mixture on each bun half. Place the lettuce, tomato, 1 patty, and red onion slices on each bottom half of the bun; top each with the other half of the bun.

TENT TALK

What are the dimensions of the field numbers in college football?

A. 4 feet tall and 3 feet wide
B. 6 feet tall and 4 feet wide
C. 7 feet tall and 4½ feet wide
D. Each university's graphic designer gets to decide

GAME-DAY HOT BROWN TURKEY SLIDERS

SERVES 8 // HANDS-ON **45 MINUTES** // TOTAL **1 HOUR, 5 MINUTES**

Our take on the classic Kentucky sandwich reconstructs the traditional hot brown into a Parker House roll format, with the melted cheese, white Béchamel sauce, and fillings inside warm, buttery rolls. They're super easy to pick up and bite, so tailgaters won't need a fork and knife.

¾ cup (6 ounces) plus 2 tablespoons unsalted butter

2 tablespoons all-purpose flour

1¼ cups whole milk, warmed

½ teaspoon kosher salt

¼ teaspoon black pepper

1 (11-ounce) package frozen Parker House yeast rolls, thawed (such as Sister Schubert's)

8 ounces sliced deli smoked turkey breast, torn into 1-inch pieces

8 ounces thinly sliced Swiss cheese

2 large plum tomatoes, sliced

1 tablespoon Dijon mustard

1 teaspoon Worcestershire sauce

2 tablespoons chopped fresh flat-leaf parsley

1 Preheat the oven to 350°F. Melt 2 tablespoons of the butter in a small saucepan over medium-high. Add the flour, and cook, stirring constantly, until a paste forms and begins to bubble, about 1 minute. Add the warm milk, whisking constantly, until the mixture thickens, about 1 minute. Remove from the heat, and whisk in the salt and pepper. Set aside to cool slightly.

2 Remove the rolls from the aluminum pan, and place on a flat surface. Using a bread knife, cut the rolls crosswise, creating tops and bottoms. Transfer the bottoms of the rolls to the aluminum pan, cut side up, and layer with half of the turkey pieces. Using half of the cooled white sauce, dollop each roll bottom with about a spoonful. Layer evenly with half of the cheese slices. Repeat the layers once. Top each with a tomato slice, and cover with the tops of the rolls.

3 Combine the Dijon, Worcestershire, and remaining ¾ cup butter in a microwavable bowl; microwave on HIGH until the mixture is melted, about 30 seconds, stirring after 15 seconds. Stir in the parsley, and pour the mixture evenly over the rolls in the pan.

4 Bake at 350°F until the rolls are golden brown and the fillings are bubbly, about 20 minutes. Keep warm, and serve warm or at room temperature.

SLOW-COOKER BEEF SLIDERS
WITH PICKLED PEPPERS

MAKES **16** // HANDS-ON **30 MINUTES** // TOTAL **7 HOURS, INCLUDES PEPPERS**

EXTRA
POINT

You can keep the beef mixture warm in a slow cooker set on WARM up to 2 hours.

Rev up your slow cooker the night before, and on game day, tote it to your tailgate, plug it in, and let your crowd build their own sandwiches. (Pictured on page 2, top right)

1 (3¼- to 3¾-pound) **boneless chuck roast,** trimmed
2 teaspoons **kosher salt,** plus more to taste
1½ teaspoons **freshly ground black pepper,** plus more to taste
1 tablespoon **vegetable oil**
1 medium-size **sweet onion,** coarsely chopped
2 **carrots,** coarsely chopped
4 **celery stalks,** coarsely chopped
2 **garlic cloves**
2 cups **beef broth**
½ cup **dry red wine**
4 fresh **thyme sprigs**
2 tablespoons **prepared horseradish**
¼ cup loosely packed **fresh flat-leaf parsley leaves,** chopped
¼ cup **chopped fresh chives**
16 **hearty dinner rolls,** split

PICKLED PEPPERS

2 cups sliced **red and yellow sweet mini bell peppers**
1 cup sliced **pepperoncini salad peppers**
1 teaspoon **pepperoncini juice** from jar
¼ cup loosely packed **fresh flat-leaf parsley leaves**
¼ cup thinly sliced **fresh chives**
1 teaspoon **extra-virgin olive oil**
Kosher salt
Freshly ground black pepper

1 Rub the roast with 2 teaspoons of the salt and 1½ teaspoons of the pepper. Heat the oil in a Dutch oven or large cast-iron skillet over medium-high. Add the roast to the hot oil, and cook 2 to 3 minutes on all sides until browned. Place the roast, onion, carrots, celery, garlic, broth, wine, and thyme in a 6-quart slow cooker.

2 Cover and cook on HIGH until the meat is tender, 6 to 8 hours. Remove the roast and vegetables; discard the vegetables. Shred the meat. Pour the liquid from the slow cooker through a fine mesh strainer into a 4-cup measuring cup, and let stand about 15 minutes.

3 Meanwhile, make the Pickled Peppers: Stir together the bell peppers, salad peppers, pepperoncini juice, parsley, chives, and olive oil in a medium bowl. Add the salt and pepper to taste.

4 Remove the fat from the cooking liquid, and discard. Stir together the shredded meat, horseradish, parsley, chives, and 1 cup of the reserved cooking liquid; discard the remaining liquid. Add the salt and pepper to taste. Serve on the dinner rolls with the Pickled Peppers.

NOTE: We tested with Pepperidge Farm Stone Baked Artisan French Rolls.

LOADED BRISKET NACHOS

SERVES 10 // HANDS-ON 25 MINUTES // TOTAL 25 MINUTES

We can just about guarantee that this will be a new favorite dish to feed your friends. The brisket and avocado make these nachos filling, while the vegetables give it freshness. Serve it straight from the pan and let everyone dip in.

1½ cups cherry tomatoes, halved

¾ cup thinly sliced red onion (from 1 onion)

2 teaspoons fresh lime juice (from 1 lime)

1 teaspoon chili powder

¼ teaspoon kosher salt

¼ teaspoon black pepper

1 jalapeño chile, thinly sliced (about 1 tablespoon)

¼ cup chopped fresh cilantro, plus more for garnish (optional)

1 (13-ounce) bag tortilla chips

4 cups shredded, cooked beef brisket, warmed (about 1 pound)

4 ounces sharp Cheddar cheese, shredded (about 1 cup)

4 ounces Monterey Jack cheese, shredded (about 1 cup)

¾ cup sour cream

1 ripe avocado, diced

Hot sauce (optional)

1 Toss together the tomatoes, onion, lime juice, chili powder, salt, pepper, jalapeño slices, and ¼ cup of the cilantro in a large bowl.

2 Preheat the broiler with the oven rack 6 inches from the heat. Line a large rimmed baking sheet with aluminum foil; lightly coat the foil with cooking spray. Arrange the tortilla chips in a single layer on the prepared baking sheet. Top the chips evenly with the shredded beef and tomato mixture. Sprinkle with the cheeses. Broil, rotating the baking sheet often, until the cheese is melted and bubbly, about 1 minute.

3 Top the nachos with dollops of the sour cream and diced avocado. Garnish with the additional cilantro and a few dashes of hot sauce, if desired.

THE ULTIMATE BULLY BURGER
WITH DILL PICKLE SAUCE

SERVES **8** // HANDS-ON **30 MINUTES** // TOTAL **30 MINUTES, INCLUDES SAUCE**

Named for the Mississippi State University bulldog mascot, Bully, this burger is food fit for champions. Half beef, half pork, this toothsome burger has a balance of rich flavors and gives State fans staying power through the fourth quarter. Don't skip the Dill Pickle Sauce—it's a must-have on this (and any) burger.

1½ pounds ground sirloin
1½ pounds ground pork
¼ cup finely chopped sweet onion
    (from 1 small onion)
1 tablespoon Worcestershire sauce
1½ teaspoons table salt
¾ teaspoon black pepper

8 Cheddar cheese slices (optional)
Dill Pickle Sauce (recipe follows)
8 hamburger buns, toasted
Toppings: green leaf lettuce, tomato
    slices, thinly sliced red onion, cooked
    bacon slices

EXTRA POINT

These patties can be made ahead and refrigerated. Transport layered between wax paper on a baking sheet stored in a cooler. Grill the patties at the tailgate.

1   Preheat the grill to medium (350°F to 400°F). Place the ground sirloin, ground pork, onion, Worcestershire, salt, and pepper in a large bowl; gently combine using your hands. Shape the mixture into 8 (5-inch) patties. Slightly press the center of each patty with your thumb, making a small indentation. (This creates a flat hamburger instead of one with a domelike shape when cooked.)

2   Place the patties on the grate, and grill, covered, until the patties are no longer pink in the center, 5 to 6 minutes per side. Top each patty with 1 cheese slice, if desired. Remove from the grill.

3   Spread 1 to 2 tablespoons of the Dill Pickle Sauce on the cut sides of the buns; top the bottom of each with a patty. Layer the patties with the desired toppings; serve warm.

DILL PICKLE SAUCE

MAKES **ABOUT 1¹/₂ CUPS** // HANDS-ON **5 MINUTES** // TOTAL **5 MINUTES**

Tart, creamy, and slightly spicy from the mustard, this sauce is always a winner.

1 cup mayonnaise
⅓ cup dill pickle relish, drained

1½ tablespoons spicy brown mustard
¼ teaspoon paprika

Stir together all the ingredients until blended; cover and chill until ready to serve.

SALSA VERDE CORN CHIP PIE

SERVES 6 // HANDS-ON 35 MINUTES // TOTAL 35 MINUTES

This Friday-night-football favorite is also a smart quick-fix meal for a college-game day Saturday. For a fun twist and practical on-the-go eating solution, serve in small, individual corn chip bags.

5 teaspoons olive oil

2 cups frozen whole kernel yellow corn, thawed

1 (9-ounce) package garlic pork sausage links, casings removed

1 medium-size sweet onion, chopped

2 teaspoons chili powder

1 teaspoon ground cumin

1 (16-ounce) bottle salsa verde

2 (4.5-ounce) cans chopped green chiles

1 (16-ounce) can navy beans, drained and rinsed

2 tablespoons fresh lime juice

6 cups original corn chips

4 ounces pepper Jack cheese, shredded (about 1 cup)

Toppings: chopped fresh cilantro, sliced radishes, diced avocado, lime wedges

1 Heat 3 teaspoons of the oil in a large skillet over medium. Add the corn; cook until the corn begins to char, 3 to 4 minutes. Remove the corn from the skillet.

2 Cook the sausage in the skillet over medium-high until browned, 6 to 8 minutes. Remove from the skillet, and drain on paper towels.

3 Heat the remaining 2 teaspoons oil in the skillet over medium-high. Add the onion; cook until tender, 4 to 5 minutes. Stir in the chili powder and cumin; cook, stirring often, 2 to 3 minutes. Stir in the salsa, chiles, and sausage. Cook over medium, stirring often, until slightly thickened, 7 to 8 minutes. Remove from the heat; stir in the beans, lime juice, and corn.

4 Divide the chips among 6 plates. Spoon the sausage mixture over the chips; top with half of the cheese. Serve with the desired toppings and remaining cheese.

NOTE: We tested with Herdez Salsa Verde and Fritos Original Corn Chips.

HONEY-AND-SOY LACQUERED RIBS

SERVES **6 TO 8** // HANDS-ON **30 MINUTES** // TOTAL **2 HOURS, 35 MINUTES**

Bake these sweet and spicy ribs up to 2 days ahead. Then simply reheat and broil before serving.

2 (2- to 2½-pound) slabs St. Louis-style pork ribs
1 tablespoon kosher salt
2 teaspoons freshly ground black pepper
½ cup honey
2 tablespoons soy sauce

2 tablespoons Asian chili-garlic sauce
1 tablespoon fresh lime juice
1 tablespoon butter
1 teaspoon dry mustard
1 teaspoon ground ginger

1 Preheat the oven to 325°F. Rinse the slabs, and pat dry. Remove the thin membrane from the back of the slabs by slicing into it with a knife and pulling it off. (This makes the ribs more tender.) Sprinkle the salt and pepper over the slabs; wrap each slab tightly in aluminum foil. Place the slabs on a jelly-roll pan, and bake at 325°F until tender and the meat pulls away from bone, 2 to 2½ hours.

2 Bring the honey, soy sauce, chili-garlic sauce, lime juice, butter, mustard, and ginger to a boil in a saucepan over high, stirring occasionally. Reduce the heat to medium-low; simmer until reduced by half, about 5 minutes. Transfer to a bowl.

3 Remove the slabs from the oven. Increase the oven temperature to broil on high. Carefully remove the slabs from the foil; place on a foil-lined baking sheet. Brush each slab with 3 tablespoons of the honey mixture.

4 Broil until browned and sticky, 5 to 7 minutes. Brush with the remaining honey mixture.

SWEET *AND* SPICY MIZZOU RIBS

SERVES **8** // HANDS-ON **30 MINUTES** // TOTAL **6 HOURS, INCLUDES 2 HOURS CHILLING**

EXTRA POINT

If you prefer your ribs to be "fall off the bone" tender, add 30 minutes to the cook time when the slabs are wrapped in foil and first cooked.

We give you two ways to prepare these saucy ribs—in the oven or on the grill—to simplify prep, whether you're tailgating on campus or in the comfort of your home.

½ cup paprika

½ cup packed dark brown sugar

½ cup kosher salt

2 teaspoons garlic powder

2 teaspoons onion powder

2 teaspoons crushed red pepper

2 teaspoons black pepper

4 (about 2½-pound) slabs St. Louis-style pork ribs

8 tablespoons Dijon mustard

2 cups ketchup

⅔ cup honey

½ cup Worcestershire sauce

½ cup finely grated yellow onion (from 1 medium onion)

6 tablespoons white vinegar

1   Stir together the paprika, brown sugar, salt, garlic powder, onion powder, red pepper, and black pepper in a small bowl. Remove the thin membrane from the back of each slab by slicing into it with a knife and pulling it off. Rub both sides of each slab with 2 tablespoons of the Dijon mustard. Sprinkle 3 to 4 tablespoons of the paprika mixture evenly on both sides. Stack the slabs on top of each other; wrap with plastic wrap, and chill 2 to 8 hours.

2   Stir together the ketchup, honey, Worcestershire, onion, and vinegar in a small saucepan over medium. Cook, stirring occasionally, until the mixture comes to a simmer. Reduce the heat to medium-low, and cook until slightly reduced and thickened, about 20 minutes. Remove from the heat, and set aside.

// IF USING AN OVEN

3   Preheat the oven to 250°F. Tightly wrap each slab in aluminum foil; place on a rimmed baking sheet. Bake 2 hours. Remove the slabs from the oven; remove and discard the foil. Return the ribs, bone side down, to the baking sheet, and bake until a wooden pick can be inserted into the meat with little resistance, about 1 hour and 30 minutes. Remove the ribs, and increase the oven temperature to broil.

4   Turn the slabs over to bone side up, and brush generously with the barbecue sauce. Broil until browned and caramelized, 4 to 5 minutes. Turn the slabs, brush the meaty side generously with the barbecue sauce, and broil until browned and caramelized, 4 to 5 minutes. Remove the ribs from the oven, and let stand 10 minutes. Cut the ribs between the bones, and serve with the remaining barbecue sauce.

// IF USING A GRILL

5   Preheat a gas grill to low (250°F to 300°F) on 1 side; keep the other side unlit. Tightly wrap each slab in aluminum foil. Place the slabs on the grates on the unlit side of the grill; grill, covered, 2 hours. Remove the slabs from the grill; remove and discard the foil. Return the slabs, bone side down, to the unlit side; grill, covered, until a wooden pick can be pressed into the meat with little resistance, about 1 hour and 30 minutes. Remove the slabs; increase the grill temperature to medium-high (450°F to 500°F).

6   Place the slabs, bone side up, on the lit side of the grill, and brush generously with the barbecue sauce. Grill, covered, until browned and caramelized, 4 to 5 minutes. Turn the slabs, brush the meaty side generously with the barbecue sauce, and grill, covered, until browned and caramelized, 4 to 5 minutes. Remove the ribs, and let stand 10 minutes. Cut the ribs between the bones, and serve with the remaining barbecue sauce.

SMOKED PORK BUTT

SERVES 8 // HANDS-ON 30 MINUTES
TOTAL 13 HOURS, 10 MINUTES, INCLUDES SAUCE AND CHOWCHOW

TENT TALK

Three of the founding members of the SEC are no longer part of the conference. Which three are they?

A. North Carolina, Furman, and Virginia
B. Florida State, Samford, and Miami
C. Georgia Tech, Sewanee, and Tulane
D. Texas, Troy, and West Virginia

Make the rub, sauce, and chowchow in advance, and prepare the meat the day before or start early in the morning of game day. To turn this smoked pork into sandwiches, don't forget to bring hamburger buns! To assemble, place the shredded pork butt on the bottom halves of the buns. Top with the Sweet-and-Tangy Tomato Barbecue Sauce, Chowchow, and top halves of the buns. Serve with Grilled Jalapeño-Lime Corn on the Cob (see page 210 for the recipe), if desired. (Also pictured on the cover.)

SMOKY-SWEET BARBECUE RUB

¼ cup kosher salt
¼ cup packed dark brown sugar
2 tablespoons plus 2 teaspoons smoked paprika
2 tablespoons granulated sugar
2 teaspoons garlic powder
2 teaspoons freshly ground black pepper

1 teaspoon dry mustard
1 teaspoon ground cumin
1 teaspoon ground ginger

ADDITIONAL INGREDIENT

1 (4- to 5-pound) bone-in pork shoulder roast (Boston butt)

1 Make the Smoky-Sweet Barbecue Rub: Stir together all the ingredients in a small bowl.

2 Trim the pork roast. Rinse and pat dry. Sprinkle with ¼ cup of the Smoky-Sweet Barbecue Rub; let stand at room temperature 30 minutes.

3 Bring the internal temperature of a smoker to 225°F to 250°F according to the manufacturer's directions, and maintain the temperature 15 to 20 minutes.

4 Place the pork, fattier side up, on the cooking grate directly over the coals in the center of the smoker. Cover with the lid, and adjust the ventilation to maintain the temperature between 225°F and 250°F. Smoke, covered and maintaining the temperature, 5 hours; turn the pork, fattier side down, and smoke 2 to 3 more hours or until a meat thermometer inserted into the thickest portion registers 195°F.

5 Transfer to a cutting board; cool 15 minutes. Shred the pork.

SWEET-AND-TANGY TOMATO BARBECUE SAUCE

MAKES ABOUT 2 CUPS // HANDS-ON 10 MINUTES // TOTAL 45 MINUTES

Serve this over Smoked Pork Butt—and every other smoked or grilled meat, for that matter.

1 cup ketchup
1 cup water
⅓ cup apple cider vinegar
¼ cup packed light brown sugar
1 tablespoon onion powder

1 tablespoon chili powder
2 tablespoons tomato paste
1½ tablespoons dark molasses
2 teaspoons freshly ground black pepper

Bring all the ingredients to a boil in a large saucepan over medium, stirring occasionally. Reduce the heat to low; cover and cook, stirring occasionally, 25 minutes or until slightly thickened. Cool 10 minutes. Cover and chill until ready to serve. Store in the refrigerator up to 1 week.

CHOWCHOW

MAKES **ABOUT 3 CUPS** // HANDS-ON **25 MINUTES**
TOTAL **3 HOURS, 55 MINUTES, INCLUDES 3 HOURS CHILLING**

These pickled veggies bring pleasing brightness to the sandwich, cutting the
fatty, rich pork, and syrupy sauce.

3 cups chopped fresh cabbage
¾ cup chopped onion (from 1 onion)
**¾ cup chopped green tomatoes (from
   1 tomato)**
**½ cup chopped green bell pepper (from
   1 bell pepper)**
**½ cup chopped red bell pepper (from
   1 bell pepper)**
1 tablespoon pickling salt

¾ cup granulated sugar
½ cup white vinegar
¼ cup water
¾ teaspoon mustard seeds
¼ teaspoon celery seeds
¼ teaspoon ground turmeric
½ teaspoon crushed red pepper (optional)
**1 jalapeño chile, seeded and finely
   chopped (optional)**

Stir together the cabbage, onion, tomatoes, bell peppers, and pickling salt. Cover and
chill 2 to 8 hours. Transfer the mixture to a Dutch oven. Stir in the sugar, vinegar,
water, mustard seeds, celery seeds, turmeric, and, if desired, red pepper. Bring to
a boil over medium-high; reduce the heat to medium, and simmer 3 minutes. Cool to
room temperature, about 30 minutes. Stir in the jalapeño, if desired. Cover and chill
1 to 8 hours before serving.

CORNMEAL BISCUIT-SMOKED PORK SANDWICHES *WITH* PEACH JAM

SERVES **10** // HANDS-ON **25 MINUTES** // TOTAL **1 HOUR, 50 MINUTES**

These cornmeal biscuits are buttery, fluffy, and a bit peppery—everything a biscuit should be! The jam and pickled jalapeños (we really do recommend you include them) balance the rich and juicy pork butt perfectly. What's more, the biscuits can be made a day in advance, and the jam and pork can be made several days in advance, making day-of prep a cinch—just assemble. Serve with Georgian Cabbage Slaw (pictured at left), if desired; see recipe on page 196.

PEACH JAM

4 cups peeled, chopped ripe fresh peaches (about 1¾ pounds) or chopped frozen peaches, thawed

1 (1.75-ounce) package powdered fruit pectin

1 teaspoon lemon zest plus ¼ cup fresh juice (from 1 large lemon)

5 cups granulated sugar

CORNMEAL BISCUITS

2 cups (about 8 ounces) self-rising flour

½ cup (about 2½ ounces) self-rising cornmeal mix

1 teaspoon black pepper

½ cup (4 ounces) cold salted butter, cut into pieces

1¼ cups whole buttermilk, cold

2 tablespoons salted butter, melted

3 tablespoons Dijon mustard

Smoked Pork Butt (recipe page 174)
Pickled jalapeños (optional)

EXTRA POINT

Use Bonne Maman peach preserves if you don't want to make the jam. The biscuits can be made and frozen. From frozen, bake at 425°F a few more minutes.

1 Make the Peach Jam: Combine the peaches, pectin, zest, and juice in a Dutch oven, and bring to a boil over medium. Boil, stirring constantly, until thick and syrupy, about 1 minute. Gradually add the sugar, stirring constantly, until the sugar dissolves. Cook, stirring often, until syrupy, about 5 minutes. Let the jam cool completely, about 1 hour. Store in an airtight container for up to 2 weeks in the refrigerator.

2 Make the Cornmeal Biscuits: Preheat the oven to 425°F. Combine the flour, cornmeal mix, and black pepper in a large bowl. Add the cold butter pieces, and toss to fully coat with the flour mixture. Cut the butter into the flour mixture with a pastry blender until the size of small peas. Cover and chill 10 minutes. Add the buttermilk, stirring with a wooden spoon just until the dry ingredients are moistened. Turn the dough out onto a floured surface, and knead 3 or 4 times, gradually sprinkling in self-rising flour as needed. With floured hands, pat the dough into a ¾-inch-thick rectangle (about 9 x 5 inches); dust the top with flour. Fold the dough in thirds, as you would a letter, starting with the short end. Repeat 2 more times.

3 Pat the dough to ½-inch thickness. Cut with a 2½-inch round cutter, and place on a baking sheet lined with parchment paper.

4 Bake at 425°F until lightly browned, 13 to 15 minutes. Remove from the oven; brush with the melted butter. The biscuits can be made up to 1 day ahead and stored in an airtight container.

5 Assemble the Smoked Pork Sandwiches: Stir together the Dijon mustard and 1 cup of the Peach Jam until combined. Split the biscuits; spread the jam mixture evenly on the bottom half of the biscuits. Top with the Smoked Pork Butt and, if desired, top with the pickled jalapeños. Top with the top biscuit halves.

FRIED OYSTER PO'BOY SLIDERS

SERVES 10 // HANDS-ON 35 MINUTES // TOTAL 50 MINUTES

EXTRA
POINT

The mayo sauce can be made in advance and stored in an airtight container in the refrigerator. If you're tailgating at home, you can crisp the bread in the oven instead.

These crispy oysters are so tasty. The mayonnaise has a hint of spice from the hot sauce, and the iceberg lettuce and tomatoes give the sandwich bite. If you can't find French-style dinner rolls, any slider-style roll will work.

10 French-style dinner rolls or slider rolls, split

¼ cup (2 ounces) salted butter, at room temperature

1⅓ cups mayonnaise

3 tablespoons Dijon mustard

1 teaspoon Louisiana hot sauce

1 teaspoon lime zest plus 2 tablespoons fresh lime juice (about 1 lime)

Vegetable or canola oil

1 cup whole buttermilk

1 cup (about 5⅓ ounces) fine yellow cornmeal

⅔ cup (about 2⅞ ounces) all-purpose flour

½ teaspoon black pepper

½ teaspoon cayenne pepper

1¼ teaspoons kosher salt

2 pints fresh shucked oysters (about 30 oysters), drained

2 cups shredded iceberg lettuce (about ¼ head lettuce)

2 plum tomatoes (about 3½ ounces each), cut into thin slices

⅔ cup bread-and-butter pickle chips

1 Preheat the grill to medium-high (450°F to 500°F). Scoop out the soft centers of the roll halves, leaving a ½-inch-thick shell. Spread the butter evenly on the cut side of the roll halves, and set aside. Stir together the mayonnaise, Dijon, hot sauce, and lime juice in a small bowl; chill until ready to use.

2 Pour the oil to a depth of about 3 inches in a medium Dutch oven; heat to 360°F over medium. Meanwhile, place the buttermilk in a medium bowl. Combine the cornmeal, flour, black pepper, cayenne pepper, lime zest, and 1 teaspoon of the salt in a medium bowl. Dip the oysters in the buttermilk, and dredge in the cornmeal mixture, shaking to remove the excess cornmeal mixture.

3 Add the oysters, in 2 to 3 batches, to the hot oil, and fry until golden and just done, 2 to 3 minutes, turning over halfway through cooking. Drain the oysters on paper towels; sprinkle with the remaining ¼ teaspoon salt.

4 Place the rolls, buttered side down, on the grill grate (or in a hot grill pan over medium-high), and grill just until crisp and grill marks appear, about 3 minutes. Spread the mayonnaise mixture evenly on the grilled sides of the rolls. Divide the lettuce, tomatoes, pickles, and fried oysters evenly among the bottom halves of the rolls; cover with the tops.

GRILLED CLAMBAKE FOIL PACKETS
WITH HERB BUTTER

SERVES **6** // HANDS-ON **20 MINUTES** // TOTAL **40 MINUTES**

TENT
TALK

When a quarterback calls an *audible*, what is he doing?

A. Scolding a teammate
B. Changing the play at the line of scrimmage
C. Shouting hello to his mother
D. None of the above

There's something perfect about the combination of college football and the low-country style of communal feasting. Assemble these foil packets in the morning, refrigerate, and throw on the grill when tailgate guests arrive, or let guests assemble their own packets and toss on the grill as they're ready to eat.

1½ cups (12 ounces) unsalted butter, softened
¼ cup finely chopped shallot (about 1 shallot)
2 tablespoons chopped fresh flat-leaf parsley
1 tablespoon chopped fresh dill
1 teaspoon lemon zest (from 1 lemon)
3 tablespoons Old Bay seasoning
12 small red potatoes (about 2 pounds), cut into ½-inch wedges
¼ cup water

3 ears corn, husks removed, each ear cut into 4 pieces
24 unpeeled raw medium shrimp (about ⅔ pound)
24 littleneck clams in shells, scrubbed (about 1 pound, 3 ounces)
1 pound smoked sausage (such as Conecuh), cut diagonally into 1-inch-thick slices
3 lemons, cut into quarters
6 fresh thyme sprigs
Grilled French bread

1 Stir together the butter, shallot, parsley, dill, lemon zest, and 1 tablespoon of the Old Bay seasoning in a medium bowl until well blended.

2 Combine the potatoes and water in a medium-size microwavable bowl; cover with plastic wrap. Microwave on HIGH until tender and a knife can be inserted easily in center of the potatoes, about 5 minutes. Drain and let stand 5 minutes.

3 Preheat a grill to medium (350°F to 450°F). Cut 12 (12-inch) square pieces of heavy-duty aluminum foil. Place 6 squares of the foil in a single layer on a work surface. Divide the potato wedges and corn evenly among the foil sheets. Top each with 4 shrimp and 4 clams. Top evenly with the sausage slices and lemon wedges. Dollop each with about ¼ cup of the butter mixture. Top each with 1 thyme sprig, and sprinkle each with 1 teaspoon of Old Bay. Top each with 1 foil square, and crimp all the sides to seal tightly.

4 Grill the packets, covered, until the shrimp are done and the clams open, 8 to 10 minutes, rotating the packets on the grill halfway through the cooking time. Discard any clams that do not open. Serve with the grilled French bread.

SHRIMP *AND* FONTINA GRITS

SERVES 10 // HANDS-ON **30 MINUTES** // TOTAL **30 MINUTES**

Consider this your new go-to recipe for making shrimp and grits for a crowd. This dish is suited for crisp fall days spent outdoors when warm and hearty food is desired. Transport the hot cooked grits in a slow cooker to your tailgate site, and keep on the WARM setting for serving. Cook the shrimp just before heading to your tailgate, and transport in a heatproof covered casserole dish.

1 quart water

1 quart plus 1 cup unsalted chicken stock

2 teaspoons kosher salt

2 cups uncooked regular white grits

¾ cup whole milk

8 ounces fontina cheese, shredded (about 2 cups)

2 teaspoons chopped fresh thyme

1 teaspoon black pepper

1 tablespoon olive oil

3 pounds peeled and deveined raw medium shrimp

1 bunch scallions, finely chopped (about 1½ cups)

2 (4-ounce) jars diced pimientos, drained

1 tablespoon minced garlic (about 3 garlic cloves)

1 tablespoon fresh lemon juice (from ½ lemon)

¼ cup (2 ounces) cold unsalted butter

1 Bring the water, 1 quart of the chicken stock, and 1 teaspoon of the salt to a boil in a stockpot over medium-high. Pour in the grits, and cook, whisking constantly, 1 minute. Cover, reduce the heat to medium-low, and cook until the grits are tender and the liquid has been absorbed, 15 to 20 minutes.

2 Remove from the heat, and stir in the milk, cheese, thyme, and ½ teaspoon of the black pepper.

3 Heat the oil in a large skillet over medium-high. Add the shrimp, and cook, stirring often, just until pink, 2 to 3 minutes. Remove the shrimp from the skillet. Add the remaining 1 cup chicken stock to the skillet, stirring to loosen the browned bits from the bottom of the skillet. Stir in the scallions, pimientos, and garlic, and cook, stirring often, 1 minute. Cook until the liquid is reduced by about half, 2 to 3 minutes. Remove from the heat, and stir in the lemon juice and remaining 1 teaspoon salt and ½ teaspoon pepper; swirl in the butter. Return the shrimp to the skillet, tossing to coat. Serve over the grits.

FRIED CATFISH FINGERS
WITH COMEBACK SAUCE

SERVES **8** // HANDS-ON **20 MINUTES** // TOTAL **50 MINUTES**

This recipe is great to make for a crowd. Fry the catfish in batches so tailgaters can get fish hot from the fryer, and serve a batch of cold beverages as folks mingle and wait for their crispy, crunchy food. The tangy sauce is addictively good and can also be served with chicken fingers, burgers, or fries.

EXTRA POINT

You can make the sauce in advance, and even bring the dry flour-cornmeal mixture premixed to your tailgate site to save time.

CATFISH

3 cups whole buttermilk
2 tablespoons hot sauce
3 pounds catfish fillets, cut into strips
Peanut oil
1 cup plain yellow cornmeal
1 cup masa harina
1 cup (about 4¼ ounces) all-purpose flour
2 teaspoons garlic powder
2 teaspoons onion powder
2 teaspoons black pepper
1 teaspoon cayenne pepper
5 teaspoons kosher salt

COMEBACK SAUCE

1 cup mayonnaise
2 tablespoons Sriracha chili sauce
1½ tablespoons apple cider vinegar
½ teaspoon kosher salt
½ teaspoon garlic powder
½ teaspoon onion powder
½ teaspoon dry mustard
½ teaspoon black pepper

1 Make the Catfish: Whisk together the buttermilk and hot sauce in a large bowl. Place the catfish in the buttermilk mixture, and let stand 30 minutes.

2 Pour the oil to a depth of 5 inches into a large Dutch oven over medium, and heat to 330°F. Stir together the cornmeal, masa, flour, garlic powder, onion powder, black pepper, cayenne pepper, and 4 teaspoons of the salt in a shallow dish.

3 Remove the fillets in batches from the buttermilk mixture, allowing the excess to drip off. Dredge in the cornmeal mixture, shaking off the excess.

4 Fry the fish, in batches, until golden brown, about 2 minutes on each side. Transfer to a wire rack on a baking sheet lined with paper towels; sprinkle with the remaining 1 teaspoon salt. Cover and keep warm until ready to serve.

5 Make the Comeback Sauce: Whisk together all the ingredients in a bowl until smooth. Serve with the Catfish.

GRILLED GATOR KEBAB BANH MI

SERVES **8** // HANDS-ON **45 MINUTES** // TOTAL **1 HOUR**

EXTRA POINT

If you have difficulty threading the gator meat onto the skewers, try folding thinner pieces over onto themselves and then skewering.

To some passionate Florida fans, only gator meat on game day will do; however, for others, this recipe works beautifully with cubed chicken breast or pork tenderloin—just reduce the marinating time to 15 minutes. If you go with gator, source the freshest gator meat possible, preferably something never frozen, from your local grocer or butcher.

1 cup water
½ cup rice vinegar
¼ cup granulated sugar
1 tablespoon kosher salt
2 cups very thinly sliced English cucumber (from 1 large cucumber)
1 cup matchstick carrots
8 (10-inch) wooden skewers
¼ cup frozen, thawed orange juice concentrate
¼ cup fish sauce

¼ cup packed light brown sugar
2 teaspoons crushed red pepper
¼ cup fresh lime juice (from 3 limes)
2 pounds alligator meat, cut into 2-inch pieces
2 (16-ounce) French bread loaves, split horizontally, each loaf cut into 4 pieces
1 cup mayonnaise
2⅔ cups watercress (about 3 ounces)
2 cups cilantro sprigs (from 2 bunches)
Sriracha chili sauce

1 Stir together the water, vinegar, sugar, and salt in a saucepan; bring to a boil over high. Place the cucumbers and carrots in a large heatproof bowl; pour the hot vinegar mixture over the vegetables. Let stand at least 30 minutes. (The mixture can be made a day ahead of time and refrigerated.)

2 Soak the skewers in water at least 30 minutes.

3 Stir together the juice concentrate, fish sauce, brown sugar, red pepper, and lime juice in a bowl. Add the alligator meat; toss to coat. Let stand 30 minutes.

4 Preheat the grill to medium-high (about 450°F) or heat a grill pan over medium-high.

5 Thread the meat onto the skewers. Place the kebabs on lightly greased grates, and grill, uncovered, turning often so the meat doesn't char too much, until the meat is done, 7 to 9 minutes, basting with the leftover marinade the first 5 minutes of grilling. Remove from the grill.

6 Place the bread pieces on the grill grate, cut sides down, and grill until lightly toasted, 1 to 2 minutes. Spread the mayonnaise evenly on the cut sides of the bread, and top with the alligator pieces. Using a slotted spoon, top each with about ¼ cup of the pickled vegetables. Sprinkle each with ⅓ cup of the watercress and ¼ cup of the cilantro. Drizzle with the sriracha.

SIDES THAT SCORE

MOVE OVER, MAIN DISHES! THESE STELLAR SIDES MAY JUST BE THE NEW TAILGATE MVPS. CHOOSE FROM SAUCY COLA BAKED BEANS, SWEET-HOT POTATO SALAD, GRILLED JALAPEÑO-LIME CORN ON THE COB, PIMIENTO CHEESE HUSH PUPPIES WITH DILLY TARTAR SAUCE, AND MORE TO ROUND OUT YOUR SPREAD.

WEATHERING A SANDSTORM

A musical miscue gave rise to
South Carolina's newest football tradition.

On September 24, 2009, Ole Miss rolled into Columbia ranked No. 4 in the country. With just two minutes remaining in the game, a mere six points separated the Gamecocks and the Rebels. That's when someone in the press box pushed play on "Sandstorm," an infectious musical composition by Finnish DJ and record producer Darude.

Instantly, fans began to bounce up and down, waving their arms in circles over their heads and chanting, "U-S-C, U-S-C, U-S-C!" The Fighting Gamecocks strutted away with a 16-10 win, and fans discovered a new way to celebrate their team.

Today, "Sandstorm" has become a song fans love and opponents love to hate. The music is played at The Cock Pit before kickoffs and after touchdowns. Fans have taken to waving white towels and sandstorming to spur on the team.

Of course, it's not like South Carolina needed anyone to throw gasoline on the fire of its passions. The Gamecocks already own one of the most thrilling entrances in college football. Inspired by an Elvis concert, the show features billowing smoke, a caged Cocky, and a stunning highlight reel, all choreographed to the theme song of the movie 2001: *A Space Odyssey*.

Fans predictably go wild when the song begins, and the stadium reaches a fever pitch by the time the team storms the field. Some say that if you look closely, you'll see the upper east deck sway, a phenomenon that once prompted former coach Joe Morrison to proclaim: "If it ain't swayin', we ain't playin'!"

There's still plenty of swaying going on at Williams-Brice Stadium these days. It's just harder to see during a "Sandstorm."

FUN FACT

The Fighting Gamecocks' name dates back to the Revolutionary War. Brigadier General Thomas Sumter was named the "Carolina Gamecock" for his fierce fighting style.

// COCK OF THE WALK

Evening settles over the campus at the University of South Carolina in Columbia like a soft, warm blanket.

Overhead, ribbons of pink unfurl in the cerulean sky, a celestial celebration of the sun's late return after a long, rainy day. Soaring trees cast long shadows over the Horseshoe, a wide green lawn at the historic heart of campus. The mournful wail of a southbound train echoes in the distance while the campus hubbub begins to subside for the day.

"The trees, the brick pathways, the buildings—the South Carolina campus is so pretty," says Makenzie Myers, who is lucky enough to live in one of the upperclassman dorms on the Horseshoe this year. "It definitely makes the hard classes more bearable when you have such a pretty walk to get there."

// ALL ABOARD FOR RAILGATING

Williams-Brice Stadium sits more than a mile from this oh-so-Southern campus, yet it might as well be on another planet. Gamecocks fans are notoriously passionate—wild about football and all the hoopla surrounding it. They're so feisty, in fact, that some say you can actually see the stadium sway during a game.

This single-minded devotion is also evident at parties that surround the stadium on game day. The crème de la crème of tailgating takes place at South Carolina's Cockaboose Railroad, just a stone's throw from the southeast side of Williams-Brice Stadium. In 1990, a real estate developer bought cabooses from Illinois Central Railroad and picked up an abandoned rail spur from CSX. Then he started selling spots.

From the outside, the shiny garnet-red cabooses look virtually the same.

FUN FACT

Three SEC schools are located in capital cities—LSU, South Carolina, and Vanderbilt.

South Carolina

Railroad

SIR BIG SPUR
THE MOST INVOLVED MASCOT IN SPORTS

GO COCKS

SPUR'S ROOST

Inside, they're customized party palaces. Each owner decorates to his or her own taste—hardwood floors, granite countertops, chandeliers, big-screen TVs, sports memorabilia. Today, these 30-foot by 9-foot metal boxes sell for thousands.

// CAROLINA PRIDE

But those famous cockabooses can only hold so many people. Tailgaters spread out and occupy every inch of available space around the stadium, including the nearby State Fairgrounds.

On Friday afternoon, Mary Shriner and her husband, Bill, from Santee, South Carolina, roll into town in their RV, where they'll stay until Sunday afternoon. The couple shares breakfast, lunch, and dinner with 25 people or more on game day. "If you go hungry," says Mary, "it's your own fault."

Mary doesn't even bother going into the stadium anymore. She says she'd rather hang out by the RV, watch college football on TV, and let others use the tickets; these days, that includes granddaughter Brice, named for the stadium: "One of the first things she could say was, 'Go, Cocks!'"

The university upped its tailgating game by opening beautiful Gamecock Park, just across the street from Williams-Brice. In addition to spots for boosters, there are food trucks, games, and music. USC coaches and players

march along Garnet Way at the center of the park on their way to the stadium two-and-a-half hours before each game.

// WE HAIL THEE, CAROLINA!

Win or lose, Carolina fans are faithful. But they smile when they talk about recent successes. Many point to the Steve Spurrier years from 2005 to 2015 as their best yet. From 2011 to 2013, the head ball coach led USC to three consecutive 11-2 finishes, landing them among the country's Top 10 teams each of those years. He also posted five consecutive wins over archrival Clemson, from 2009 to 2013. By the time he "fired himself" in October 2015, Spurrier had amassed a record of 86-49, the school's best.

Longtime Carolina fans point out that Williams-Brice sits on George Rogers Drive. As a senior, Rogers led USC to two consecutive 8-4 seasons, rushing for 100 yards or more in each of his final 22 games at South Carolina. He ended his career with 5,204 yards rushing, 31 touchdowns, and a Heisman Trophy. After being drafted No. 1 by the New Orleans Saints, Rogers rushed for more than 7,000 yards in the NFL, winning a Super Bowl ring with the Washington Redskins.

In 2015, the school unveiled a statue on the northwest corner of Springs Brooks Plaza depicting Rogers standing on a bench, cheering on his teammates.

// HERE'S A HEALTH, CAROLINA!

Tailgating is the warm-up for what unfolds inside Williams-Brice—aka The Cockpit. Gamecocks are aggressive and territorial. Regardless of size or ability, they're ready to fight at a moment's notice, and SEC opponents know it, especially when they play in Columbia. Fans holler. They wave towels, and they jump up and down tirelessly. They even bring a live rooster to the game, and their battle cry is a crowing cock. It's Saturday in South Carolina, and these fans will do whatever it takes to spur on their team.

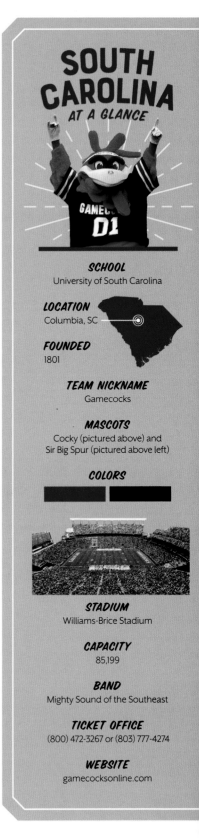

SOUTH CAROLINA
AT A GLANCE

GAMEC
D1

SCHOOL
University of South Carolina

LOCATION
Columbia, SC

FOUNDED
1801

TEAM NICKNAME
Gamecocks

MASCOTS
Cocky (pictured above) and Sir Big Spur (pictured above left)

COLORS

STADIUM
Williams-Brice Stadium

CAPACITY
85,199

BAND
Mighty Sound of the Southeast

TICKET OFFICE
(800) 472-3267 or (803) 777-4274

WEBSITE
gamecocksonline.com

MINI REPLICAS OF GAMECOCK HELMETS WILL LEAVE PASSERSBY NO DOUBT ABOUT WHICH TEAM YOU CLAIM.

CHOOSE DEEP RED DHALIAS AND CRYSANTHEMUMS PAIRED WITH A FEATHER OR TWO—A NOD TO THE GAMECOCKS.

A TABLECLOTH MADE OF GARNET-STRIPED GRAIN SACK MATERIAL LOOKS CASUAL YET COLLECTED.

SOUTH CAROLINA
GAMECOCKS

Boiled Peanut
Hummus with
Pork Rinds
P. 91

Shrimp and
Fontina Grits
P. 181

Sweet-and-Smoky
Collard Greens
P. 199

Pineapple Upside-
Down Skillet Cake
P. 232

SERVES 10

EMBELLISH WITH FOOTBALL
CUTOUTS AND PALMETTO
LEAVES FROM THE OFFICIAL
SOUTH CAROLINA STATE TREE.

WATERMELON-SATSUMA SALAD
WITH GOAT CHEESE AND MINT

SERVES 8 // HANDS-ON 20 MINUTES // TOTAL 20 MINUTES

Cool mint and watermelon make this delicious salad an excellent option when tailgating on a hot day.

½ cup fresh lime juice (from 4 limes)

2 tablespoons rice vinegar

2 tablespoons minced shallots (from 2 shallots)

1½ tablespoons light agave nectar

1 teaspoon Tajín seasoning (or ¼ teaspoon cayenne pepper plus 1½ teaspoons kosher salt), plus more for serving

3 tablespoons chopped fresh mint

⅔ cup grapeseed oil

6 cups cubed seedless watermelon (about 7 pounds watermelon)

½ English cucumber, cut into half moons

1½ cups satsuma orange sections (about 4 medium satsuma oranges)

4 ounces goat cheese, crumbled (about 1 cup)

3 tablespoons toasted sesame seeds

EXTRA POINT

Make sure the goat cheese is well chilled before crumbling it. Make the dressing and prep the remaining ingredients a day ahead; assemble the salad at your tailgate.

1 Whisk together the lime juice, vinegar, shallots, agave, Tajín, and 1 tablespoon of the mint in a bowl. Let stand until the shallots are softened, about 10 minutes. Gradually whisk in the oil.

2 Place the watermelon and cucumber in a large bowl. Add half of the dressing; toss to coat. Place the watermelon mixture on a platter. Drizzle with the remaining dressing. Sprinkle with the orange sections, goat cheese, sesame seeds, and remaining 2 tablespoons mint. Serve with additional Tajín, if desired.

FRESH FRUIT SALAD
WITH MINT-LIME SIMPLE SYRUP

SERVES 8 TO 10 // HANDS-ON 15 MINUTES
TOTAL 4 HOURS, 45 MINUTES, INCLUDES 4 HOURS CHILLING

Any fruit can be jazzed up with this refreshing Mint-Lime Simple Syrup.

MINT-LIME SIMPLE SYRUP

1 cup granulated sugar

1 cup loosely packed fresh mint leaves

1 cup water

¼ cup fresh lime juice

FRUIT SALAD

2 (16-ounce) containers fresh strawberries, halved

1 (6-ounce) container fresh raspberries

2 cups seedless green grapes

2 kiwifruit, peeled and thinly sliced

1 Make the Mint-Lime Simple Syrup: Stir together the sugar, mint leaves, and water in a saucepan over medium-high. Bring to a boil, stirring occasionally, and boil 1 minute or until the sugar dissolves. Remove from the heat. Stir in the lime juice, and cool 30 minutes.

2 Pour the mixture through a fine mesh strainer into an airtight container. Cover and chill the syrup 4 hours.

3 Make the Fruit Salad: Gently toss together the strawberries, raspberries, grapes, and kiwifruit in a large bowl. Add ½ cup of the Mint-Lime Simple Syrup, and gently stir to coat. Serve immediately, or cover and chill up to 1 week. Store the remaining simple syrup in the refrigerator.

APPLE-PECAN SLAW ▶

SERVES **8** // HANDS-ON **25 MINUTES** // TOTAL **25 MINUTES**

Apples, apple cider vinegar, and mustard infuse this slaw with sweet tanginess that pairs brilliantly with heavier entrées like hot chicken or ribs. After tossing all the ingredients, let the dish chill in the refrigerator or a cooler for about an hour. This softens the kale and gives it a traditional coleslaw texture.

¾ cup canola mayonnaise

3 tablespoons apple cider vinegar

1 tablespoon coarse-grained mustard

1 tablespoon honey

1½ teaspoons kosher salt

¾ teaspoon black pepper

6 cups thinly sliced kale (from 2 bunches)

2 cups thinly sliced crisp red apple (such as Jazz, Honeycrisp, or Gala) (about 1 large)

1 cup chopped toasted pecans

1 cup matchstick carrots

2 tablespoons chopped fresh tarragon

2 tablespoons thinly sliced fresh chives

Whisk together the mayonnaise, vinegar, mustard, honey, salt, and pepper in a large bowl. Add the kale, apple slices, pecans, carrots, tarragon, and chives, and toss to coat.

GEORGIAN CABBAGE SLAW

SERVES **10** // HANDS-ON **10 MINUTES** // TOTAL **20 MINUTES**

Creamy, briny, and sweet, this slaw is a fantastic side dish for burgers, stew, or barbecue. It even makes a tasty relish for hotdogs. We recommend using pickled okra from the Wickles Pickles brand; it's absolutely delicious and has a bit of spice. (Pictured on pages 80 and 176)

1 head green cabbage (about 2 pounds), coarsely chopped (about 12 cups)

½ cup finely chopped celery (from 2 celery stalks)

¾ cup mayonnaise

½ cup coarsely chopped pickled okra (such as Wickles Pickles)

¼ cup pickled okra liquid from jar

1 teaspoon kosher salt

1 Place the cabbage, in batches, in a food processor, and pulse until finely chopped (but not juiced), about 5 pulses. Transfer to a large bowl; add the celery, and toss.

2 Process the mayonnaise, okra, okra liquid, and salt in a food processor. Pulse until finely chopped and blended, about 5 pulses. Add to the cabbage, and toss to coat. Let stand at least 10 minutes before serving.

WEDGE SALAD *ON A* STICK

SERVES 8 // HANDS-ON 10 MINUTES // TOTAL 10 MINUTES

Creative and satisfying, this reimagined, no-fork-needed "salad" couldn't be more perfect for game-day feasting. Serve the salad sticks to tailgate guests and be ready for a blitz upon the tray. (Pictured on pages 146 and 208)

1 romaine lettuce heart (about 8 ounces)
½ cup mayonnaise
¼ cup whole buttermilk
2 tablespoons fresh lemon juice (from 1 lemon)
½ teaspoon black pepper
¼ teaspoon kosher salt

4 ounces blue cheese, crumbled (about 1 cup)
1 pint cherry tomatoes
1 medium-size red onion, roughly chopped
8 (6-inch) wooden skewers
4 cooked bacon slices, crumbled (about ⅓ cup)

1 Cut the romaine lettuce heart in half lengthwise. Place the romaine halves on a cutting board, flat-side down, and cut in half lengthwise again. Cut each long quarter into 4 (2-inch) pieces to create 16 "cubes."
2 Stir together the mayonnaise, buttermilk, lemon juice, pepper, salt, and half of the blue cheese in a small bowl.
3 Alternately thread the romaine cubes, cherry tomatoes, and red onions evenly onto 8 (6-inch) skewers. Place the skewers on a platter. Drizzle with the dressing. Sprinkle with the bacon crumbles and remaining blue cheese.

EXTRA **POINT**

Using romaine lettuce hearts is a must in order to create ideal "cubes" for sliding onto the skewers.

◁ SWEET-AND-SMOKY COLLARD GREENS

SERVES 10 // HANDS-ON 15 MINUTES // TOTAL 2 HOURS, 25 MINUTES

Collard greens and college football—these things go hand in hand in the South, especially at the University of South Carolina, where collards are the official state vegetable. Due to their tough leaves, collard greens hold up well when braised. Here, they're cooked with smoked ham hocks, mustard powder, hot sauce, cider vinegar, and sweet tea to give them their unique zing.

1 tablespoon canola oil
2 sweet onions, chopped (about 2 cups)
4 garlic cloves, finely chopped (about 2 tablespoons)
1½ pounds smoked ham hocks (about 2 hocks)
3 pounds fresh collards, trimmed and washed (about 10 cups)

2 (32-ounce) containers low-sodium chicken broth
4 cups brewed sweet tea
½ cup apple cider vinegar
2 teaspoons kosher salt
1 teaspoon dry mustard
2 teaspoons hot sauce
1 teaspoon black pepper

Heat the oil in a 10-quart stockpot over medium. Add the chopped onions, and cook, stirring often, until softened, about 8 minutes; add the garlic, and cook, stirring often, until fragrant, about 1 minute. Add the ham hocks and collard greens. Stir in the broth, tea, vinegar, salt, mustard, hot sauce, and pepper, and cook until tender, about 2 hours. Carefully remove the ham hocks from the pot, and let stand until cool enough to handle, about 10 minutes. Remove and discard the bones and fat from the ham hock; roughly chop the meat, and stir into the collard green mixture.

GREEN BEAN BENEDICTINE SALAD

SERVES **8** // HANDS-ON **30 MINUTES** // TOTAL **30 MINUTES**

Blanching and shocking the beans keep them tender and bright green, and the combination of Castelvetrano olives, green beans, and almonds creates a buttery and nutty flavor. This salad can be made a day in advance and transported to your tailgate site in a cooler.

TENT *TALK*

True or False: On a kicking play, it is illegal to hit or tackle the kicker when his leg is extended.

4 ounces cream cheese, softened
½ cup peeled, chopped English cucumber (from 1 small cucumber)
¼ cup olive oil
2 tablespoons fresh lemon juice (from 1 lemon)
¼ cup water
2 tablespoons chopped fresh flat-leaf parsley

1 teaspoon kosher salt
½ teaspoon black pepper
2 (8-ounce) packages haricots verts (French green beans), trimmed
¼ cup pitted Castelvetrano olives, halved lengthwise
¼ cup sliced toasted almonds
¼ cup thinly sliced scallion (from 1 medium scallion)

1 Combine the cream cheese, cucumber, olive oil, and lemon juice in a mini food processor; process until smooth. With the processor running, gradually pour the water through the food chute until emulsified and the desired consistency is reached. Pour the dressing into a bowl, and stir in the parsley, salt, and pepper. Set aside.

2 Bring a large pot of water to a boil. Add the green beans, and boil until tender-crisp, 3 to 4 minutes. Drain and plunge into ice water to stop the cooking process. Pat the green beans dry with a paper towel. Transfer to a platter, and drizzle the dressing over the beans. Quarter the olive halves lengthwise; sprinkle the olives, almonds, and scallions over the beans. Keep refrigerated or cool until ready to serve.

STREET CORN SALAD

SERVES **8** // HANDS-ON **20 MINUTES** // TOTAL **20 MINUTES**

Bright in color and flavor, street corn salad takes any party up a notch. (Also pictured on page 150)

½ cup chopped fresh cilantro
3 tablespoons fresh lime juice
1 teaspoon kosher salt
½ teaspoon black pepper
2 tablespoons olive oil

4 cups fresh corn kernels
1 cup thinly sliced radishes
1 cup cherry tomato halves
⅓ to ½ cup crumbled Cotija cheese
  (or feta cheese)

1   Combine the cilantro, lime juice, salt, and pepper; whisk in the olive oil.
2   Stir together the corn, radishes, and tomatoes in a medium bowl. Gently stir in the dressing; spoon the mixture onto a serving platter, and sprinkle with the cheese.

SAUCY COLA BAKED BEANS

SERVES **8** // HANDS-ON **30 MINUTES** // TOTAL **1 HOUR, 5 MINUTES**

Baked beans are a classic accompaniment with any tailgate spread. Here, the flavor is kicked up a notch with hickory-smoked bacon, jalapeño chiles, cola soft drink, and hot sauce, ensuring that tailgaters will make multiple returns to the serving dish. You can make this dish ahead, transfer it to a slow cooker, and reheat at your tailgate site.

6 thick-cut hickory-smoked bacon slices
1 large sweet onion (about 8 ounces),
  chopped (about 1½ cups)
1 cup chopped green bell pepper (about
  4 ounces)
2 medium jalapeño chiles, seeded and
  chopped (about ½ cup)
2 teaspoons minced garlic
1 (16-ounce) can light red kidney beans,
  drained and rinsed
1 (16-ounce) can dark red kidney beans,
  drained and rinsed

1 (16-ounce) can navy beans, drained
  and rinsed
1 (15-ounce) can black beans, drained
  and rinsed
1 cup cola soft drink
½ cup ketchup
⅓ cup packed dark brown sugar
¼ cup apple cider vinegar
2 tablespoons spicy brown mustard
1 teaspoon hot sauce
1 teaspoon table salt

1   Preheat the oven to 375°F. Cook the bacon in a Dutch oven over medium until crisp; remove to paper towels to drain, reserving 2 tablespoons of the bacon drippings in the pan. Crumble the bacon.
2   Add the onion, bell pepper, and jalapeños to the hot drippings in the pan, and cook, stirring often, until the vegetables are soft, about 8 to 10 minutes. Add the garlic, and cook, stirring constantly, 1 minute. Stir in the beans, cola, ketchup, brown sugar, vinegar, mustard, hot sauce, and salt, and bring the mixture to a simmer. Remove from the heat, and stir in the crumbled bacon. Spoon the mixture into a lightly greased 11- x 7-inch (2-quart) baking dish.
3   Bake at 375°F until the mixture is thickened and bubbly, 30 to 35 minutes. Serve warm.

IN THE NAVY

Maybe it was an aha moment. Or maybe it was frustration with Knoxville's game-day traffic. We'll never really know. But when UT play-by-play announcer George Mooney fired up his runabout and boated to work one autumn Saturday, he launched one of Tennessee's finest traditions— the Volunteer Navy.

As it turns out, good ole Rocky Top has a soggy bottom. By fate or by design, UT's cavernous Neyland Stadium sits in a bend on the banks of the Tennessee River. Long before a game starts in Knoxville, hundreds of boats float upstream, tie together, and settle in for a fun-filled football weekend. A few die-hard fans drop anchor in August and stay until icicles hang from their hulls.

And yet, to say that boating to a game is merely a form of transportation is like saying former UT quarterback Peyton Manning is just another guy who played football. The Vol Navy is tradition and a way of life for those who have reached the pinnacle of Tennessee tailgating.

With more than 100,000 fans attending every home game, tailgates aren't confined to the water. The party spreads out all over campus, from Circle Park to Cumberland Avenue. But it's all just a teaser for the main event on Neyland Drive.

Hours before a game starts, the University of Tennessee campus is awash in a sea of orange and white. This sea parts for the Vol Walk and again for the Pride of the Southland Marching Band's procession to the stadium, but little else can stem the tide.

Tennessee fans flood the stadium just in time to see Smokey lead the team through the Power T. At last, it's football time in Tennessee!

FUN FACT

It took Boudleaux and Felice Bryant just 10 minutes to write the song "Rocky Top." It's not UT's official fight song, but it is one of Tennessee's 10 official state songs.

TENNESSEE
AT A GLANCE

SCHOOL
University of Tennessee

LOCATION
Knoxville, TN

FOUNDED
1794

TEAM NICKNAME
Volunteers

MASCOT
A Bluetick Coonhound
named Smokey

COLORS

STADIUM
Neyland Stadium

CAPACITY
102,455

BAND
Pride of the Southland
Marching Band

TICKET OFFICE
(800) 332-8657 or
(865) 656-1200

WEBSITE
utsports.com

// THE HEART OF A VOLUNTEER

The eternal flame of the Volunteer spirit burns bright on UT's flagship campus in Knoxville, Tennessee.

Adopted as the university's official symbol in 1932, the Volunteer Statue—affectionately known as the Torchbearer—stands proudly at the intersection of Circle Park and Volunteer Boulevard. The chiseled young Volunteer looks boldly toward the future, the Goddess of Winged Victory in one hand and a torch held aloft in the other.

On graduation day, students stand in long lines at Torchbearer Plaza to have photos taken. When returning to campus, alumni linger at the base of the 9-foot statue, inspired once again by the values that define a Volunteer.

For other visitors, a plaque bearing the Volunteer Creed illuminates the statue's significance. It reads: "One that beareth a torch shadoweth oneself to give light to others."

// A QUARTERBACK'S LASTING LEGACY

On game day, buses stop at the Torchbearer Statue to let members of the Tennessee football team disembark for the traditional Vol Walk. Flush with adrenaline and giddy with excitement, players walk down Peyton Manning Pass, through a gauntlet of cheering fans, to reach Gate 21A and enter their beloved Neyland Stadium.

Few embody the Volunteer Spirit better than Manning, a quarterback who wore the orange and white from '94 to '97 on his way to becoming the most prolific passer in Tennessee football history. Manning was 39-6 as a starter at UT, was the No. 1 pick in the 1998 NFL draft, and went on to become one of the greatest quarterbacks in league history.

When he announced his retirement in 2016, after 18 years in the NFL and just days after leading the Denver Broncos to victory in Super Bowl L, Manning thanked the Volunteer faithful, saying that staying for his senior year was the smartest decision he ever made. "I cherish my time in Knoxville, especially my senior year, and I want Vol fans everywhere to know the unique role you have played in my life," he said, fighting back tears.

// THE GENERAL'S HOUSE

Fittingly, the Pass—a sloping, narrow thoroughfare that connects Volunteer Boulevard with Phillip Fulmer Way—leads directly to the house that Robert Neyland built.

Now the fifth-largest stadium in the country, Neyland Stadium sits on the bank of the Tennessee River at the edge of downtown Knoxville. It is a towering monument to a man whose legacy lives large in college football history.

A West Point graduate who played three sports and earned the rank of brigadier general in the U.S. Army, Robert Neyland twice interrupted his coaching career for military service. That he was a man of war suited Tennessee. The team's nickname comes from the state's reputation for sending volunteers to fight for their country.

General Robert Neyland, right, talks to his players during a game at Neyland Stadium in Knoxville, Tennessee, circa the 1950s.

In three separate stints at UT—1926 to 1934, 1936 to 1940, and 1946 to 1952—he amassed a record of 173-31-12. This includes undefeated streaks of 33, 28, 23, 19, and 14 games, as well as seven conference championships and four national titles. The General remains the winningest coach in Tennessee history.

Neyland Stadium not only carries his name, but also his stamp of approval. The General designed the stadium, as well as the expansions that helped it grow to its current official capacity of 102,455. He served as athletic director until his death in 1962, and Volunteer players still recite Neyland's seven maxims of football before each game.

// IT'S GAME DAY!

The Volunteers' tapestry of traditions is colorful and ever-changing.

Tennessee's signature orange and white colors reflect the wild daisies that are said to have once grown in abundance on The Hill, the heart of UT's old campus, where Ayres Hall still stands today. Neyland's checkerboard end zones echo the architecture of Ayres' Gothic tower, which sits on a hill overlooking the stadium. Before every game, the Pride of the Southland Marching Band stops on its way to the game for a musical salute at the base of The Hill.

The team's mascot is a Bluetick Coonhound named Smokey. This extraordinary hound dog is not named for the nearby Smoky Mountains, as many think, but for the original mascot, Brooks' Blue Smokey, who barked his way into the hearts of students during a 1953 halftime howling contest. It's Smokey and his handler who lead the way when the team runs onto the field, running through the Power T formed by the Pride of the Southland.

Just minutes before the team runs onto the field, a tradition unseen by many takes place deep in the belly of Neyland Stadium. On their way out of the locker room, each player touches a state-shaped sign above the door, declaring, "I will give my all for Tennessee today."

On the field, in the classroom, throughout life, the indomitable Volunteer spirit prevails.

SALUTE NEYLAND STADIUM'S
CHECKERBOARD END ZONES
WITH A MATCHING TABLECLOTH
AND SOLID ORANGE RUNNER.

ORANGE LILLIES AND ANY
SMALL WHITE FLOWERS,
SUCH AS FEVERFEW, MAKE A
STUNNING TABLE BOUQUET.

TENNESSEE
VOLUNTEERS

T

Sloppy Joe Dip	BBQ Chicken Drumsticks	Wedge Salad on a Stick	Elvis Bars
P. 84	P. 147	P. 199	P. 243

SERVES 8

A YARN TASSEL GARLAND AND FOOTBALL AND COCKTAIL NAPKINS WITH THE ICONIC "T" INSIGNIA TOP IT OFF.

SWEET-HOT POTATO SALAD ▸

SERVES **10** // HANDS-ON **15 MINUTES** // TOTAL **1 HOUR, 5 MINUTES**

EXTRA
POINT

You can make this dish up to 2 days in advance and transport it in a cooler to your tailgate site. Serve chilled or at room temperature.

The sweet-hot pickles and mustard give this mayonnaise-based dish pleasing acidity. Be sure to bring the potatoes to a boil with the water for even cooking.

10 cups water
1½ pounds small Yukon Gold potatoes
1½ pounds small red potatoes
2 tablespoons kosher salt
4 large eggs
¾ cup mayonnaise
⅓ cup juice from 1 (16-ounce) jar sweet-hot pickles (such as Wickles)

2 tablespoons coarse-grained mustard
1 teaspoon granulated sugar
½ teaspoon black pepper
¾ cup chopped sweet-hot pickles (such as Wickles)
⅔ cup thinly sliced red onion (from 1 small onion)
3 tablespoons chopped fresh dill

1 Place the water, potatoes, and 1½ tablespoons of the salt in a large saucepan, and bring to a boil over high. Reduce the heat to medium; simmer the potatoes until tender, 20 to 25 minutes. Using a slotted spoon, transfer the potatoes to a plate. (Do not discard the cooking water.) Cool the potatoes completely, about 30 minutes. Cut the potatoes into ¾-inch pieces.

2 Return the water to a boil over high. Carefully add the eggs with a slotted spoon, and cook 8 minutes; immediately plunge into a bowl of ice water to stop the cooking process. Cool completely, about 5 minutes. Peel the eggs, and roughly chop.

3 Stir together the mayonnaise, pickle juice, mustard, sugar, pepper, and remaining ½ tablespoon salt in a large bowl. Add the potatoes, eggs, pickles, onion, and dill; stir well. Serve at room temperature or chilled.

GRILLED JALAPEÑO-LIME
CORN *ON THE* COB

SERVES **8** // HANDS-ON **30 MINUTES** // TOTAL **30 MINUTES**

Serve sweet-hot corn on the cob when in need of a dish to please a crowd. Pull the corn off the grill, cut into thirds, and let guests top the pieces with as much or as little of the butter mixture as they please. To make the butter mixture hotter, leave a few seeds intact in the jalapeño. (Pictured on the cover and page 175)

8 ears fresh corn, husks removed
Cooking spray
Kosher salt
Freshly ground black pepper
½ cup (4 ounces) butter, softened
1 jalapeño chile, seeded and minced

1 small garlic clove, pressed
1 tablespoon lime zest, plus more for serving
1 tablespoon fresh lime juice
2 teaspoons chopped fresh cilantro

1 Preheat the grill to medium-high (400°F to 450°F). Coat the corn lightly with cooking spray. Sprinkle with the desired amount of salt and pepper. Grill the corn, covered, 15 minutes or until golden brown, turning occasionally.

2 Meanwhile, stir together the butter, jalapeño, garlic, 1 tablespoon of the lime zest, lime juice, and cilantro. Remove the corn from the grill, and cut into thirds. Serve the corn with the butter mixture. Garnish with the additional lime zest, if desired.

CREAMY MEXICAN-STYLE CORN *ON THE* COB

SERVES 10 // HANDS-ON 10 MINUTES // TOTAL 20 MINUTES

This corn on the cob is finger-licking good. The lightly charred ears are slathered in a tangy mayo and sprinkled with Cotija cheese and a chipotle mixture. If chipotle chile powder isn't available, use regular chili powder.

½ cup mayonnaise
2 teaspoons fresh lime juice (from 1 lime)
6 garlic cloves, minced (about 2 tablespoons)
1 teaspoon kosher salt
1½ teaspoons chipotle chile powder

1 teaspoon black pepper
10 ears fresh corn
2½ ounces Cotija cheese, crumbled (about ½ cup)
⅓ cup packed fresh cilantro leaves
2 limes, cut into wedges

1 Preheat the grill to medium-high (400°F to 450°F). Whisk together the mayonnaise, lime juice, garlic, and ¼ teaspoon of the salt in a small bowl; set aside. Combine the chipotle powder, black pepper, and remaining ¾ teaspoon salt in a separate bowl.

2 Place the corn on lightly oiled grates; grill, uncovered, turning often, until lightly charred, about 10 minutes. Brush the corn with the mayo mixture; sprinkle with the Cotija cheese, chipotle mixture, and cilantro. Squeeze the limes evenly over the corn before serving.

MIKE'S MAQUE CHOUX SALAD

SERVES 10 // HANDS-ON 20 MINUTES // TOTAL 50 MINUTES

Maque choux is a classic Louisiana dish that contains corn, bell pepper, and onion. Adding orzo to this salad along with a tangy dressing makes this a perfect game-day pasta salad. The flavor is sweet from the corn but rounded out by the salty bacon drippings and dressing.

1½ cups (about 9 ounces) uncooked orzo
1 tablespoon bacon drippings or melted salted butter
1 small yellow onion, chopped (about 1 cup)
1 medium-size red bell pepper, chopped (about 1 cup)
2 garlic cloves, minced (about 2 teaspoons)
3 cups fresh yellow corn kernels plus milky liquid scraped from corncobs (from 4 ears corn)

1 teaspoon kosher salt
¼ cup sliced scallions (about 2 scallions)
1 pint multicolored cherry tomatoes, quartered
2 tablespoons white balsamic vinegar
2 teaspoons Dijon mustard
½ teaspoon black pepper
¼ cup olive oil
¼ cup French fried onions (such as French's) (optional)
3 tablespoons chopped fresh flat-leaf parsley (optional)

EXTRA POINT

Make this up to 2 days in advance; store covered in the refrigerator. Take it out 30 minutes prior to serving. Garnish with the crispy fried onions at serving time.

1 Cook the orzo according to the package directions; drain and run under cold water to cool.

2 Heat the bacon drippings in a large skillet over medium. Add the onion and bell pepper, and cook, stirring occasionally, until soft, 5 to 7 minutes. Add the garlic, and cook, stirring often, until fragrant, about 1 minute. Add the corn and milky liquid, and cook, stirring occasionally, until the vegetables are tender, about 8 minutes. Stir in ½ teaspoon of the salt; remove from the heat, and cool to room temperature, about 20 minutes.

3 Combine the corn mixture, orzo, scallions, and cherry tomatoes in a large bowl. Whisk together the vinegar, Dijon, pepper, and remaining ½ teaspoon salt in a small bowl. Slowly drizzle in the oil, whisking until combined. Add to the corn mixture, and toss to combine. Sprinkle the fried onions and chopped parsley over the top of the mixture, if desired.

PIMIENTO CHEESE HUSH PUPPIES *WITH* DILLY TARTAR SAUCE ▶

SERVES 10 // HANDS-ON 20 MINUTES // TOTAL 20 MINUTES

EXTRA POINT

Use an ice-cream scoop to get the hush puppy batter into perfect rounds. Roasted red peppers will work in place of pimientos.

Crispy outer edges and soft centers with a creamy and tangy dill sauce make this the gold standard for hush puppies. You can make the tartar sauce in advance so it's ready to go when you pull the hot hush puppies out of the fryer.

PIMIENTO CHEESE HUSH PUPPIES
Vegetable oil
2¼ cups (about 9.6 ounces) plain yellow cornmeal
¾ cup (about 3¼ ounces) all-purpose flour
2 teaspoons kosher salt
1½ teaspoons baking powder
¾ teaspoon baking soda
¾ cup whole buttermilk
¾ cup water
3 large eggs, lightly beaten
5 ounces sharp Cheddar cheese, shredded (about 1¼ cups)

1 (4-ounce) jar diced pimientos, drained well
⅓ cup thinly sliced scallions

DILLY TARTAR SAUCE
1½ cups mayonnaise
1 cup finely chopped dill pickles
3 tablespoons fresh lemon juice (from 1 lemon)
2 tablespoons chopped fresh dill, plus more for garnish
2 tablespoons coarse-grained mustard
¼ teaspoon cayenne pepper

1 Make the Pimiento Cheese Hush Puppies: Pour the oil to a depth of 5 inches into a large Dutch oven over medium; heat to 330°F. Combine the cornmeal, flour, salt, baking powder, and baking soda in a bowl. Stir together the buttermilk, water, and eggs in a large bowl. Add the dry ingredients to the wet ingredients, and stir just until smooth. Fold in the cheese, pimientos, and scallions.

2 Spoon the batter, in batches (about 3 tablespoonfuls per hush puppy), into the hot oil, and cook until golden brown, about 4 minutes per batch, rotating occasionally. Place on a platter lined with paper towels.

3 Make the Dilly Tartar Sauce: Stir together all the tartar sauce ingredients until combined. Garnish with the additional dill, if desired. Serve with the hush puppies.

PIMIENTO CHEESE ROLLS

MAKES 1 DOZEN ROLLS // HANDS-ON 15 MINUTES // TOTAL 1 HOUR, 15 MINUTES

Three-ingredient rollups are just the ticket to a no-hassle tailgate.

1 (25-ounce) package frozen Southern-style biscuits

All-purpose flour
2 cups pimiento cheese

1 Arrange the biscuits, sides touching, in 3 rows of 4 biscuits on a lightly floured surface. Let stand 30 to 45 minutes or until the biscuits are thawed but cool to the touch.

2 Preheat the oven to 375°F. Sprinkle the biscuits with the flour. Press the edges together; pat to form a 12- x 10-inch rectangle; spread the dough with the cheese.

3 Roll up, starting at one long end; cut into 12 (1-inch-thick) slices. Place 1 slice into each muffin cup of a lightly greased 12-cup muffin pan.

4 Bake at 375°F until golden, 20 to 25 minutes. Let cool in the pan on a wire rack 5 minutes; remove from the pan, and serve immediately.

LOADED GOLDEN RAVIOLI NACHOS

SERVES 8 // HANDS-ON 30 MINUTES // TOTAL 30 MINUTES

A nontraditional take on the classic tailgate food, these "nachos" are made with ravioli instead of tortilla chips. The breaded, fried, and baked preparation of the ravioli is original to St. Louis, making this a perfect dish to serve at (but not limited to) Missouri games. Piled with fresh toppings such as tomato, cilantro, avocado, and a creamy glaze, the cheesy goodness that results will have you blissfully swaying to the Marching Mizzou's "Missouri Waltz."

EXTRA POINT

Be sure to have a candy thermometer on hand for measuring the temperature of the oil in Step 1.

6 cups canola or vegetable oil

2 large eggs

7 to 8 tablespoons whole milk

1½ cups panko (Japanese-style breadcrumbs)

2 (9-ounce) packages refrigerated four-cheese ravioli

3 ounces sharp Cheddar cheese, shredded (about ¾ cup)

3 ounces white Cheddar cheese, shredded (about ¾ cup)

1 cup chopped tomato (from 1 medium tomato)

¼ cup sliced scallions (about 2 scallions)

¼ cup cilantro leaves

¼ cup diced red onion (from 1 small onion)

1 small ripe avocado, diced

1 small jalapeño chile, seeded and sliced

¾ cup sour cream

½ teaspoon kosher salt

Lime wedges

1 Place the oil in a Dutch oven; heat to 325°F over medium. Whisk together the eggs and ¼ cup of the milk in a medium bowl. Place the breadcrumbs in a separate medium bowl.

2 Dip the ravioli in the egg mixture; dredge in the breadcrumbs, shaking to remove any excess breadcrumbs.

3 Add the ravioli, in 2 to 3 batches, to the hot oil, and fry until golden brown, 2 to 3 minutes, flipping, if necessary, to brown evenly. Remove from the oil, and let stand on paper towels to drain.

4 Preheat the broiler to high with the oven rack 8 inches from the heat. Place the ravioli in a single layer on a rimmed baking sheet, and sprinkle evenly with the cheeses.

5 Broil until the cheeses are melted and the ravioli starts to crisp around the edges, 2 to 3 minutes. Sprinkle with the tomato, scallions, cilantro, red onion, avocado, and jalapeño. Stir together the sour cream and 3 tablespoons of the milk, adding the remaining 1 tablespoon milk, if necessary, to reach the desired consistency. Drizzle over the nachos; sprinkle with the salt. Serve with the lime wedges.

SWEET VICTORIES

IT'S THE MUST-HAVE IN TIMES OF CELEBRATION. IT'S THE CONSOLATION
IN MOMENTS OF DEFEAT. IT'S DESSERT. THIS SELECTION OF PUDDING,
CAKE, COBBLER, AND MORE WILL ENSURE THAT EVERY GAME DAY ENDS
ON A HIGH NOTE, NO MATTER WHAT THE SCOREBOARD SAYS.

FUN FACT

Today, A&M students never sit during a game, signaling their willingness to be the 12th Man.

MIDNIGHT YELL

They don't have a fight song; they have a war hymn. They poke fun at opponents. And yes, they yell. The night before every home game, members of the 12th Man follow Texas A&M's Yell Leaders and the Fightin' Texas Aggie Band into Kyle Field. What commences at midnight is quite possibly the most passionate display of fan loyalty in college football.

This is Midnight Yell. You can thank Peanut Owens and his buddies for this tradition. Yell Practice had long been an after-dinner ritual for the cadets at what was then an all-male military school. But someone in Peanut's cadre thought the freshmen should meet at midnight for more work. Word spread, and Midnight Yell was born. The year: 1931.

Today, over 20,000 people make their way to Kyle Field to experience the tradition of Midnight Yell before each home game. Part pep rally, part comedy show, part sing-along, it features military-inspired "yells" with intricate arm gestures, cannon fire, and fireworks. And when the game isn't at home, the Aggies still don't miss a beat. Two nights before an away game, there's an evening Yell Practice at the Quadrangle. Then, the night before the game, Yell Leaders hold their Midnight Yell in or near the city they're about to invade.

Every Midnight Yell also includes an exercise called "mugging down." When the Aggies score, every Aggie scores—or so it's said in College Station. As the lights go out at Midnight Yell, the Aggies kiss their dates, just so they'll know what to do on game day when A&M scores a touchdown. Kissing takes practice, too!

TEXAS A&M
AT A GLANCE

SCHOOL
Texas A&M University

LOCATION
College
Station, TX

FOUNDED
1876

TEAM NICKNAME
Aggies

MASCOT
Reveille (pictured)

COLORS

STADIUM
Kyle Field

CAPACITY
102,733

BAND
Fightin' Texas Aggie Band

TICKET OFFICE
(888) 992-4443 or (979) 845-2311

WEBSITE
12thman.com

// THE 12TH MAN

No Texas Aggie stands alone.

It doesn't matter where they go or what they do—on the football field, the battlefield, in the game of life. Whenever an Aggie needs reinforcement, other Aggies stand ready to help.

This time-honored tradition dates back to January 2, 1922, when A&M played the top-ranked Centre College Praying Colonels in the Dixie Classic, a post-season matchup that would eventually become the Cotton Bowl. Injuries had depleted Coach Dana X. Bible's reserves, leaving only the 11 players on the field to finish the game. He needed someone—anyone—to suit up in case another on his team went down.

The coach found E. King Gill, a former reserve player who had left the team to play basketball, working in the press box as a spotter for the local paper. Gill changed into an injured player's uniform beneath the stands and joined Bible on the A&M sideline. Though Gill didn't play in the Maroon and White's 22-14 victory, he was eager to go into the game. He was the Aggies' 12th Man.

// A SPIRIT CAN NE'ER BE TOLD

The 12th Man is one of A&M's most treasured traditions. A statue outside Kyle Field pays tribute to Gill. But no statue will ever capture the full spirit of Aggieland.

No fan base is more loyal than Texas A&M's. During the game, Aggies will sing *The Aggie War Hymn* and then link arms and sway left to right to "saw Varsity's horns off," making it look as if the entire stadium is moving. As long as there are seconds on the clock, A&M fans stand, wave their 12th Man towels, and yell.

During the 2007 Fresno State game, Aggies in the student section left their seats and clustered near the end zone, trying to help prevent the Bulldogs from scoring. A&M won that game 47-45 in triple overtime.

// KEEPERS OF THE SPIRIT

Many of the school's traditions can be traced directly to the Texas A&M Corps of Cadets. More than a thousand student organizations operate on campus at A&M, but the Corps is the largest and the oldest—as old as the school itself.

Texas A&M opened as an all-male military school in 1876, and service in the Corps was mandatory for male students until 1965. Today, not all students who attend A&M are in the Corps; however, A&M's Corps of Cadets still commissions more military officers than any other institution outside the service academies.

Members of the Fightin' Texas Aggie Band, the country's largest military band, are selected from the Corps ranks. A&M's mascot, a full-blooded rough collie named Reveille, attends classes with her Cadet handler and prowls the sidelines with the team. With her five diamonds, Miss Rev is also the highest ranking member of the Corps of Cadets. The Corps commander gets only four.

// GIG 'EM, AGGIES!

Texas A&M football has given fans plenty to yell about. The Aggies have claimed three national championships—1919, 1927, and 1939. Not a single team scored on Coach Bible's undefeated 1919 squad. They outscored opponents by a whopping 275 to 0.

Paul "Bear" Bryant's grueling 1954 summer football camp was the subject of the ESPN movie "The Junction Boys." Two of his players—Jack Pardee and Gene Stallings—went on to coach in the NFL, and Stallings won a national championship at Alabama. In Bryant's last season as A&M's coach, John David Crow brought the 1957 Heisman back to College Station.

R.C. Slocum ended his coaching career at Texas A&M with a record of 123-47–2, the school's best. The Aggies lost only four times at Kyle Field in the 1990s under his direction—the Aggies' Wrecking Crew defense was legendary.

In 2012, the university joined the Southeastern Conference, becoming its 13th member and beginning a bright new chapter. The team took the SEC by storm, ending the season with an 11-2 record, ranked No. 5 in the nation. Quarterback Johnny Manziel won the Heisman that year, becoming the first freshman to receive the award. Thanks to Johnny Football, A&M also became the first team in SEC history to log more than 7,000 yards of total offense in a season.

// A-G-G-I-E-S

They say everything is bigger in Texas, and that's true at A&M. The massive campus covers 5,200 acres and enrolls nearly 70,000 students, a fifth of whom live on campus. At capacity, Kyle Field holds 102,733 screaming fans. It's the largest stadium in the SEC and the third largest in the country. From the air, the stadium looks like a battleship afloat in a sea of maroon when A&M is playing.

Aggies have hearts as big as Texas, too. "Howdy" is the preferred greeting on campus, and students will answer any question a visitor might ask.

"I have never walked on a campus that is so open and friendly," says one out-of-towner. "And on game day, they are willing to treat you like family and long-lost friends, even if you are pulling for the other team."

HOME OF THE 12TH MAN

FUN FACT

The player wearing No. 12 on the Aggies' football team embodies the spirit of the 12th Man.

A SOLID WHITE TABLECLOTH MAKES THE DECOR AND FOOD POP. PATTERNED NAPKINS AND LEAVES ADD INTEREST.

TEXAS A&M
AGGIES

ATM

Red Grapefruit Punch	Cowboy Caviar	Loaded Brisket Nachos	Sopapilla Cheesecake Bars
P. 66	P. 93	P. 167	P. 250

SERVES 10

PAINTED WOODEN "A&M"
LETTERS MAKE AN IMPACT.
A WOODEN TEXAS CUTOUT
IS A CREATIVE FOOD DISPLAY.

POLISHED COASTERS
SHOWCASING THE SCHOOL
LOGO ECHO THE GRAPHIC
VIBE OF THE TABLE.

CHOCOLATE-AND-PEANUT BUTTER BANANA PUDDING

SERVES 8 // HANDS-ON 30 MINUTES
TOTAL 2 HOURS, 50 MINUTES, INCLUDES 2 HOURS CHILLING

You won't go wrong serving tailgate guests this creamy peanut butter-flavored custard layered with chocolate and bananas. The combination of the bananas and peanuts with the chocolate cookies and cocoa gives it a subtle black and gold appearance—a salute to the mighty Vanderbilt Commodores.

⅓ cup (about 1½ ounces) all-purpose flour
¼ teaspoon table salt
¾ cup plus 6 tablespoons granulated sugar
3 cups whole milk
3 large eggs
⅔ cup creamy peanut butter
1 tablespoon unsalted butter

2½ teaspoons vanilla extract
6 medium-size ripe bananas
1½ (9-ounce) packages chocolate wafer cookies (such as Nabisco Famous)
3 cups heavy cream
¼ cup finely chopped roasted, salted peanuts
1 tablespoon unsweetened cocoa

EXTRA POINT

You can make this dish a day in advance and store it covered in the refrigerator. Garnish right before serving.

1 Stir together the flour, salt, and ¾ cup of the sugar in a large saucepan. Whisk together the milk and eggs in a bowl, and add to the sugar mixture. Cook over medium-low, whisking constantly, until thickened, 15 to 20 minutes. Remove from the heat; stir in the peanut butter, butter, and 1½ teaspoons of the vanilla until the mixture is smooth.

2 Fill a large bowl with ice. Place the saucepan in the ice, and let stand, stirring occasionally, until the mixture is thoroughly chilled, about 30 minutes.

3 Meanwhile, cut the bananas into ¼-inch slices. Crumble 4 cookies; set aside.

4 Beat the cream and remaining 1 teaspoon vanilla in the bowl of a heavy-duty stand mixer fitted with the whisk attachment on high speed until foamy; gradually add the remaining 6 tablespoons sugar, 1 tablespoon at a time, and beat at medium-high speed until stiff peaks form. (Do not overbeat.)

5 Line the bottom of a 13- x 9-inch baking dish with the cookies slightly overlapping. Top with half of the bananas and half of the pudding mixture. Repeat the layers once. Top with the sweetened whipped cream. Cover and chill 2 to 24 hours. Top with the reserved crumbled cookies and peanuts. Sift the unsweetened cocoa over the top.

MISSISSIPPI MUD PIE TRIFLE

SERVES 12 // HANDS-ON 20 MINUTES // TOTAL 1 HOUR

EXTRA POINT

This can be made a day in advance and chilled in the refrigerator. Sub any chocolate cookie or brownie for the Oreos, if desired.

You've heard of Mississippi Mud Pie, but this Mississippi Mud Pie Trifle is on a whole new level of decadence, one fit for tailgating at the legendary Grove in Oxford, Mississippi. The Oreos are crunchy, but they also soak up some of the pudding, making them deliciously spongy and dirt-like in the way that all Mississippi Mud fans love.

4½ cups whole milk
1 cup granulated sugar
¼ teaspoon table salt
6 tablespoons unsweetened cocoa
¼ cup cornstarch
6 large egg yolks
10 ounces semisweet baking chocolate, finely chopped

¼ cup (2 ounces) unsalted butter, cut into pieces
2 teaspoons vanilla extract
4½ cups coarsely crushed creme-filled chocolate sandwich cookies (such as Oreos) (from 1 [19.1-ounce] pack)
4 cups sweetened whipped topping (such as Cool Whip)

1 Combine 4 cups of the milk and ½ cup of the sugar in a saucepan; stir in the salt. Cook over medium, stirring often, until the sugar is dissolved, 7 to 8 minutes. Remove from the heat.

2 Stir together the cocoa, cornstarch, and remaining ½ cup sugar in a bowl. Add the remaining ½ cup milk; whisk until smooth. Whisk the cocoa mixture into the hot milk mixture. Return to the heat, and bring to a boil over medium, whisking constantly. Reduce the heat to medium-low, and simmer, whisking constantly, until the pudding is thickened, about 2 minutes.

3 Place the egg yolks in a bowl; whisk until smooth. Gradually whisk 1 cup of the hot cocoa pudding into the eggs. Pour the egg mixture into the saucepan. Bring the pudding to a boil over medium, whisking constantly, 2 minutes. Remove from the heat.

4 Place the chopped chocolate, butter, and vanilla in a large bowl; add the hot pudding, and whisk until the chocolate and butter are melted and incorporated and the pudding is smooth, about 2 minutes. Cool completely.

5 Place 2 cups of the crushed cookies in the bottom of a trifle dish. Spread half of the pudding over the cookie bottom. Top with 2 cups of the whipped topping, and sprinkle with 2 cups of the crushed cookies. Spread with the remaining half of the pudding, and top with the remaining 2 cups whipped topping; sprinkle with the remaining ½ cup crushed cookies.

APPLE-SPICE BUNDT CAKE
with CARAMEL FROSTING

SERVES **12** // HANDS-ON **35 MINUTES** // TOTAL **3 HOURS, 55 MINUTES**

Incorporating the beloved fall flavors of apple, pumpkin, and caramel, this decadent delight will have tailgaters playing zone coverage at your cake table.

CREAM CHEESE FILLING

1 (8-ounce) package cream cheese, softened
¼ cup granulated sugar
1 large egg
2 tablespoons all-purpose flour
1 teaspoon vanilla extract

APPLE-SPICE BATTER

1 cup packed light brown sugar
1 cup vegetable oil
½ cup granulated sugar
3 large eggs
2 teaspoons vanilla extract
2 teaspoons baking powder
2 teaspoons pumpkin pie spice
1½ teaspoons ground cardamom
1 teaspoon kosher salt

½ teaspoon baking soda
½ teaspoon ground coriander
3 cups (about 12¾ ounces) all-purpose flour
3 large Granny Smith apples (about 1½ pounds), peeled and grated

CARAMEL FROSTING

½ cup packed light brown sugar
¼ cup heavy cream
¼ cup (2 ounces) salted butter
1 teaspoon vanilla extract
1¼ cups (about 5 ounces) powdered sugar, sifted

TOPPING

⅔ cup roughly chopped toasted pecans

TENT TALK

On what yard line is the ball placed in overtime?

A. 20 yard line
B. 25 yard line
C. 30 yard line
D. 40 yard line

1. Make the Cream Cheese Filling: Preheat the oven to 350°F. Beat the cream cheese, granulated sugar, egg, flour, and vanilla with an electric mixer on medium speed until smooth.

2. Make the Apple-Spice Batter: Beat the brown sugar, oil, and granulated sugar with the mixer on medium speed until well blended. Add the eggs, 1 at a time, beating well after each addition. Stir in the vanilla. Whisk together the baking powder, pumpkin pie spice, cardamom, salt, baking soda, coriander, and flour. Gradually add to the brown sugar mixture, beating on low speed just until blended. Add the apples, and beat on low speed just until combined.

3. Spoon half of the batter into a greased and floured 14-cup Bundt pan. Dollop the Cream Cheese Filling over the apple mixture, leaving a 1-inch border around the edges of the pan. Swirl the filling through the batter using a knife. Spoon the remaining batter over the filling.

4. Bake at 350°F until a long wooden pick inserted in the center comes out clean, 50 minutes to 1 hour. Cool the cake in the pan on a wire rack 20 minutes; remove from the pan to the wire rack, and cool completely, about 2 hours.

5. Meanwhile, make the Caramel Frosting: Bring the brown sugar, cream, and butter to a boil in a 2-quart heavy saucepan over medium, whisking constantly; boil, whisking constantly, 1 minute.

6. Remove the pan from the heat; stir in the vanilla. Gradually whisk in the powdered sugar until smooth. Gently stir until the mixture begins to cool and thicken, 4 to 5 minutes.

7. Spoon the Caramel Frosting immediately over the cooled cake; sprinkle with the pecans.

PINEAPPLE UPSIDE-DOWN SKILLET CAKE

SERVES 10 // HANDS-ON 20 MINUTES // TOTAL 1 HOUR, 20 MINUTES

This old-fashioned upside-down cake takes on a new twist with a crunchy coconut chip topping while still including iconic pineapple. Because pineapple is a motif of hospitality throughout South Carolina, this dish is especially appropriate when tailgating at USC's Williams-Brice Stadium.

TENT TALK

The goalposts at the back of each end zone measure 18'6" wide and 30' tall. How far off the ground is the crossbar?

A. 10 feet
B. 11 feet
C. 12 feet
D. 15 feet

⅔ cup honey

1 (15.25-ounce) can pineapple slices in juice, drained

1 (10-ounce) jar maraschino cherries without stems, drained (optional)

1⅓ cups granulated sugar

¾ cup (6 ounces) unsalted butter, softened

1 teaspoon vanilla extract

1 teaspoon rum extract

2 cups (about 8½ ounces) all-purpose flour

1 teaspoon baking powder

½ teaspoon table salt

¼ teaspoon baking soda

¾ cup well-shaken and stirred canned coconut milk

3 large eggs

½ cup sweetened toasted coconut chips (such as Bare)

1 Preheat the oven to 350°F. Pour the honey into a buttered 10-inch cast-iron skillet, tilting the skillet to spread evenly. Place the pineapple in a single layer on the honey. Place a cherry in the center of each pineapple slice, if desired. Reserve the remaining cherries for another use.

2 Combine the sugar and butter in the bowl of a heavy-duty electric stand mixer; beat on medium speed until fluffy. Stir in the vanilla and rum extracts. Whisk together the flour, baking powder, salt, and baking soda in a medium bowl. Whisk together the coconut milk and eggs in a small bowl. Add the flour mixture to the sugar mixture alternately with the coconut milk mixture, beginning and ending with the flour mixture. Beat on low speed just until blended after each addition. Spread the batter over the pineapple in the skillet.

3 Bake at 350°F until a wooden pick inserted in the center comes out clean, about 50 minutes, shielding with aluminum foil after 45 minutes to prevent excessive browning, if necessary. Cool in the skillet on a wire rack 10 minutes.

4 Invert the cake onto a serving platter, and sprinkle with the coconut chips.

PEACH COBBLER BREAD PUDDING

SERVES **10** // HANDS-ON **20 MINUTES** // TOTAL **2 HOURS**

This marriage of two classic desserts—cobbler and bread pudding—is delicious enough to unite all who gather at your tailgate tent, even arch gridiron rivals. The pecan mixture crumbled over the top makes this treat a contender for one of our favorite desserts ever.

2 (16-ounce) cans refrigerated jumbo biscuits (such as Pillsbury Grands! Flaky Layers Original Biscuits)
5 large eggs, lightly beaten
5 cups half-and-half
1½ tablespoons vanilla extract
½ teaspoon kosher salt
½ teaspoon ground ginger
¼ teaspoon ground nutmeg
1¾ cups packed light brown sugar
1 cup chopped pecans
¼ cup (about 1 ounce) all-purpose flour
¼ cup (2 ounces) unsalted butter, melted
2½ pounds fresh peaches, peeled and sliced
Whipped cream (optional)

1 Cook the biscuits according to the package directions. Cool completely, about 15 minutes; cut each biscuit into quarters.
2 Preheat the oven to 350°F.
3 Whisk together the eggs, half-and-half, vanilla extract, salt, ginger, nutmeg, and 1 cup of the brown sugar in a large bowl. Add the biscuit quarters; toss to coat. Let stand 20 minutes, stirring occasionally.
4 Stir together the pecans, flour, butter, and remaining ¾ cup brown sugar in a small bowl; set aside.
5 Gently stir the peaches into the biscuit mixture. Place the mixture in a buttered 13- x 9-inch baking dish.
6 Bake the cobbler at 350°F until bubbly around the edges and firm in the center, 35 to 40 minutes. Sprinkle the pecan mixture over the top, and bake until the topping is browned, about 15 more minutes. Let stand 25 minutes before serving. Serve warm, or cool completely. Top with the whipped cream, if desired.

TENT TALK

Regulation footballs are approximately 11 inches tall, 21 inches around the middle, and 28 inches long. How many pounds of air do they contain?

A. 10 to 11 pounds
B. 12.5 to 13.5 pounds
C. 14 to 15 pounds
D. The quarterback gets to decide

SWEET POTATO BREAD PUDDING CUPS

SERVES 12 // HANDS-ON **40 MINUTES** // TOTAL **2 HOURS, INCLUDES 1 HOUR CHILLING**

EXTRA POINT

These treats are great served warm or at room temperature. Buy caramel sauce in a squeeze bottle so it's easy to drizzle over the cups at the tailgate.

These individual bread puddings are moist and sweet with crunch from the pecans and silkiness from the sweet potato. The vanilla cream poured into the center of each bread pudding cup gains it extra points. Be careful when you transport the bread puddings; they are very delicate. You can actually transport them in the muffin cups, covered with plastic.

2 medium-size sweet potatoes (about 10 ounces each)
½ teaspoon ground cinnamon
½ teaspoon kosher salt
½ cup (4 ounces) unsalted butter
2 large eggs
½ cup granulated sugar
1¼ teaspoons vanilla bean paste

½ cup heavy cream
1½ cups whole milk
1 (14-ounce) soft brioche or French bread loaf, torn into 2-inch pieces
½ cup chopped pecans
3 large egg yolks
⅓ cup bottled caramel syrup

1 Pierce the sweet potatoes several times with a fork. Wrap each potato in a damp paper towel; microwave on HIGH until cooked through, 8 to 10 minutes, turning each potato halfway through the cook time. Remove from the microwave, and let stand until cool enough to handle. Peel the potatoes, and place in a medium bowl. Add the cinnamon, salt, and ¼ cup of the butter; mash with a potato masher or fork until thoroughly mashed.

2 Whisk together the eggs, ¼ cup of the sugar, and ¼ teaspoon of the vanilla bean paste until well combined. Whisk in the cream and ½ cup of the milk until blended.

3 Spray a 12-cup muffin pan with cooking spray. Place 2 bread pieces in each muffin cup. Pour ½ cup of the egg mixture over the bread in the muffin cups; top each with 2 tablespoons of the sweet potato mixture, and sprinkle evenly with the pecans. Top each evenly with the remaining bread pieces. Pour the remaining egg mixture evenly over the bread in the muffin cups; dot each evenly with the remaining ¼ cup butter. Chill 1 hour.

4 Meanwhile, preheat the oven to 300°F. Bake the chilled bread pudding cups in the preheated oven until the custard is set, about 25 minutes. Let cool in the muffin pan on a wire rack 10 minutes. Remove the pudding cups to the rack, and let cool completely, about 30 minutes. Store in an airtight container up to 1 day.

5 Stir together the remaining 1 cup milk and 1 teaspoon vanilla bean paste in a medium saucepan over medium, and cook until warm, about 5 minutes. Whisk together the egg yolks and remaining ¼ cup sugar in a medium bowl until slightly thickened and pale. Gradually whisk half of the warm milk mixture into the yolk mixture until combined. Add the yolk-milk mixture to the remaining warm milk mixture in the pan, stirring constantly. Cook over medium-low, stirring constantly with a wooden spoon, until thickened and the mixture coats the back of the spoon, about 10 minutes. (Don't let the mixture boil.)

6 Pour the vanilla sauce into a small bowl; place the bowl over an ice bath, and stir until completely cool, about 5 minutes. Store covered in the refrigerator up to 2 days. To serve the bread pudding cups, use the handle of a wooden spoon to poke a hole in the center of each pudding cup. Pour the vanilla sauce evenly into each hole in the cups; drizzle the tops with the caramel syrup.

OLD-FASHIONED BLACKBERRY COBBLER

SERVES **8** // HANDS-ON **20 MINUTES** // TOTAL **1 HOUR, 20 MINUTES**

Serve with whipped cream or vanilla ice cream kept cool in a cooler, if desired.

6 cups fresh blackberries (about 2 pounds) (or frozen blackberries, thawed)
2 teaspoons fresh lemon juice (from 1 lemon)
2 cups granulated sugar
½ cup (4 ounces) salted butter, melted

2½ cups (about 10⅝ ounces) all-purpose flour
1 tablespoon baking powder
½ teaspoon kosher salt
1¼ cups whole milk
2 teaspoons vanilla extract

1 Preheat the oven to 350°F. Lightly grease a 13- x 9-inch baking dish with cooking spray.
2 Place the blackberries in a large bowl, and sprinkle with the lemon juice and ½ cup of the sugar; toss to coat. Let stand until the juices begin to release, about 10 minutes, stirring occasionally. Stir in ¼ cup of the melted butter. Spread the blackberry mixture on the bottom of the prepared baking dish.
3 Whisk together the flour, baking powder, salt, and remaining 1½ cups sugar in a clean bowl. Stir in the milk, vanilla, and remaining ¼ cup melted butter until combined. Pour the batter over the blackberry mixture in the baking dish.
4 Bake at 350°F until the crust is golden brown and the blackberry mixture is bubbly, about 50 minutes. Let stand 10 minutes before serving.

CLASSIC APPLE COBBLER

SERVES **6** // HANDS-ON **1 HOUR** // TOTAL **2 HOURS, 10 MINUTES**

September means the arrival of more than college football. Welcome the fall with a bubbling cobbler made with seasonal sweet-tart Granny Smith and Braeburn apples. You could use any kind of apple here, but you'll get the best results if you combine two or more types as different kinds keep the flavor and texture from being one-note.

2½ pounds Granny Smith apples (about 5 large), peeled and cut into ½-inch-thick wedges

2½ pounds Braeburn apples (about 5 large), peeled and cut into ½-inch-thick wedges

1¼ cups packed light brown sugar

¼ cup (about 1 ounce) all-purpose flour

6 tablespoons (3 ounces) salted butter

2 cups (about 8 ounces) self-rising soft wheat flour (such as White Lily)

3 tablespoons granulated sugar

½ cup (4 ounces) cold salted butter, cut into small cubes

1 teaspoon lemon zest plus 2 tablespoons fresh juice (from 1 lemon)

¾ teaspoon ground cinnamon

½ teaspoon table salt

¾ to 1 cup cold heavy cream

Vanilla ice cream

1   Preheat the oven to 425°F. Toss together the apples, brown sugar, and all-purpose flour in a large bowl. Melt 4 tablespoons of the butter in a large skillet over medium-high. Add the apple mixture, and cook, stirring often, until the apples are tender and the syrup thickens, 20 to 25 minutes.

2   Meanwhile, stir together the self-rising flour and 2 tablespoons of the granulated sugar in a large bowl. Cut the ½ cup cold butter cubes into the self-rising flour mixture with a pastry blender or fork until the mixture is crumbly and resembles small peas; freeze 10 minutes.

3   Remove the apples from the heat; stir in the lemon zest and juice, cinnamon, and salt. Spoon the apple mixture into a lightly greased 8-inch square (2-quart) baking dish. Bake at 425°F for 15 minutes, placing a baking sheet on the oven rack directly below the dish to catch any drips.

4   Meanwhile, make a well in the center of the flour mixture. Add ¾ cup of the cream; stir just until the dough comes together, adding the additional cream up to 1 cup, 1 tablespoon at a time, if needed. Turn the dough out onto a lightly floured surface, and knead lightly 3 or 4 times. Roll or pat the dough to ¾- to 1-inch thickness. Cut with a 2½-inch round cutter; reroll the scraps once, and repeat the process to make 9 biscuits.

5   Place the biscuits on top of the hot apple mixture in the baking dish. Melt the remaining 2 tablespoons butter, and brush over the biscuits. Sprinkle the biscuits with the remaining 1 tablespoon granulated sugar. Return the cobbler to the oven, and bake until the biscuits are golden and done, 15 to 17 minutes. Cool 30 minutes; top the servings with the ice cream.

TIGER STRIPES FROZEN CUSTARD

SERVES 8 // HANDS-ON 20 MINUTES

TOTAL 5 HOURS, 20 MINUTES, INCLUDES 2 HOURS CHILLING AND 2 HOURS FREEZING

EXTRA POINT

It's best to churn the ice cream at home, where you can be sure that it gets cold enough to freeze. For best results, freeze for at least 2 hours before serving.

Creamy frozen custard that's not too sweet and pairs marvelously with a hot fudge topping will put pep in your step on warm-weather game days. The chocolate layers create "tiger stripes" in the custard as it curls in the ice-cream scoop, and yellow food coloring gives the dish a black-and-gold appearance, making the dessert a Mizzou fan favorite. Enjoy it with additional hot fudge topping or whipped cream on top, if desired.

6 large egg yolks
⅓ cup granulated sugar
2 tablespoons light corn syrup
1½ cups heavy cream
¾ cup whole milk
½ teaspoon vanilla extract

¼ teaspoon table salt
3 to 4 drops yellow food coloring gel (optional)
½ cup hot fudge topping, warmed according to jar directions

1 Whisk together the egg yolks, sugar, and corn syrup in a heavy-bottomed saucepan until well combined. Whisk in the cream and milk until well combined, and cook over medium-low until a candy thermometer registers 170°F, whisking often. Stir in the vanilla, salt, and, if desired, 3 to 4 drops of the food coloring gel. (If any solids form in the cream mixture, pour it through a fine mesh strainer, and discard the solids.) Pour the cream mixture into a chilled bowl; place the bowl in an ice bath, and let stand 1 hour, stirring occasionally. Remove the bowl, cover, and chill at least 2 hours or up to 24 hours.

2 Pour the cream mixture into the bowl of a 2-quart ice-cream maker, and prepare it according to the manufacturer's directions (instructions may vary). Transfer half of the custard mixture to an 8- x 4-inch loaf pan. Drizzle evenly with ¼ cup of the fudge topping. Top with the remaining custard mixture, and drizzle with the remaining ¼ cup fudge topping. Cover and freeze until firm, at least 2 hours. Serve with an ice-cream scoop to make the best "tiger stripes."

ELVIS BARS

SERVES **16** // HANDS-ON **15 MINUTES** // TOTAL **1 HOUR, 45 MINUTES**

Inspired by the favorite sandwich of one of Tennessee's most iconic personalities, these bars are made of peanut butter, bananas, and bacon. They're easy to transport and can be made up to 2 days in advance.

½ cup (4 ounces) unsalted butter, softened

½ cup creamy peanut butter

½ cup granulated sugar

½ cup packed dark brown sugar

2 medium-size ripe bananas, mashed (about ¾ cup)

1 large egg

1 teaspoon vanilla extract

2 cups (about 8½ ounces) all-purpose flour

½ teaspoon baking powder

½ teaspoon kosher salt

½ teaspoon ground cinnamon

4 cooked bacon slices, crumbled

1 cup semisweet chocolate chips

1 Preheat the oven to 350°F. Grease a 9-inch square baking pan, and line with parchment paper. Combine the butter, peanut butter, granulated sugar, and brown sugar in the bowl of a heavy-duty stand mixer fitted with the paddle attachment, and beat on medium-high speed until fluffy and well combined, 3 to 5 minutes, stopping to scrape down the sides of the bowl as needed.

2 Add the mashed bananas, egg, and vanilla. Beat on medium speed, just until combined, 30 seconds to 1 minute.

3 Whisk together the flour, baking powder, salt, and cinnamon in a small bowl. Gradually add the dry ingredients to the wet ingredients, beating on medium speed just until combined. Fold in the bacon and chocolate chips. Pour the batter into the prepared pan, smoothing the top with a spatula.

4 Bake at 350°F until golden brown and a wooden pick inserted into the center comes out clean, 30 to 35 minutes. Let cool completely, about 1 hour, before cutting into squares.

AYE, AYE, COMMODORE!

Blindfold a stranger, drop him in the middle of Vanderbilt Stadium, and he'll probably expect to see the sea when the blinder comes off.

The Admiral, a naval horn atop the Vanderbilt Stadium press box, blares as the home team takes the field and whenever Vanderbilt scores. With his mutton chop sideburns, cutlass-wielding mascot Mr. Commodore looks for all the world like a 19th-century naval officer. Players chosen for their character and leadership carry an anchor to every game, home and away.

Though Nashville sits on the banks of the Cumberland River, the nearest ocean is almost 500 miles away. But you only have to examine the school's history to find the genesis of the naval traditions. They pay tribute to the universty's benefactor, Cornelius Vanderbilt.

His is the ultimate rags-to-riches story. This son of a ferryboat captain quit school at age 11 and by 16 was operating his own boat, ferrying goods and passengers between Staten Island and Manhattan. So tireless and driven was he that other New York captains began jokingly calling him the Commodore.

Shrewd investments in steamships and railroads propelled Vanderbilt to the ranks of the world's richest men. His $1 million gift, which he hoped would help heal the wounds of the Civil War, established the university—yet the Commodore never actually set foot in the South.

Today, Vanderbilt is the only private school in the SEC and the smallest, but it plays David to the conference's Goliaths often enough to be taken seriously. Sea or no sea, Commodore teams embody the indomitable spirit and work ethic of the man whose name they wear.

FUN FACT

Quarterback Jay Cutler is undeniably one of the best to play the game at Vanderbilt. During his senior year, he took home 2005 SEC Offensive Player of the Year honors.

// ROOTED IN TRADITION

A majestic oak stands at the heart of the Vanderbilt University campus in Nashville, its immense canopy shading students as they walk to and from classes.

The students seem lost in their own thoughts, unaware of their leafy companion. But this tree—the school's Bicentennial Oak—took root before the American Revolution and has stood watch over generations of students who have trod these hallowed grounds.

So magnificent and treasured are Vanderbilt's old-growth trees that the entire campus is an arboretum. The school's 333 acres are home to more than 6,000 trees and shrubs (190 species), with more planted each year to preserve the historic ecosystem.

As soon as the school was formed in 1873, its new chancellor, Bishop Holland McTyeire, began to plan. Subsequent leaders continued to tend the trees. Now some of Tennessee's largest and oldest trees thrive at Vanderbilt, creating a peaceful oasis at the heart of the campus. Though it's not necessary to visit the interior of the campus to get to Vanderbilt Stadium, which sits on the far western edge of campus, many alumni and fans stroll through on game day anyway.

// AMONG GIANTS

The red-bricked splendor of Kirkland Hall is a must-see. The cornerstone was laid in 1874, but the original building burned in 1905. The school didn't close a single day while Kirkland (then called Old Main) was rebuilt. A one-ton bronze bell marks the hours and calls students to class, just as it has since the building reopened in 1906.

Some passersby nod to the statue of benefactor Cornelius Vanderbilt, just inside the gates of the official entrance. Vanderbilt had a vision of a place that would "contribute to strenghtening the ties that should exist between all sections of our common country" when he gave $1 million to create a university in 1873. Some believe the Commodore's second wife—Frank Armstrong Crawford Vanderbilt, a Mobile native—convinced her husband to make the gift. Her cousin

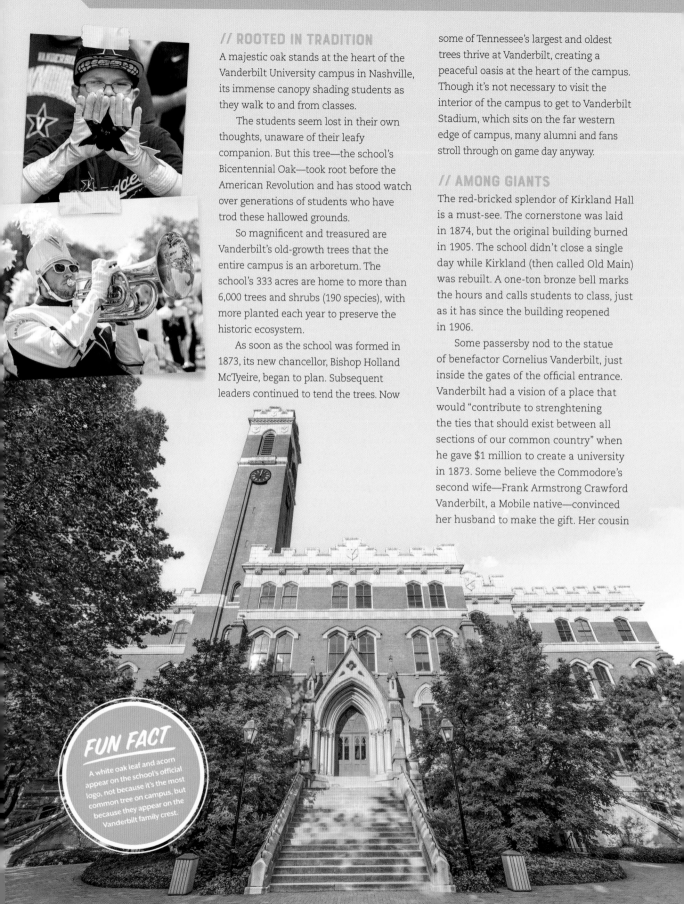

FUN FACT
A white oak leaf and acorn appear on the school's official logo, not because it's the most common tree on campus, but because they appear on the Vanderbilt family crest.

Amelia was Bishop McTyeire's wife, suggesting an additional influence on the New York shipping and railroad magnate.

// CONQUER AND PREVAIL

Trees are not the only giants here. Vanderbilt, the SEC's only private school, is selective and academically rigorous. Vanderbilt alumni can be found in Congress, on the judicial bench, in the pulpit, leading corporations, conducting innovative medical research, serving in their communities, and playing in the NFL, MLB, PGA, and LPGA.

Vanderbilt also had a hand in building the SEC into the powerhouse it is today. Dr. William Dudley, for whom the original Dudley Field was named, helped organize both the Southern Intercollegiate Athletic Association (predecessor to the SEC) and the NCAA, in addition to serving as Vanderbilt's dean of medicine.

The most successful coach in Vanderbilt's history was Dan McGugin, with a record of 197–55–19. Under his guidance, Vandy claimed 29 winning seasons and 10 conference championships (and 1 co-championship in 1903). His 1904 team scored 474 points while allowing just 4 and finished 9-0.

A number of McGugin's players became coaches, including Jess Neely, who was captain and halfback of Vandy's undefeated 1922 team. A Tennessee native, Neely returned to Vanderbilt in 1967 to serve as athletic director. You'll find him on the short list of coaches who notched 200 or more career wins.

// ANCHOR DOWN

In more recent years, players like quarterback Jay Cutler have carried the standard for the Commodores. The Santa Claus, Indiana, native set numerous school records, including total passing yards and touchdowns, and was the 11th overall pick in the 2006 NFL draft.

Still, it wasn't Cutler who became the school's first unanimous All-American. That honor goes to linebacker Zach Cunningham, who graduated in 2016 and was chosen in the second round of the 2017 NFL draft.

Vandy fans love their 'Dores, win or lose. The parking lots adjacent to the stadium become Vandyville on game day. From this sea of black tents, fans move to Jess Neely Drive to join the Spirit of Gold Marching Band and cheer on the team as they walk from the McGugin Center to Vanderbilt Stadium.

Two seniors chosen to lead each Star Walk carry a gold anchor symbolizing team unity. The foghorn named The Admiral that's mounted atop the press box celebrates every score, and a black "victory flag" emblazoned with Vanderbilt's Athletics' Star V symbol flies above the west side of the stadium for seven days after every conquest.

Best of all, Vandy's campus is just a mile and a half from Nashville's historic Lower Broadway. With Nashville being the only city with an SEC team and an NFL team, it's possible to see the Commodores play on Saturday and the Tennessee Titans kick off on Sunday. When the games are over, fans and foes alike sample all the good eats and great tunes that Music City has to offer.

VANDERBILT
AT A GLANCE

SCHOOL
Vanderbilt University

LOCATION
Nashville, TN

FOUNDED
1873

TEAM NICKNAME
Commodores

MASCOT
Mr. Commodore (pictured), typically shortened to Mr. C

COLORS

STADIUM
Vanderbilt Stadium

CAPACITY
40,550

BAND
Spirit of Gold Marching Band

TICKET OFFICE
(877) 448-2639 or
(615) 322-4653

WEBSITE
vucommodores.com

SPRAY-PAINT REAL OR FAUX
LEAVES GOLD. ARRANGE
THEM WITH BRANCHES OF
BLACK PRIVET FOR A TWIST.

VANDERBILT
COMMODORES

V

SERVES 8

USE A SIMPLE GOLD PLASTIC
TABLECLOTH. GUSSY IT UP
WITH A SHINY TASSEL BANNER
BORDERING THE EDGES.

VINTAGE COASTERS AND
CARDBOARD ANCHORS
PAINTED BLACK AND GOLD
CREATE A SIGNATURE LOOK.

SOPAPILLA CHEESECAKE BARS

SERVES **16** // HANDS-ON **15 MINUTES** // TOTAL **2 HOURS, 5 MINUTES**

EXTRA
POINT

Make these bars a day in advance and transport to your tailgate site in an airtight container inside a cooler.

Traditional sopapilla is a fried pastry with a cinnamon-sugar topping. Our version calls for baking the pastry and filling it with sweetened cream cheese, resulting in decadent bars. Serve with ice-cold milk or coffee to balance the richness.

1 (17.3-ounce) package frozen puff pastry sheets, thawed

2 (8-ounce) packages cream cheese, softened

2 tablespoons sour cream

¾ cup plus 2 tablespoons granulated sugar

2 large eggs

2 teaspoons lemon zest (from 1 lemon)

1 teaspoon vanilla extract

2 teaspoons ground cinnamon

2 tablespoons salted butter, melted

1 Preheat the oven to 400°F. Roll out 1 of the puff pastry sheets into a 13- x 9-inch rectangle, and press into the bottom of a 13- x 9-inch baking pan. Prick all over with a fork, and bake at 400°F until well browned, 15 to 20 minutes. Let cool 20 minutes. Reduce the oven temperature to 350°F.

2 Beat the softened cream cheese, sour cream, and ¾ cup of the sugar with an electric mixer on medium speed until well combined and creamy, 3 to 5 minutes. Add the eggs, 1 at a time, and beat just until combined. Stir in the lemon zest and vanilla until combined. Spread the cream cheese mixture on top of the cooled pastry.

3 Stir together the cinnamon and remaining 2 tablespoons sugar in a small bowl.

4 Roll out the second puff pastry sheet into a 13- x 9-inch rectangle. Place on top of the cream cheese layer; brush edge to edge with the melted butter, and sprinkle with the cinnamon-sugar.

5 Bake at 350°F until golden brown, 30 to 35 minutes. Cool completely on a wire rack, about 1 hour; cut into 16 bars.

CHERRY PIE BARS

SERVES **24** // HANDS-ON **15 MINUTES** // TOTAL **2 HOURS, 15 MINUTES**

A classic cherry dessert is baked into a crowd-pleasing, portable treat. Make and store these bars, wrapped in aluminum foil, for up to three days. Keep this dish cool until ready to serve.

3 cups (12 ounces) all-purpose flour
¾ cup granulated sugar
½ teaspoon table salt
1½ cups (12 ounces) cold butter, cubed
3 cups canned cherry pie filling (about 1½ [21-ounce] cans)

¾ cup chopped pecans
1 cup (about 4 ounces) powdered sugar
4 to 5 teaspoons whole milk
¼ teaspoon almond extract

1 Preheat the oven to 350°F. Line the bottom and sides of a 13- x 9-inch baking pan with heavy-duty aluminum foil, allowing 2 to 3 inches to extend over the sides; lightly grease the foil with cooking spray.

2 Pulse the flour, granulated sugar, and salt in a food processor until combined. Add the butter cubes, and pulse until the mixture is crumbly. Reserve 1 cup of the flour mixture. Press the remaining flour mixture onto the bottom of the prepared pan.

3 Bake at 350°F until lightly browned, 25 to 30 minutes. Spread the cherry pie filling over the crust in the pan. Toss together the reserved 1 cup flour mixture and pecans. Sprinkle the pecan mixture evenly over the filling.

4 Bake at 350°F until golden brown, 40 to 45 minutes. Cool completely in the pan on a wire rack, about 1 hour. Lift the baked bars from the pan, using the foil sides as handles.

5 Stir together the powdered sugar, 4 teaspoons of the milk, and almond extract. Add the remaining 1 teaspoon milk to reach the desired consistency, if needed. Drizzle over the pecan mixture. Cut into 24 bars.

PEANUT BRITTLE PUPPY CHOW

MAKES **14 CUPS** // HANDS-ON **15 MINUTES** // TOTAL **55 MINUTES**

Call the Dawgs—we've got puppy chow! The sweet and salty combination from the brittle, peanut butter, salt, and cereal makes this the perfect dessert snack. Warning: This treat is highly addictive. After your friends have been introduced to it, they may ask you to bring it to every gathering henceforth.

1 (12-ounce) package rice cereal squares
   (such as Rice Chex) (about 10 cups)
1 cup white chocolate chips
1 cup semisweet chocolate chips
¾ cup creamy peanut butter
¼ cup (2 ounces) salted butter
1 teaspoon kosher salt
1 teaspoon vanilla extract

2 cups (about 8 ounces) powdered sugar
8 ounces peanut brittle, broken into bite-size pieces (about 2 cups)
2 cups candy-coated chocolate-covered peanuts (such as M&M's) (preferably red and brown for UGA, or different colors to suit your team of choice)

EXTRA POINT

Using a double boiler to melt the chocolate-peanut butter mixture ensures a smooth consistency to make coating the cereal easy.

1   Place the cereal in a large bowl. Set aside.
2   Combine the white chocolate chips, semisweet chocolate chips, peanut butter, butter, and salt in a heatproof bowl, and place over a saucepan of simmering water. Melt over medium-low, stirring occasionally, until smooth, about 10 minutes. Stir in the vanilla. Pour the chocolate mixture over the cereal, stirring constantly, until fully coated. Let cool until the chocolate has set, about 10 minutes.
3   Transfer the cereal mixture to 2 large ziplock plastic bags. Sift the powdered sugar evenly into the bags, and shake to coat the cereal. Pour the mixture onto 1 or 2 large rimmed baking sheets lined with wax paper. Let cool completely, about 30 minutes. Toss with the peanut brittle and M&M's. Store in an airtight container up to 1 week.

MAROON-AND-WHITE BUTTER COOKIES

MAKES **ABOUT 2 DOZEN** // HANDS-ON **20 MINUTES**
TOTAL **8 HOURS, 48 MINUTES, INCLUDES 8 HOURS CHILLING**

These cookies, which showcase the colors of Mississippi State University, are buttery with a slight chew from the cranberry and have a nice herbaceous finish.

2 cups granulated sugar
1 cup (8 ounces) unsalted butter, softened
1 tablespoon vanilla extract
2 large eggs
3½ cups (about 14⅞ ounces) all-purpose flour

½ teaspoon baking soda
½ teaspoon table salt
1 cup finely chopped sweetened dried cranberries
2 tablespoons minced fresh rosemary
2 teaspoons lemon zest (from 1 lemon)

1 Beat the sugar, butter, and vanilla in the bowl of a heavy-duty electric stand mixer on medium speed until fluffy. Add the eggs, 1 at a time, beating well after each addition.

2 Stir together the flour, baking soda, and salt; gradually add to the butter mixture, beating just until blended after each addition. Stir in the cranberries, rosemary, and lemon zest.

3 Shape the dough into 4 (about 2 inches in diameter) logs; wrap each log in plastic wrap. Chill 8 hours or up to 3 days.

4 Preheat the oven to 350°F. Cut each log into ¼-inch-thick slices; place on parchment paper-lined baking sheets. Bake until lightly browned, 8 to 12 minutes. Remove from the baking sheets to wire racks, and cool completely, about 20 minutes. Store in an airtight container.

KEY LIME-WHITE CHOCOLATE COOKIES

MAKES **ABOUT 4 DOZEN** // HANDS-ON **20 MINUTES** // TOTAL **1 HOUR, 15 MINUTES**

With a deliciously chewy interior and a slightly crispy exterior, these cookies are everything you love about white chocolate-macadamia cookies, with a special lime note. Look for Key lime juice in the juice aisle of the grocery store, or sub regular lime juice instead.

EXTRA
POINT

These cookies can be made up to a day in advance and stored in an airtight container.

3 cups (about 12¾ ounces) all-purpose
   flour
1 teaspoon baking soda
½ teaspoon baking powder
½ teaspoon table salt
1 cup (8 ounces) unsalted butter, softened
1⅓ cups granulated sugar
2 large egg whites

1 tablespoon Key lime zest plus
   3 tablespoons fresh juice
   (from 5 Key limes)
1 teaspoon vanilla extract
12 ounces white baking chocolate,
   chopped (about 2 cups)
1 cup chopped toasted macadamia nuts
   (optional)

1   Preheat the oven to 350°F. Whisk together the flour, baking soda, baking powder, and salt in a medium bowl.

2   Beat the butter and sugar with an electric mixer on high speed until light and fluffy, about 2 minutes.

3   Add the egg whites, zest, juice, and vanilla. Beat on medium speed until combined, about 1 minute. Gradually add the flour mixture, beating on low speed just until incorporated after each addition. Stir in the white chocolate and, if desired, the nuts.

4   Scoop the dough by 2-tablespoonful portions onto parchment paper-lined baking sheets. Bake at 350°F until barely browned around the edges, about 12 minutes. Cool the cookies on the pan on a wire rack 5 minutes. Transfer the cookies to the rack, and serve warm or let cool completely.

WHOOPIE PIES

MAKES **24 TO 26 WHOOPIE PIES** // HANDS-ON **45 MINUTES** // TOTAL **1 HOUR, 45 MINUTES**

Everybody will love these cute sandwich cookies stuffed with buttercream filling. The cookie dough comes together in a snap, and the cookies bake quickly; just 7 minutes per pan. See pages 257-259 for how to customize these treats for your favorite team.

½ cup (4 ounces) salted butter, softened
1 cup granulated sugar
3 large eggs, at room temperature
1 teaspoon vanilla extract
2 cups (about 8½ ounces) all-purpose flour

1 teaspoon baking powder
½ teaspoon baking soda
½ teaspoon table salt
¼ cup whole milk
Whoopie Pie Filling (recipe follows)

1 Preheat the oven to 400°F. Combine the butter and sugar in the bowl of a heavy-duty stand mixer; beat on medium speed until well blended, about 3 minutes. Add the eggs, 1 at a time, beating well after each addition. Stir in the vanilla.

2 Stir together the flour, baking powder, baking soda, and salt in a medium bowl. Add the flour mixture to the butter mixture alternately with the milk, beginning and ending with the flour mixture. Beat on low speed just until blended after each addition.

3 Using a 1-inch cookie scoop, drop the dough about 3 inches apart onto parchment paper-lined baking sheets.

4 Bake at 400°F until the cookies are just set and beginning to brown, 7 to 8 minutes. Transfer the baking sheets to wire racks, and cool the cookies on the baking sheets 5 minutes. Transfer the cookies from the baking sheets to the wire racks, and cool completely, about 20 minutes.

5 Spread the Whoopie Pie Filling on the flat side of half of the cookies (about 2 tablespoons per cookie). Cover with the remaining half of the cookies, flat side down, and gently press together.

WHOOPIE PIE FILLING

MAKES **ABOUT 2¾ CUPS** // HANDS-ON **10 MINUTES** // TOTAL **10 MINUTES**

This filling gives the Whoopie Pies a wonderfully smooth and creamy texture.

½ cup (4 ounces) salted butter, softened
4 ounces cream cheese, softened
2 teaspoons vanilla extract

½ teaspoon table salt
1 (16-ounce) package powdered sugar
3 tablespoons heavy cream

Beat the butter and cream cheese with an electric mixer on medium speed until creamy; add the vanilla and salt, and beat until blended. Gradually add the powdered sugar, beating on low speed until blended and smooth after each addition. Add the cream, and beat on low speed until smooth.

SEC TEAM WHOOPIE PIES

Don't leave anyone wondering which team you're rooting for.
Make it loud and deliciously clear by whipping up a batch of these
whoopie pies and customizing them according to your team of choice.

ROLL TIDE WHOOPIE PIE

Omit Whoopie Pie Filling. Prepare Whoopie Pies as directed through Step 4. Beat 1 cup heavy cream and ¼ cup powdered sugar with an electric mixer on high speed until stiff peaks form. Pat ½ cup chopped strawberries dry with paper towels, and gently fold berries into whipped cream. Spread whipped cream filling evenly on flat side of half of cookies, and top with remaining cookies.

WOOO PIG WHOOPIE PIE

Prepare Whoopie Pies as directed through Step 3, sprinkling ½ cup chopped pecans evenly over tops of unbaked cookies (about ½ tsp. per cookie). Bake and cool as directed. Spread jarred hot-fudge topping on flat side of half of cookies (about ½ Tbsp. per cookie). Proceed with recipe as directed in Step 5.

WAR EAGLE WHOOPIE PIE

Prepare Whoopie Pies as directed, stirring 1 tsp. lemon zest and 1 Tbsp. fresh juice into dough with vanilla in Step 1 and reducing milk to 3 Tbsp. in Step 2. Bake and cool as directed. Prepare Whoopie Pie Filling as directed, omitting vanilla, reducing cream to 2 Tbsp., and stirring in 2 tsp. lemon zest and 2 Tbsp. fresh juice. Stir 5 to 6 drops of yellow food coloring into filling. Spread filling evenly on flat side of half of cookies, and top with remaining cookies.

= TIE 'EM UP =

These treats make excellent take-home gifts! Purchase cellophane bags and place three whoopie pies in each. Tie each bag with twine or ribbon in your team's colors. Store the packages in a cooler in a way that the bags won't get wet. As guests leave, offer them a sweet surprise for the road.

ORANGE GROVE WHOOPIE PIE

Prepare Whoopie Pies as directed, omitting vanilla and stirring in 2 tsp. orange zest and 1 Tbsp. fresh juice in Step 1, and sprinkling tops of unbaked cookies with orange-colored nonpareils in Step 3. Bake and cool as directed. Prepare Whoopie Pie Filling as directed, reducing cream to 2 Tbsp. and stirring in 1 tsp. orange zest and 1 Tbsp. fresh juice. Spread filling evenly on flat side of half of cookies, and top with remaining cookies.

GEORGIA PEACH WHOOPIE PIE

Prepare Whoopie Pies as directed through Step 4. Spread peach preserves on flat side of half of cookies (about 2 tsp. per cookie). Proceed with recipe as directed in Step 5.

WILDCAT WHOOPIE PIE

Prepare Whoopie Pies as directed through Step 3, sprinkling ½ cup mini semisweet chocolate chips evenly over tops of unbaked cookies. Proceed with recipe as directed in Steps 4 and 5. Roll edges of filled cookies in 1 cup finely chopped toasted walnuts.

HOTTY TODDY WHOOPIE PIE

Prepare Whoopie Pies as directed through Step 4, stirring 2 Tbsp. each red and blue nonpareils into dough in Step 2. Bake and cool as directed. Prepare Whoopie Pie Filling as directed, omitting heavy cream and stirring in 2 Tbsp. honey and 2 Tbsp. fresh lemon juice. Spread filling evenly on flat side of half of cookies, and top with remaining cookies.

COCKY COCONUT WHOOPIE PIE

Prepare Whoopie Pies as directed through Step 3, sprinkling ½ cup finely chopped sweetened dried cranberries evenly over tops of unbaked cookies. Proceed with recipe as directed in Steps 4 and 5. Roll edges of filled cookies in 1½ cups toasted sweetened shredded coconut.

SMOKEY WHOOPIE PIE

Prepare Whoopie Pies as directed, reducing sugar to ¾ cup in Step 1, omitting milk, and adding 3 Tbsp. sorghum syrup in Step 2. Proceed with recipe as directed in Steps 4 and 5. Roll edges of filled cookies in 1 cup chopped, crisply cooked bacon (about 6 to 7 slices).

LSU

M STATE

(Missouri Tigers)

TIGER ROAR WHOOPIE PIE

Prepare Whoopie Pies as directed. Stir together 1 cup powdered sugar and 2½ Tbsp. whole milk in a small bowl until glaze is smooth. Brush glaze on tops of filled cookies, and sprinkle with purple, green, and gold sanding sugar, using predominantly purple and gold.

BULLY WHOOPIE PIE

Prepare Whoopie Pies as directed through Step 3, reducing flour to 1¾ cups, adding ¼ cup unsweetened cocoa to flour mixture, and stirring ½ cup chopped toasted walnuts into dough in Step 2. Bake and cool as directed. Prepare Whoopie Pie Filling as directed, increasing butter to 1 cup, omitting cream cheese, reducing heavy cream to 2 Tbsp., and adding 1 (7-oz.) jar marshmallow crème. Spread filling on half of cookies; top with other half.

GOOEY BUTTER WHOOPIE PIE

Prepare Whoopie Pies as directed through Step 4. Prepare Whoopie Pie Filling as directed, increasing butter to 1 cup and omitting cream cheese. Spread filling evenly on flat side of half of cookies, and top with remaining cookies. Lightly dust tops of cookies with powdered sugar.

A&M

V

WRECKING CREW WHOOPIE PIE

Stir together ½ cup granulated sugar and 2 tsp. ground cinnamon. Prepare Whoopie Pies as directed through Step 3, sprinkling sugar mixture over unbaked cookies. Proceed with Steps 4 and 5. Microwave 8 oz. bittersweet chocolate baking bar and 2 Tbsp. vegetable shortening on HIGH until melted, stirring every 20 seconds. Dip cookies halfway in melted chocolate. Place cookies on a wax paper-lined baking sheet, and chill until set.

MR. COMMODORE WHOOPIE PIE

Prepare Whoopie Pies as directed through Step 3, sprinkling ½ cup chopped honey-roasted peanuts over tops of unbaked cookies. Bake and cool as directed. Prepare Whoopie Pie Filling as directed, reducing butter to 6 Tbsp. and beating in 2 Tbsp. creamy peanut butter with butter and cream cheese. Spread filling on flat side of half of cookies, and top with remaining cookies. Insert a sword-shaped cocktail pick in each filled Whoopie Pie.

METRIC EQUIVALENTS

The recipes that appear in this cookbook use the standard United States method for measuring liquid and dry or solid ingredients (teaspoons, tablespoons, and cups). The information in the following charts is provided to help cooks outside the U.S. successfully use these recipes. All equivalents are approximate.

METRIC EQUIVALENTS FOR DIFFERENT TYPES OF INGREDIENTS

A standard cup measure of a dry or solid ingredient will vary in weight depending on the type of ingredient. A standard cup of liquid is the same volume for any type of liquid. Use the following chart when converting standard cup measures to grams (weight) or milliliters (volume).

Standard Cup	Fine Powder (ex. flour)	Grain (ex. rice)	Granular (ex. sugar)	Liquid Solids (ex. butter)	Liquid (ex. milk)
1	140 g	150 g	190 g	200 g	240 ml
¾	105 g	113 g	143 g	150 g	180 ml
⅔	93 g	100 g	125 g	133 g	160 ml
½	70 g	75 g	95 g	100 g	120 ml
⅓	47 g	50 g	63 g	67 g	80 ml
¼	35 g	38 g	48 g	50 g	60 ml
⅛	18 g	19 g	24 g	25 g	30 ml

USEFUL EQUIVALENTS FOR LIQUID INGREDIENTS BY VOLUME

¼ tsp				=	1 ml
½ tsp				=	2 ml
1 tsp				=	5 ml
3 tsp	=	1 Tbsp	= ½ fl oz	=	15 ml
	2 Tbsp	= ⅛ cup	= 1 fl oz	=	30 ml
	4 Tbsp	= ¼ cup	= 2 fl oz	=	60 ml
	5⅓ Tbsp	= ⅓ cup	= 3 fl oz	=	80 ml
	8 Tbsp	= ½ cup	= 4 fl oz	=	120 ml
	10⅔ Tbsp	= ⅔ cup	= 5 fl oz	=	160 ml
	12 Tbsp	= ¾ cup	= 6 fl oz	=	180 ml
	16 Tbsp	= 1 cup	= 8 fl oz	=	240 ml
	1 pt	= 2 cups	= 16 fl oz	=	480 ml
	1 qt	= 4 cups	= 32 fl oz	=	960 ml
			= 33 fl oz	= 1000 ml	= 1 l

USEFUL EQUIVALENTS FOR DRY INGREDIENTS BY WEIGHT

(To convert ounces to grams, multiply the number of ounces by 30.)

1 oz	=	¹⁄₁₆ lb	=	30 g
4 oz	=	¼ lb	=	120 g
8 oz	=	½ lb	=	240 g
12 oz	=	¾ lb	=	360 g
16 oz	=	1 lb	=	480 g

USEFUL EQUIVALENTS FOR LENGTH

(To convert inches to centimeters, multiply the number of inches by 2.5.)

1 in			=	2.5 cm	
6 in	=	½ ft	=	15 cm	
12 in	=	1 ft	=	30 cm	
36 in	=	3 ft	= 1 yd =	90 cm	
40 in			=	100 cm	= 1 m

USEFUL EQUIVALENTS FOR COOKING/OVEN TEMPERATURES

	Farenheit	Celsius	Gas Mark
Freeze water	32°F	0°C	
Room temperature	68°F	20°C	
Boil water	212°F	100°C	
Bake	325°F	160°C	3
	350°F	180°C	4
	375°F	190°C	5
	400°F	200°C	6
	425°F	220°C	7
	450°F	230°C	8
Broil			Grill

RECIPE INDEX

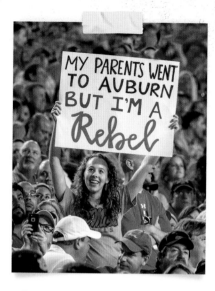

TEAM MENUS INDEX

ALABAMA CRIMSON TIDE, 23

Rammer Jammer Coffee Punch, 70
Fried Chicken, Green Tomato, and
    Waffles with Sriracha Syrup, 25
Cheese Grits and Greens Casserole, 26
Sweet Crimson Roll Tide Rolls, 41

ARKANSAS RAZORBACKS, 37

Arkancider-Honeybee Grape Cider, 69
Razorback Breakfast Casserole, 30
Ham-and-Cheddar Pinwheels, 38
Mini Biscuits with Chocolate Gravy, 38

AUBURN TIGERS, 53

Watermelon-Mint Lemonade, 55
Smoked War Eagle Wings with White
    Sauce, 148
Sweet-Hot Potato Salad, 210
Peach Cobbler Bread Pudding, 235

FLORIDA GATORS, 65

Cuban Black Bean Salsa with Avocado-
    Lime Dressing, 88
Florida Citrus Seafood Chowder, 118
Grilled Gator Kebab Banh Mi, 184
Key Lime-White Chocolate Cookies, 255

GEORGIA BULLDOGS, 81

Chicken and Smoked Sausage Brunswick
    Stew, 122
Cornmeal Biscuit-Smoked Pork
    Sandwiches with Peach Jam, 177
Georgian Cabbage Slaw, 196
Peanut Brittle Puppy Chow, 253

KENTUCKY WILDCATS, 101

Kentucky Lemon-Mint Punch, 55
Loaded Potato Skins, 94
Game-Day Hot Brown Turkey Sliders, 165
Green Bean Benedictine Salad, 200

LSU FIGHTING TIGERS, 115

Tiger Tasso Skewers, 95
Creole Gumbo, 117
Fried Oyster Po'boy Sliders, 178
Mike's Maque Choux Salad, 213

MISSISSIPPI STATE BULLDOGS, 133

Sweet Heat Pimiento Cheese, 92
The Ultimate Bully Burger with Dill Pickle
    Sauce, 169
Saucy Cola Baked Beans, 203
Maroon-and-White Butter Cookies, 254

MISSOURI TIGERS, 145

Caramel-Walnut Snack Mix, 105
Sweet and Spicy Mizzou Ribs, 172
Loaded Golden Ravioli Nachos, 217
Tiger Stripes Frozen Custard, 240

OLE MISS REBELS, 161

Sweet Magnolia, 59
Fried Catfish Fingers with Comeback
    Sauce, 183
Pimiento Cheese Hush Puppies with Dilly
    Tartar Sauce, 214
Mississippi Mud Pie Trifle, 228

SOUTH CAROLINA GAMECOCKS, 193

Boiled Peanut Hummus with Pork
    Rinds, 91
Shrimp and Fontina Grits, 181
Sweet-and-Smoky Collard Greens, 199
Pineapple Upside-Down Skillet Cake, 232

TENNESSEE VOLUNTEERS, 209

Sloppy Joe Dip, 84
BBQ Chicken Drumsticks, 147
Wedge Salad on a Stick, 199
Elvis Bars, 243

TEXAS A&M AGGIES, 225

Red Grapefruit Punch, 66
Cowboy Caviar, 93
Loaded Brisket Nachos, 167
Sopapilla Cheesecake Bars, 250

VANDERBILT COMMODORES, 249

Sausage and Cheddar Deviled Eggs, 102
Memphis-Style BBQ Chili, 125
Nashville Hot Chicken Sliders, 154
Chocolate-and-Peanut Butter Banana
    Pudding, 227

TENT TALK ANSWERS

OPENING DRIVE

p. 27: A. Auburn and Georgia first played one another in 1892.

p. 30: A. Birmingham, Alabama

p. 38: D. The ball is placed on the 35-yard line for a kickoff.

p. 44: True. The NCAA suggests that quarterbacks and running backs wear numbers below 50 and receivers wear numbers above 79. That makes players wearing the numbers 50 through 79 ineligible receivers, or linemen, who are not allowed to catch forward passes.

LIBATIONS

p. 55: C. A team must have 7 players on the line of scrimmage for every play.

p. 59: D. A total of 13 schools joined forces to charter the Southeastern Conference.

p. 66: D. A football field is 53⅓ yards wide.

p. 69: False. From 1883 to 1898, a touchdown was worth only 4 points; in 1898, the point value became 5. Since 1912, however, a touchdown has been worth 6 points.

p. 70: False. The chains are placed on the field opposite the press box, typically the visitors' side, to make them easier for broadcasters to read.

DINK & DUNK

p. 83: B. Returning the ball after a blocked extra point or a failed two-point conversion yields only two points.

p. 87: B. Former Dawgs Terrell Davis, Jake Scott, and Hines Ward have all been named Most Valuable Player in an NFL Super Bowl game.

p. 91: B. Early footballs were likely made of pig bladders, not pigskin. Today's footballs are made of cowhide.

p. 102: False. A receiver is only required to have one foot in bounds for a pass to be complete in the college game. Both feet must be in bounds in professional football.

BOWL ELIGIBLE

p. 125: False. That area of the field is known as Coffin Corner. It's very difficult for a team to score from deep in its own territory.

p. 136: B. The official capacity of Texas A&M's Kyle Field is 102,733, making it the fourth largest in the nation. Neyland Stadium in Knoxville, Tennessee, holds 102,455, while LSU's Tiger Stadium holds 102,321. Bryant-Denny Stadium in Tuscaloosa, Alabama, holds 101,821.

HOT OFF THE GRIDIRON

p. 147: C. A gridiron is a metal grate with parallel bars used for grilling. In the early days of football, fields were marked with both vertical and horizontal parallel lines, which resembled a gridiron.

p. 151: B. The line of scrimmage measures 11 inches, which equals the length of a football.

p. 153: C. The ball is placed on the 3-yard line for both point-after attempts and two-point conversions. In professional football, the ball is placed on the 2-yard line.

p. 163: B. Field numbers must measure 6 feet tall and 4 feet wide.

p. 165: True. Both opponents get one time-out and a chance to score. After the third time-out, teams are forced to try a two-point conversion by either running or throwing the ball into the end zone. The game continues in this fashion until one team has more points than the other.

p. 170: True. After a safety, the offensive team must kick the ball to the other team from their own 20-yard line.

p. 174: C. Georgia Tech, Sewanee, and Tulane. Other original members include Alabama, Auburn, Florida, Georgia, Kentucky, LSU, Mississippi State, Ole Miss, Tennessee, and Vanderbilt.

p. 180: B. When a quarterback calls an audible, he changes the play at the line of scrimmage and shouts the new play to his teammates.

SIDES THAT SCORE

p. 196: False. In college football, a player is down if any part of his body touches the ground.

p. 200: True. When a kicker has his leg extended in the kicking position, he is vulnerable to injury. This protection is also extended to the snapper and holder on a place kick.

SWEET VICTORIES

p. 231: B. The ball is placed on the 25-yard line.

p. 232: A. The crossbar is 10 feet above the ground.

p. 235: B. The NCAA and NFL both require that footballs be filled with 12.5 to 13.5 pounds of air.

p. 239: C. The University of Florida collects royalties on every bottle of Gatorade sold.

p. 243: A. The huddle was first used in the 1890s by Gallaudet, a college for the deaf in Washington, D.C. Quarterback Paul Hubbard had his team gather around him in a tight circle so they could discuss plays in sign language without the other team seeing what they were signing.

p. 256: A. Riley Smith played at Alabama. Heisman Trophy winner Jay Berwanger of the University of Chicago was selected first in the 1936 draft, but he never played professional ball.

PHOTO CREDITS

The team pennants throughout the book are from College Flags and Banners Company, **www.collegeflagsandbanners.com**. They offer a variety of products for different universities and sports teams, including a set of 12"x30" SEC team pennants.

GETTY IMAGES

Robin Alam: 261; **Andy Altenburger:** 263 (Ole Miss fan); **Jonathan Bachman:** 51 (Auburn fans); **Todd Bennett:** 191 (Williams-Brice Stadium); **Logan Bowles:** 61; **Raymond Boyd:** 247 (Vanderbilt Stadium); **Chris Brashers:** 34 (Arkansas fan with hog hat); **Frederick Breedon:** 245; **Mike Carlson:** 206 (Smokey); **Kevin C. Cox:** 129, 138, 262 (Alabama fan), 264; **Brett Deering:** 108; **Tim Dominick:** 190 (South Carolina fans with banner); **Scott Donaldson:** 4 (South Carolina fans); **Elsa:** 16; **Rob Foldy:** 62 (Albert E. Gator); **Jamie Gilliam:** 246 (Vanderbilt fan with gloves), 246 (Vanderbilt band), 247 (Vanderbilt players carrying anchor), 247 (Mr. Commodore); **Chris Graythen:** 113 (Mike the Tiger); **Sam Greenwood:** 186; **Michael Hickey:** 97, 98 (Kentucky fans), 99 (The Wildcat), 99 (Kroger Field); **Grant Halverson:** 4 (Vanderbilt cheerleaders), 190 (South Carolina band); **Wesley Hitt:** 4 (Arkansas fans), 15 (Auburn fans), 34 (Arkansas cheerleader), 35 (Frank Broyles), 35 (Donald W. Reynolds Razorback Stadium), 131 (Player holding #HAILSTATE sign), 143 (Jesse Hall and the Columns), 262 (Mississippi State player); **Icon Sportswire:** 190 (South Carolina Railroad Cockaboose); **Scott Kane:** 142 (Truman the Tiger); **Tyler Kaufman:** 112 (LSU fans); **Todd Kirkland:** 79 (Georgia fans holding "Dawg Nation" sign); **John Korduner:** 112 (LSU Golden Girl cheerleader), 112 (LSU band), 113 (Death Valley stadium); **Streeter Lecka:**

78 (Uga), 189 (South Carolina fans); **Bob Levey:** 220, 223 (Texas A&M Corp of Cadets); **lissart:** 11; **Mark LoMoglio:** 20 (Big Al), 21 (Child holding "Roll Tide" sign); **Al Messerschmidt:** 266 (South Carolina fans); **Jessica Morgan:** 99 (Jockey); **Ken Murray:** 223 (Texas A&M fans), 266 (LSU fans); **Matthew Pearce:** 35 (Big Red); **Christian Petersen:** 50 (Aubie); **Wade Rackley:** 207 (Tennessee players touching sign); **Stacy Revere:** 131 (Fans holding Dak Prescott face sign); **Joe Robbins:** 205, 207 (Tennessee players running onto field); **David Rosenblum:** 62 (Ben Hill Griffin Stadium); **Marc Serota:** 8; **Ezra Shaw:** 46; **Jamie Squire:** 270; **Tennessee/Collegiate Images:** 206 (General Robert Neyland); **Chris Trotman:** 63 (Fans at Ben Hill Griffin Stadium); **University of Georgia:** 78 (Sanford Stadium); **University of Mississippi:** 159 (Roy Lee Mullins); **Jeffrey Vest:** 79 (Georgia fans), 191 (Sir Big Spur), back endsheet; **Skip Williams:** 207 (Tennessee fans); **Tom Williams:** 14 (LSU, Alabama fans tailgating); **Mike Zarrilli:** 191 (Cocky the Gamecock); **Ed Zurga:** 143 (Cheerleaders on Truman's Taxi).

SHUTTERSTOCK

AP/REX: 4 (Texas A&M fans), 74; **Tony Gutierrez:** 22 (Reveille); **Rob Hainer:** 20 (Bryant-Denny Stadium); **Mark Humphrey:** 218; **Thomas Mcewen:** 267; **Lisovskaya Natalia:** 10; **Sean Pavone:** 246 (Kirkland Hall); **David J. Phillip:** 4 (LSU fan).

ADDITIONAL PHOTOGRAPHY BY

Paul Abell/XOS Digital: 79 (Georgia players in huddle); **Auburn University Photographic Services:** 4 (Auburn fans); **Walt Beazley:** 32; **Travis Bell/ESPN images:** 7; **R. Kevin Butts:** 222 (Kyle

Field); **Tim Casey/XOS Digital:** 265; **Kyle Coburn/XOS Digital:** 143 (Marching Mizzou band); **Gabriel Chmielewski:** 223 (Home of the 12th Man sign); **Mark Cornelison:** 98 (The Wildcat on statue); **Marlee Crawford/Ole Miss Communications:** 159 (Ole Miss tailgating); **David A. Dickey/Auburn University Photographic Services:** 51 (Auburn cheerleader); **Jeff Etheridge/Auburn University Photographic Services:** 49, 50 (Jordan-Hare Stadium); **Steve Franz/XOS Digital:** 110, 113 (LSU fan cooking); **Thomas Graning/Ole Miss Communications:** 158 ("Fins Up"); **Glen Johnson/XOS Digital:** 14 (Texas A&M fans singing); **Robert Jordan/ Ole Miss Communications:** 158 (Vaught-Hemingway Stadium at Hollingsworth Field); **Justin Kelley:** 141, 142 (Eric Waters on the rocks at Faurot Field); **Grace King:** 15 (Florida fan tailgating); **Nathan Latil/Ole Miss Communications:** 4 (Ole Miss pumpkins), 14 (Ole Miss woman setting up tailgating table), 156; **Neil Leifer/Sports Illustrated:** 18; **Michelle Lepianka/XOS Digital:** 21 (Alabama parade); **Robert Lewis:** 131 (Mississippi State fans tailgating); **Hannah Pietrick:** 63 (Woman taking photo of boy), 63 (Cheerleaders); **Kelly Price:** 14 (Mississippi State fans); **Tori Richman:** 15 (South Carolina, Clemson player arguing); **Zachary Riggins:** 21 (Fans tailgating at Denny Chimes); **Casey Sykes:** 12, 15 (Georgia player with fans), 76; **University of Arkansas/XOS Digital:** 34 (Arkansas fans); **University of Missouri/XOS Digital:** 15 (Missouri fans climbing on goalposts); **Chet White:** 98 (Kentucky players walking onto field); **Blake Williams:** 130 (Bully the Bulldog); **XOS Digital:** 51 (Fans rolling Toomer's Corner), 130 (Davis Wade Stadium at Scott Field), 142 (Faurot Field at Memorial Stadium), 206 (Neyland Stadium).

THE SEC THANKS OUR CORPORATE SPONSORS

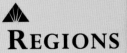

IT'S MORE THAN PASSION.

IT'S TRUE LOVE.

TAKE IT ALL IN